AMERICAN POLITICAL, ECONOMIC, AND SECURITY ISSUES

CALL FOR A NEW ERA IN THE U.S. BUDGET

AMERICAN POLITICAL, ECONOMIC, AND SECURITY ISSUES

Additional books in this series can be found on Nova's website under the Series tab.

Additional E-books in this series can be found on Nova's website under the E-book tab.

AMERICAN POLITICAL, ECONOMIC, AND SECURITY ISSUES

CALL FOR A NEW ERA IN THE U.S. BUDGET

BENJAMIN J. WALTERS
EDITOR

Nova Science Publishers, Inc.
New York

For permission to use material from this book please contact us:
Telephone 631-231-7269; Fax 631-231-8175
Web Site: http://www.novapublishers.com

LIBRARY OF CONGRESS CATALOGING-IN-PUBLICATION DATA

ISBN 978-1-60741-883-2 Call for a new era in the U.S. budget / editor, Benjamin J. Walters.
p. cm.
Includes index.
ISBN 978-1-60741-883-2 (hardcover)
1. Budget--United States. 2. United States--Economic conditions--21st century. I. Walters, Benjamin J. II. Title: Call for a new era in the US budget.
HJ2051.C26 2010
352.4'80973--dc22

2010031173

Published by Nova Science Publishers, Inc. † New York

CONTENTS

PREFACE

At this moment of economic crisis and uncertainty, the USA is being tested. This book presents a preliminary analysis of President Obama's budget and an update of the Congressional Budget Office's budget and economic outlook This book consists of public documents which have been located, gathered, combined, reformatted, and enhanced with a subject index, selectively edited and bound to provide easy access.

Chapter 1- Over the decades, the United States has grown and prospered when all Americans have shared in the opportunities created by our economy. Bottom-up growth that empowers hardworking families to climb the ladder of success and raise their children with security, opportunity, and hope for the future lies at the heart of the American dream. It is the responsibility of our elected leaders to create the conditions for our people to aim high, work hard, and realize the full promise of American life.

Yet for far too long, the resilience, optimism, and industriousness of the American people have been frustrated by irresponsible policy choices in Washington. Prudent investments in education, clean energy, health care, and infrastructure were sacrificed for huge tax cuts for the wealthy and well-connected. In the face of these trade-offs, Washington has ignored the squeeze on middle-class families that is making it harder for them to get ahead. Our Government has spent taxpayer money without making sure the numbers add up and without making it clear and understandable to the American people where their money was being spent. Tough choices have been avoided, and we have failed to make the wise investments we need to compete in a global, information-age economy.

Chapter 2- This report presents the Congressional Budget Office's (CBO's) latest projections for the budget and economic outlook, updating the projections published in early January 2009. In addition, CBO has reviewed the President's budgetary proposals contained in the February publication *A New Era of Responsibility: Renewing America's Promise,* and this report summarizes CBO's preliminary analysis of that budget plan. (CBO will review the complete plan after the Administration submits it to the Congress later this spring.)

In: Call for A New Era in the U.S. Budget
Editor: Benjamin J. Walters
ISBN: 978-1-60741-883-2

Chapter 1

A NEW ERA OF RESPONSIBILITY: RENEWING AMERICA'S PROMISE

Office of Management and Budget

INHERITING A LEGACY OF MISPLACED PRIORITIES

Over the decades, the United States has grown and prospered when all Americans have shared in the opportunities created by our economy. Bottom-up growth that empowers hardworking families to climb the ladder of success and raise their children with security, opportunity, and hope for the future lies at the heart of the American dream. It is the responsibility of our elected leaders to create the conditions for our people to aim high, work hard, and realize the full promise of American life.

Yet for far too long, the resilience, optimism, and industriousness of the American people have been frustrated by irresponsible policy choices in Washington. Prudent investments in education, clean energy, health care, and infrastructure were sacrificed for huge tax cuts for the wealthy and well-connected. In the face of these trade-offs, Washington has ignored the squeeze on middle-class families that is making it harder for them to get ahead. Our Government has spent taxpayer money without making sure the numbers add up and without making it clear and understandable to the American people where their money was being spent. Tough choices have been avoided, and we have failed to make the wise investments we need to compete in a global, information-age economy.

While middle-class families have been playing by the rules, living up to their responsibilities as neighbors and citizens, those at the commanding heights of our economy have not. They have taken risks and piled on debts that while seemingly profitable in the short-term, have now proven to be dangerous not only for their individual firms but for the economy as a whole. With loosened oversight and weak enforcement from Washington, too many cut corners as they racked up record profits and paid themselves millions of dollars in compensation and bonuses. There's nothing wrong with making money, but there is something wrong when we allow the playing field to be tilted so far in the favor of so few.

This is the legacy that we inherit—a legacy of mismanagement and misplaced priorities, of missed opportunities and of deep, structural problems ignored for too long. It's a legacy of irresponsibility, and it is our duty to change it.

A Deep and Destructive Recession

No one reading this report needs to be told that our economy is in crisis. We have lost jobs for 13 consecutive months for a total of 3.6 million jobs lost. According to the Bureau of Labor Statistics, more jobs were lost last year than in any year since data collection of this kind began in 1939 (see Figure 1, Annual Change in Payroll Employment, 1940-2008). In percentage terms, the job loss in the current recession is the worst since the early 1980s (see Figure 2, Job Losses in Five Recessions).

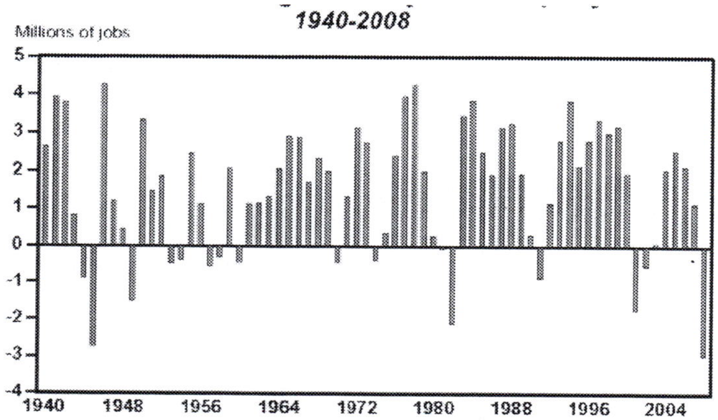

Source: Bureau of Labor Statistics.
Note: Values reflect December to December changes in seasonally-adjusted payroll employment.

Figure 1. Annual Change in Payroll Employment.

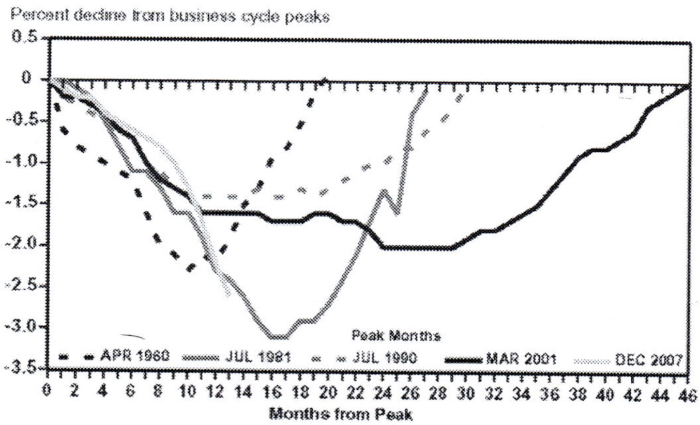

Source: Employment data from Bureau of Labor Statistics. Business cycle peak dates from National Bureau of Economic Research.

Figure 2. Job Losses in Five Recessions.

Many newly unemployed workers will be facing long odds when they try to find another good job. Since the start of the recession, the number of those unemployed for 27 weeks or more has risen by 1.3 million including a 440,000-person increase in December 2008 and January 2009. Increasingly, workers are giving up looking for work or involuntarily settling for part-time work; in fact, the underemployment rate, which measures all those out of work or underemployed for economic reasons, rose to 13.9 percent in January 2009 (see Figure 3, The Underemployment Rate).

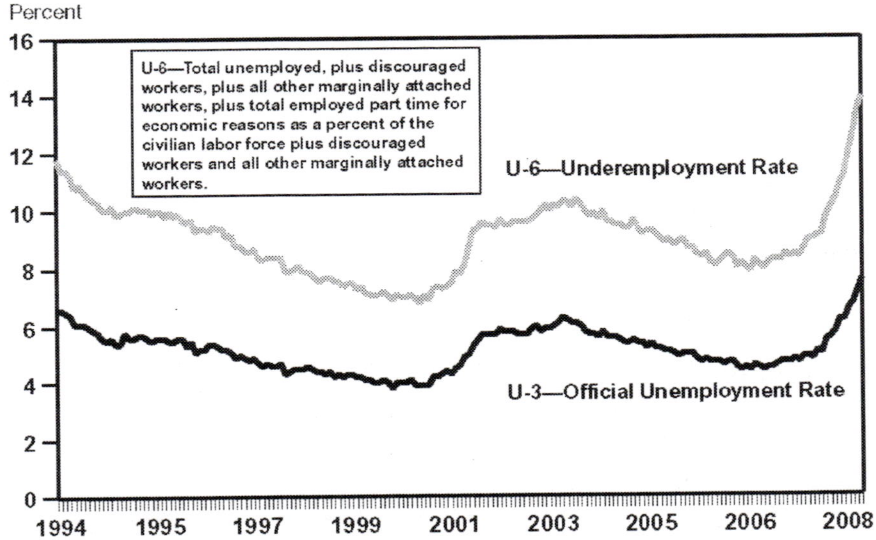

Source: Bureau of Labor Statistics.

Figure 3. The Underemployment Rate.

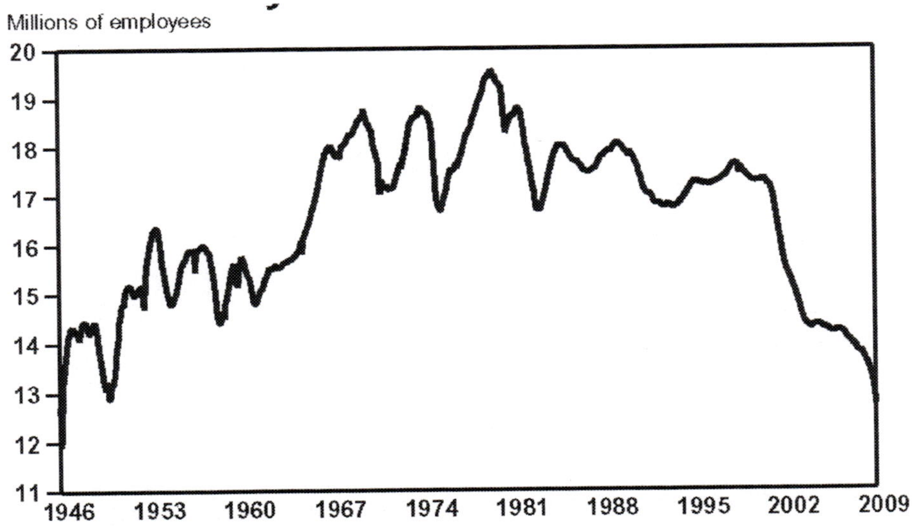

Source: Bureau of Labor Statistics.

Figure 4. Manufacturing Employment is Lower than at Any Time Since 1946.

Every sector of our economy has been affected by this recession. The automobile industry, which required a Government rescue this past winter, has shed 204,000 jobs since the start of this recession. Over the last year, the Big Three automakers have seen sales plunge anywhere between 39 and 55 percent. Manufacturing as a whole has been hard hit with employment falling to a 60-year low (see Figure 4, Manufacturing Employment). Housing starts and permits continue to fall; in fact, the U.S. Census reported that housing starts were at the lowest levels since monthly recording of these data began in 1959 (see Figure 5, Housing Starts). At the same time, mortgages in the foreclosure process increased 204 percent between October 2006 and October 2008, and over 1 million properties went into foreclosure in 2008.

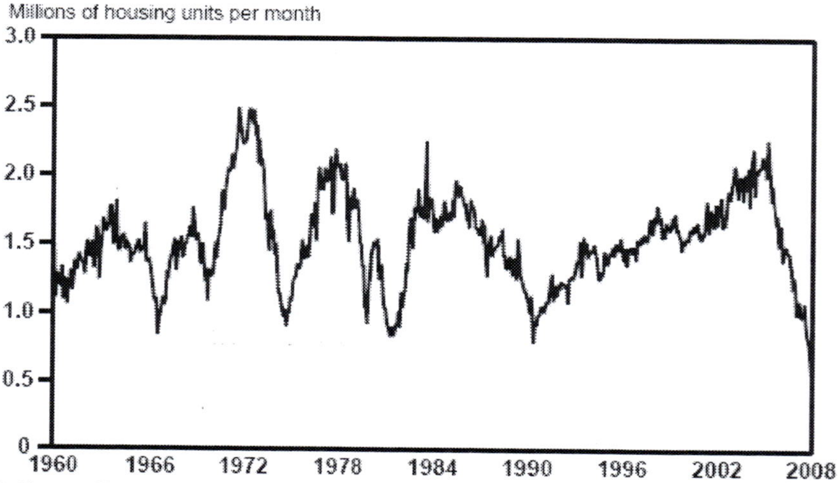

Source: U.S. Census Bureau.

Figure 5. Housing Starts have Reached an All-Time Low.

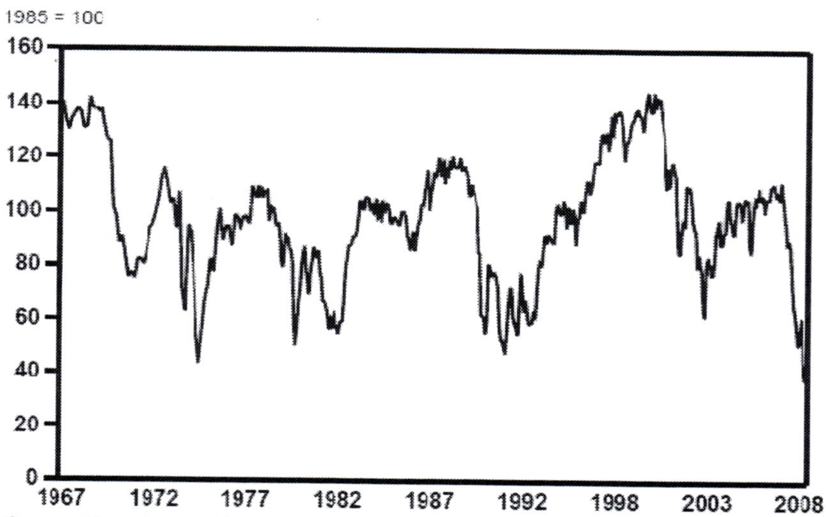

Source: Conference Board, monthly values interpolated 1966-1977.

Figure 6. Consumer Confidence Has Fallen to a Forty-Year Low.

Unsurprisingly, consumer confidence too is at an all time low (see Figure 6, Consumer Confidence). Some Americans are unable to keep up with the mounting bills and dwindling prospects: last fiscal year, personal bankruptcy filings topped 1 million, an increase of almost 30 percent from 2007. The overall picture is bleak: GDP fell at a 3.8 percent annualized rate in the last quarter of 2008, the biggest economic contraction in more than a quarter of a century.

A central cause of this sudden downturn has been a meltdown in our capital and credit markets. The subprime mortgage crisis is the result of a perfect storm of excessive risk-taking by both investors and borrowers, inadequate disclosure, non-existent or myopic oversight, market gatekeepers compromised by conflicts of interest, and irresponsible lending to thousands of Americans who, when offered the chance to own their own home, were advised to throw caution to the wind. Through sophisticated financial engineering, bad loans made on Main Street made their way onto the books of some of the largest firms on Wall Street, and then were sold to pension funds and individual investors around the world. Once the real estate market began to cool, loans defaulted at alarming numbers, these complex financial products started to lose their value, and the credit boom unraveled, erasing enormous wealth for both families and business as well as the jobs fueled by consumer spending.

The resulting collapse laid low some of the most prominent financial institutions in the American economy, and has wiped out trillions of dollars in wealth and retirement savings for millions of Americans who thought they had successfully provided for their golden years. Uncertainty about how far and wide the contagion has spread has brought our financial system to a near standstill. Loans to consumers, small businesses, and other borrowers are hard to come by, and likewise, the mortgage squeeze acts as a brake on the return of housing demand. The injection of unprecedented amounts of funds by the Federal Reserve and through the Troubled Asset Relief Program (TARP) attempted to restore confidence in the financial markets to get capital flowing once more and has slowed or perhaps halted the meltdown—but it has not been enough to fully restore confidence and the smooth operation of credit markets. A lack of trust still pervades markets. When that happens, investors pull their money out of the market, depositors make runs at banks, and banks stop lending to companies and to one another. Because of this lack of trust, our credit markets are effectively still frozen. As a result, businesses are unable to expand, families are unable to finance a new home, a new car, or a college education for their kids; and our economy suffers.

An Anemic Recovery Already Has hurt American Families

Adding insult to injury, American families have entered this recession weakened by the anemic recovery from the last downturn at the beginning of this decade. For millions of Americans, the recovery from 2001 through 2007 was hardly one at all. Measured by job gains, the economic recovery in the 2000s was the weakest one in a generation. From 2001 to 2007, the period in which the economy was expanding as measured by the growth in output, only 99,000 jobs were created each month on average. The period began with an outright decline in employment that did not end until 2003. Average job gains were more than twice as large during the expansions of the 1980s (228,000 a month) and the 1990s (200,000 a month) (see Figure 7, 2000s Economic Recovery Brought Weakest Job Gains). Real wages also showed very little improvement in the latest expansion, rising on average at an annualized rate of just 0.1 percent each month, compared with 0.7 percent during the 1990s expansion.

On top of that, this was the first economic recovery since World War II where real median household income did not rise above its previous peak (see Figure 8, Real Median Household Incomes). Between 2000 and 2007, median income among households headed by those under 65 fell by $1,951. To keep up, more and more Americans have turned to credit and debt: by 2007, household debt as a percentage of disposable personal income was 133.7 percent. And some Americans have not been able to keep up, falling out of the middle class and into poverty. From 2000 to 2007, the number of Americans living in poverty increased by nearly 5.7 million, and 1.7 more children lived in poverty in 2007 than in 2000. In fact, 18 percent of children, about 13 million in total, lived in poverty in 2007.

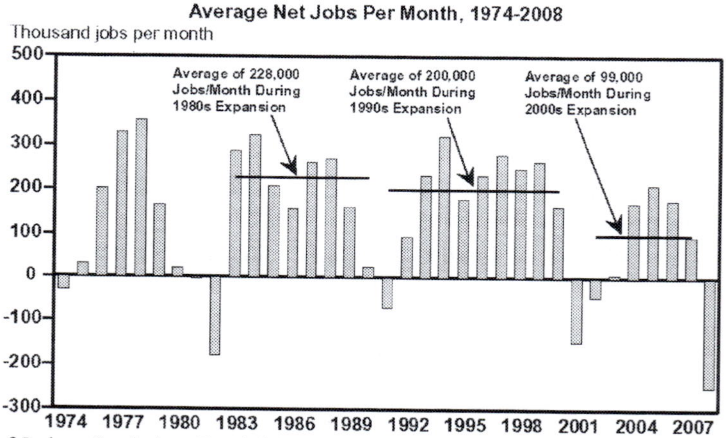

Source: Bureau of Labor Statistics, Establishment Survey, dates for expansions from National Bureau of Economic Research.

Figure 7. 2000s Economic Recovery Brought Weakest Job Gains in a Generation.

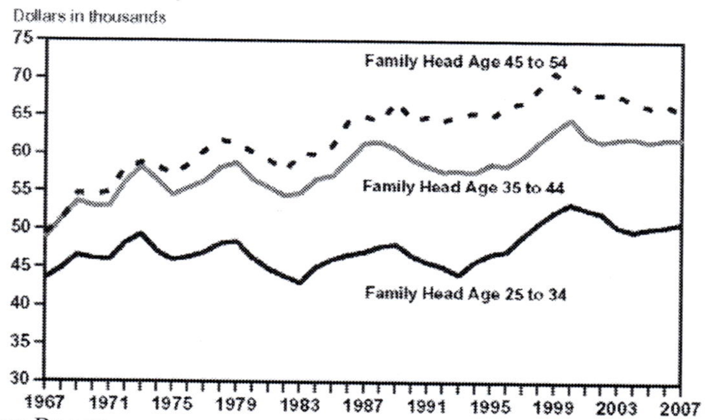

Source: U.S. Census Bureau.

Figure 8. Real Median Household Incomes Have Not Returned to the Levels Reached in the 1990s.

Ignoring our Long-Term Challenges

As the typical family saw its income decline and the underpinnings of our economic growth become increasingly unsustainable, nothing was done to address these mounting problems. These problems then were made worse by policies that benefited those at the top at the expense of almost all Americans and by a failure to tackle some of the most significant, structural impediments to long-term economic growth.

Growing Imbalance: Accumulating Wealth and Closing Doors to the Middle Class

For the better part of three decades, a disproportionate share of the Nation's wealth has been accumulated by the very wealthy. Technological advances and growing global competition, while transforming whole industries—and birthing new ones—has accentuated the trend toward rising inequality. yet, instead of using the tax code to lessen these increasing wage disparities, changes in the tax code over the past eight years exacerbated them.

According to the Internal Revenue Service, the Nation's top 400 taxpayers made more than $263 million on average in 2006, but paid income taxes at the lowest rate in the 15 years in which these data have been reported. In constant dollars, the average income of the top 400 taxpayers nearly quadrupled since 1992.

It's no surprise, then, that wealth began to be ever more concentrated at the top. By 2004, the wealthiest 10 percent of households held 70 percent of total wealth, and the combined net worth of the top 1 percent of families was larger than that of the bottom 90 percent. In fact, the top 1 percent took home more than 22 percent of total national income, up from 10 percent in 1980 (see Figure 9, Top One Percent of Earners). And these disparities are felt far beyond one's bank statement as several studies have found a direct correlation between health outcomes and personal income.

There is nothing wrong with people succeeding and making money. But there is something wrong when the opportunity for all Americans to get ahead, to enter the middle class, and to create a better life for their children becomes more and more elusive. That is what has been happening: The ladder into the middle class and beyond has become harder and harder to climb. The American dream has slowly slipped beyond the grasp of millions as we have deliberately ignored the very investments in our people that strengthen the middle class and neglected the drivers of economic growth that will sustain our economy for the long run.

Education

We know that the key to success in the 21st Century lies in investing in our people—in giving the chance to get a world-class education from cradle to career. Economists from across the spectrum agree that in this digital age, a highly educated and skilled workforce is critical not only to individual opportunity, but also to the overall success of our economy. The more people we educate to the highest standards possible, the better off all of us will be. yet too many children are not getting the world-class education that they deserve and that they need to thrive in this information-age economy.

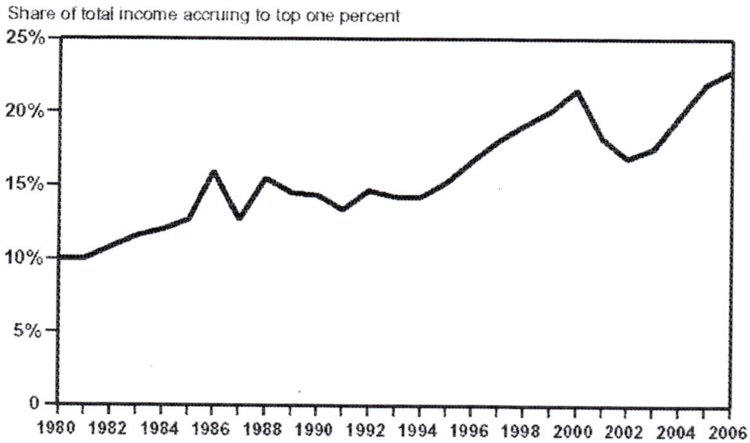

Source: Piketty and Saez (2003), updated by authors.

Figure 9. Top One Percent of Earners Have Been Increasing Their Share.

Research has shown that there is a high return for investments made in high-quality, comprehensive programs supporting disadvantaged children, and their families, from birth. Some studies show that for every dollar invested, there is a $4 to $9 return to society in higher earnings, higher graduation and employment rates, less crime, decreased need for special education services, less use of the public welfare system, and better health. However, we have yet to make a serious commitment to our youngest learners.

From kindergarten through high school, too many of our students are falling behind. According to the National Assessment of Educational Progress, the Nation's Report Card, in 2007 only one-third of fourth-graders was able to demonstrate solid academic performance in reading. Similarly, only 31 percent of eighth-graders demonstrated solid academic performance, a percentage that has remained stagnant since 1992. Achievement levels are similarly disappointing in mathematics.

We have not yet created a credible system of accountability for strong outcomes and a way to provide teachers and principals with the tools they need to get results. The problem is exacerbated by our failure to invest in the physical structures of our schools. A 2004 report by the National Center for Education Statistics found that 8.5 percent of public schools have exceeded their capacity; in almost one out of five schools, teachers have to teach in common areas such as gyms and cafeterias; and one in four schools report that teachers do not have their own classrooms in which to teach.

Another part of the problem is that when these students graduate from high school and look toward continuing their education, they face high costs of college attendance. The average tuition and fees at public, four-year institutions between the 2000-200 1 school year and 2008-2009 year increased by more than 26 percent, after adjusting for inflation and increases in tax credits and financial aid (see Figure 10, Average Annual Undergraduate Tuition). It's no surprise, then, that 60 percent of college students graduate with debt, and the typical debt load is over $20,000. Facing numbers like these, many students will simply decide that they cannot afford college, and many more already in college will decide that they cannot afford to stay. While 94 percent of high school students in the top quintile of socioeconomic status continue on to post-secondary education, only 54 percent of those in the bottom quintile do so.

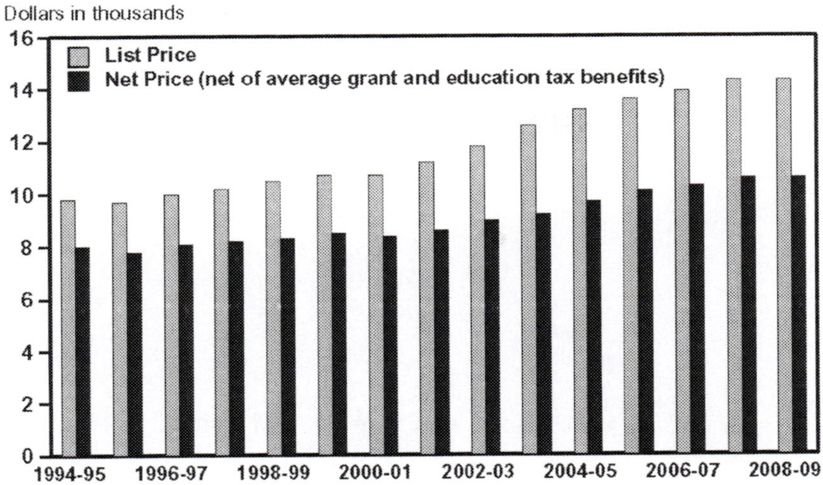

Source: College Board.

Figure 10. Average Annual Undergraduate Tuition, Room and Board for Public Four-Year Institutions (List and Net Prices).

If all our young children are not able to go to a high-quality school with modern facilities and great teachers and if older students are unable to afford to go to college and stay there until graduation, there is no way that our economy will be able to expand opportunity, strengthen the middle class, and compete in a global economy.

Health Care

One of the other big drains on family budgets and on the performance of the economy as a whole has been the increasing costs of health care. yet the evidence suggests that substantial reductions in costs could be achieved without sacrificing the quality of health care delivered. And in part because of the high costs of the current system, too many Americans remain uninsured or underinsured—causing them to forgo needed care and to bear unnecessary financial risks.

Since 2000, health insurance premiums have increased faster than worker's earnings. After adjusting for inflation, family health insurance premiums have increased by 58 percent while workers' wages have increased only 3 percent (see Figure 11, Family Health Insurance Premiums). In 2007, 17 million insured Americans spent more than 10 percent of their salary on health care, and 25 million Americans are underinsured, without enough coverage to keep costs in check.

Over the past eight years, the number of uninsured in America has jumped by 6.9 million and now totals 45.7 million Americans. Moreover, the number of people who have gone without health insurance for at least some portion of the previous 12 months tops 60 million. Many of those are people whom insurers will not cover because they have existing medical problems. Millions more have insurance, but could lose access as soon as they develop a serious medical problem. These Americans suffer, but their lack of health care options impacts all of us: every time an uninsured person walks into an emergency room because there is nowhere else to turn, a hidden tax is imposed on other citizens as premiums go up.

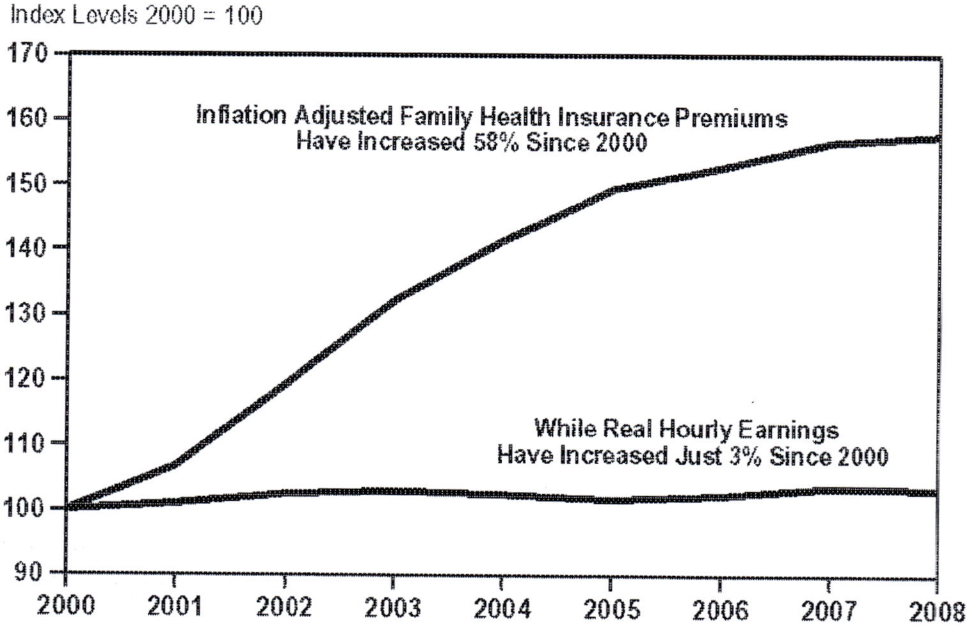

Source: Kaiser Family Foundation / Bureau of Labor Statistics.

Figure 11. Since 2000 Family Health Insurance Premiums Have Increased Much Faster than Workers' Real Earnings.

At the same time, health care costs are imposing large burdens on families—often in unexpected ways. Workers' take-home pay is constrained by health insurance costs to a degree that is both underappreciated and unnecessarily large. For instance, as mentioned earlier, at the state government level, evidence suggests that rising health care costs have crowded out support for higher education—raising tuition levels and impairing the quality of public higher education. Overall, health care is consuming an ever- increasing amount of our Nation's resources: in 1970, health care expenditures were 7 percent of GDP; now, it's 16 percent; and at this rate will hit nearly 20 percent by 2017.

We have a substantial opportunity to improve the efficiency of our health sector. Costs vary widely across areas of the United States, but evidence suggests that the high-cost areas do not generate better health outcomes than the lower-cost ones. Costs are twice as high at some of our Nation's leading medical centers than at others—and again the high-cost centers do not generate better outcomes than the lower-cost ones. Academic researchers suggest that costs could be reduced by as much as 30 percent—or roughly $700 billion a year—while protecting the quality of health care delivered if the high-cost areas and hospitals adopted the practices of the low-cost ones. According to Institute of Medicine estimates, as many as 100,000 Americans die each year due to preventable medical errors. Only four cents of every dollar spent on health care goes to preventive care. And while the United States leads the world in health care expenditures by a wide margin, our health outcomes often fall short of those achieved by other developed countries.

The bottom line is that the current path of rising health care costs is unsustainable, not only for the Federal Budget but also for family budgets.

Fai1ure to Invest in Tile Future

America's prosperity has always risen from the ground up, seeded by the hard work and ingenuity of our workers, inventors, and entrepreneurs. But germs of a good idea or a new way of doing business cannot take root and flourish without the Nation preparing the conditions for growth. That takes sound management of the economy; access to capital; and investments in science, technology, and infrastructure. That's why we built the great land-grant universities as our Nation expanded west, sent the Greatest Generation to college on the G.I. Bill, and invested in science and technology at the height of the Cold War. It's why previous generations built the Erie Canal at the start of the 19th Century, the transcontinental railroad after the Civil War, and the interstate highway system in the 1950's. It's why we electrified rural America during the depths of the Great Depression and laid fiber optic cables in our own time.

Investing in the future has been critical to long-term economic growth and creating high-paying jobs for our people throughout our history. yet, over the past several years, we've been delinquent in making these down payments on future growth.

Infrastructure

As our society becomes more mobile and interconnected, the need for 21st Century transportation networks has never been greater. As our economy slows, repairing and upgrading our infrastructure is an effective way to revive it and create new jobs. In the longer term, infrastructure investment will enable the United States to compete with the rest of the world and keep good jobs here at home. After all, in this day and age, businesses can now locate almost anywhere in the world and bring the jobs they create with them—and a modern infrastructure is critical if those jobs are to come to and stay in America.

Yet too many of our Nation's railways, highways, bridges, airports, and neighborhood streets are not keeping up with the needs of our Nation due to lack of investment and strategic longterm planning. The American Society of Civil Engineers gives our country's infrastructure the grade of a "D." The unsatisfactory condition and operational performance of our roads and bridges carries real costs from billions of dollars in car repairs to wasted fuel and time. The Texas Transportation Institute 2007 Urban Mobility Report estimates that drivers experienced over 4.2 billion hours of delay and wasted approximately 2.9 billion gallons of fuel in 2005.

Looking forward, we are behind in building the infrastructure that we need to compete in the global, information-age economy and are at risk of losing our Nation's scientific dominance. Over the last three decades, Federal funding for the physical, mathematical, and engineering sciences has declined as a percentage of GDP at a time when other countries are substantially increasing their own research budgets. At one point not long ago, the United States led the world in broadband deployment; now, that leadership is in question. Wireless networks in many countries abroad are faster and more advanced than our own. Our electrical grid is still constructed around the same model of 100 years ago, and in some places is as old. Power interruptions and outages cost Americans at least $80 billion each year. Finally, because of an insistence on putting dogma ahead of science, the United States has fallen behind in some of the most important, cutting- edge research such as stem-cell research.

Clean Energy

This lack of investment in the future is most glaring in the area of clean energy. For decades, we have talked about the security imperative we have to wean our Nation off foreign oil, which is often controlled by those whose interests are inimical to ours. And in recent years, a consensus has developed over the need to limit greenhouse gas emissions, which produce global warming and increase the risk of severe storms and weather conditions that might ruin crops, devastate cities, and destabilize whole regions. All of these facts are reason enough to invest in clean energy technologies. But there is an economic imperative to embrace these investments as well.

The clean energy sector presents us with immense promise—to develop and dominate a new industry sector and to create high-paying jobs here at home. From new, highly fuel-efficient cars to renewable sources of power, there are a host of emerging technologies that can spur the growth of new business while creating millions of new jobs. Our economic competitors know that. That's why they are racing to dominate these industries and to transform their economies.

Yet, the last Administration approached our energy needs by focusing on finding more of the fossil fuels we use now. As a result, we are still addicted to fossil fuels and more dependent on foreign oil than ever before. We have yet to make important policy changes and critical investments in the clean energy infrastructure that we'll need to transform our economy. Beyond clean energy, we have not kept up with investing in the basic science and research that will power this sector and the entire economy in decades to come. In fact, as a share of GDP, American Federal investment in the physical sciences and engineering research has dropped by half since 1970.

Eroding Trust and Accountability

Government is able to work on behalf of the people and attend to their immediate needs and long-range problems when it truly is a government of, by, and for the people. Part of what ails our economy is a profound disconnect between our leaders in Washington and the rest of the Nation.

Over the past eight years, policy was made behind closed doors. In many cases, unprecedented levels of secrecy have been invoked to block public scrutiny. In such an environment, the well connected and those who are able to hire high-priced lobbyists were able to carve out huge loopholes in our tax code, win massive subsidies that shifted the tax burden to small businesses and the middle class, and obtain exemptions from the basic rules of the road for themselves and their clients. And they did this all without paying for it or being held to account. This must change.

Fiscal Irresponsibility

Another manifestation of irresponsibility is the large budget deficits we are inheriting. These deficits, over time, will harm economic growth and impose burdens on our children and grandchildren. For the past eight years, in a time of economic growth, the Government spent recklessly on tax cuts for the few and hand-outs for the well-off and well-connected, mismanaged billions of dollars in taxpayer money, and failed to honor the responsibilities we have to future generations. Massive new programs have routinely been omitted from the Budget to mask their true cost, while a new entitlement program and massive tax cuts were proposed and signed into law without any attempt to pay for them. Between 2000 and 2008, real Government outlays increased at a 3.6 percent annual average rate, three times the 1.2 percent annual average rate between 1992 and 2000. This has helped turn a surplus of $236 billion at the end of the Clinton Administration, that was projected to grow still larger over time, into a deficit of more than $1 trillion in 2009. (see Figure 12, Surpluses Have Turned to Deficits). Furthermore, the amount of debt held by the public has nearly doubled to $6.4 trillion from 2001 to 2008. We are now living with the fallout of this deep fiscal irresponsibility.

Unfortunately, we are also inheriting the worst economic crisis since the Great Depression— which will force us to increase deficit spending temporarily as we try to jumpstart economic growth. This is an extraordinary response to an extraordinary crisis, and as we come out of this recession, we must return to the path of fiscal responsibility. It will mean tough choices—choices that are tougher because of the legacy of fiscal irresponsibility left to us.

Erosion of Market Oversight

Our Nation depends on private initiative and on free markets. But the financial crisis has re-minded us that without a watchful eye, the markets can spin out of control. In recent years, a dogmatic deregulatory approach to our capi-tal markets, driven by ideology rather than pragmatism, has now put those very markets—the envy of the world—in their most serious crisis in decades. Policymakers for-got that markets work when there is transparency of financial infor-mation for investors and consum-ers alike; independent oversight; and accountability enforced by active and uncompromised regulators. Because of deliberate policy decisions, balance sheets did not accurately reflect the risks that firms were taking; large pools of capital were left unregulated while more and more investors were exposed to them; and conflicts of interest compromised the credit rating agencies upon which investors relied. Investors and consumers ended up participating in complex transactions without full disclosure of the relevant risks, and eventually these mortgages, credit card debts, and other loans ended up costing many Americans dearly.

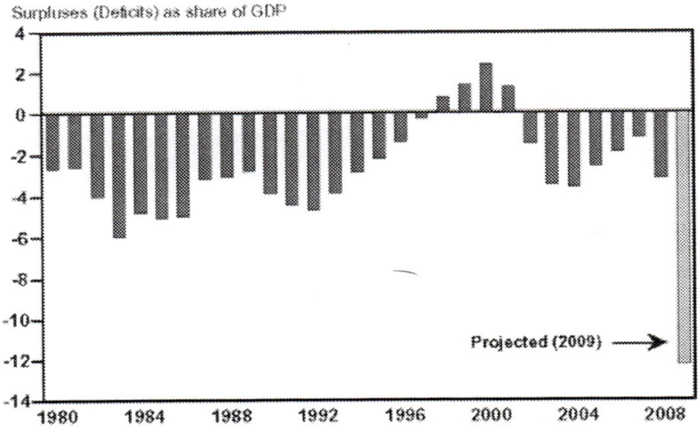

Figure 12. Surpluses Have Turned to Deficits.

Because our regulatory system atrophied and its patchwork quilt of different regulators and standard-setters was left untouched, it failed to keep pace with financial innovation. As a result, investors were led into investments that they neither understood nor were appropriate to their risk profile, and many people took on debts that they never could have hoped to pay. Corners were cut, and rules were bent. At every level, some of the most important market actors failed to live up to their responsibilities and failed to do what investors need of them to invest their hard-earned money wisely.

An Unresponsive Government

It is no coincidence that the policy failures of the past eight years have been accompanied by unprecedented Governmental secrecy and unprecedented access by lobbyists and the well-connected to policymakers in Washington. Consequently, the needs of those in the room trump those of their fellow citizens. We saw this with the Energy Task Force convened in 2002. When a Supreme Court order finally opened up its proceedings to review, it became apparent that regulatory decisions were made that reflected specific requests by industry representatives with the Government's ear.

The growth of Federal contracting is another instance where special interests benefited from special access. Federal spending on contracts more than doubled from about $208 billion in 2000 to more than $423 billion in 2006—and yet the number of contract officers overseeing these contracts remained flat. The value of contracts not subject to full and open competition grew from $48.6 billion to $112.5 billion during the same period. Cost-type contracts that are particularly vulnerable to waste since they provide no incentive to control costs increased more than 75 percent under the previous Administration.

This special-interest driven use of taxpayer dollars shows up in the billions of dollars in improper overpayments for Medicare and Medicaid, the billions that Federal taxpayers pay out to fund corporate loopholes; and in the $4 billion in Iraq-related spending auditors estimate is lost to waste and ineffective programs. Most egregiously, we see this irresponsibility in the tens of thousands of Federal contractors and Medicare service providers who make money off of the Government, but fail to pay all their taxes—costing us billions.

For the Nation to move out of this economic crisis, and to put our country on the path to productivity and growth, the American people need its leaders to live up to their responsibilities. That means opening the doors to citizen input; holding those entrusted with taxpayer dollars accountable for their use; and setting strong, enforceable rules of the road to keep our markets free and fair. With a government that is accountable to the people, we can jumpstart our economy in a way that is both quick and wise, and begin to make the long-term investments in areas long neglected.

JUMPSTARTING THE ECONOMY AND INVESTING FOR THE FUTURE

There are no quick and easy fixes to the recession plaguing our economy. This crisis has been many years in the making, and it is likely to get worse before it gets better. There is no doubt that our Nation has the creativity, capability, and industriousness to lift ourselves out of this downturn and begin the process of transforming our economy for the 21st Century. As we do this, we need to remember that throughout our history, the United States has grown and prospered when all Americans have shared in the opportunities created by our economy. While our economy has made the transition from an agrarian economy to an industrial one and on to an information-age economy, this essential truth has not changed: America thrives when all our people have the chance to succeed.

The past eight years have discredited once and for all the philosophy of trickle-down economics—that tax breaks, income gains, and wealth creation among the wealthy eventually will work their way down to the middle class. In its place, we need economic opportunity to trickle up. We need policies that will strengthen the middle class and create the conditions to spur innovation and sustainable economic growth. Some may say that in this current environment this is aiming too high. Settling never has been the American way, and now is no time to lower our sights. While we have inherited unprecedented budget deficits and a weakened economy, now is precisely the time for the country to make the long overdue investments that will fundamentally transform our economy so that we can compete and thrive in the decades ahead. As we jumpstart our economy out of this recession, the American people expect and demand that their Government does so with unprecedented transparency and accountability so that they know where their tax dollars are going and how these funds are being spent.

Immediate Relief and Economic Stimulus

As the year started, it became clear there was a wide and growing shortfall between what the economy could produce and what it was producing. If we kept on this course, economists predicted that the economy would shed millions of additional jobs, the unemployment rate could exceed 10 percent, and over the next two years, the country would lose roughly $2 trillion in income. With traditional monetary policy levers largely exhausted, the Congress passed and the President signed into law the American recovery and reinvestment Act of 2009 (the "recovery Act"), a nationwide effort to create jobs and transform our economy to compete in the 21st Century.

Because speed is of the essence when it comes to acting to save our economy and millions of jobs, approximately three-quarters of the funds in this package will be spent out over the next 18 months. Many of the long-term investments will stimulate the economy too as these elements of the package are simultaneously designed to spark economic growth, save or create 3 to 4 million jobs, and help families through these tough times. To provide immediate relief and get the economy moving again, the Administration will:

Make Permanent the $800 "Making Work Pay" Tax Cut for Workers and Their Families. The recovery Act created the Making Work Pay tax credit, a refundable income tax credit, which will offset the payroll tax on up to the first $6,450 of earnings for about 95 percent of all American workers while still preserving the important principle of a dedicated revenue source for Social Security. This helps small business owners struggling to meet expenses. And with families squeezed, this tax cut will put needed money in their pockets for them to make ends meet and cover the costs of necessities. This is the first- stage of a middle-class tax cut promised during the presidential campaign. The Budget will make Making Work Pay permanent.

Continue to Cut Taxes for the Families of Millions of Children Through an Expansion of the Child Tax Credit. By expanding the Child Tax Credit, the Recovery Act provided a new tax cut and increased the generosity of the existing credit to millions of children—fulfilling the promise that a family that works hard and plays by the rules will be able to raise their children above the poverty line. The Budget makes this tax cut permanent.

Increase Food Stamp Benefits for Over 30 Million Americans. Even in tough times, our Nation is a nation of plenty, and no one should have to go hungry. The Recovery Act will spend nearly $20 billion to increase food stamp benefits for overstretched families, and provide additional support for food banks, school lunch programs, and the Special Supplemental Nutrition Program for Women, Infants, and Children (WIC) program.

Provide Nearly 60 Million Retired and Disabled Americans an immediate $250 Through Temporarily increasing Benefits. These vulnerable populations are the first ones to feel an economic downturn. Through the Recovery Act, we will spend almost $15 billion to provide nearly 60 million retired Americans and Americans with disabilities an immediate $250 through temporarily increasing Social Security, Supplemental Security Income, and Veterans benefits.

Extend, Expand, and Reform unemployment insurance (ui) Benefits. With unemployment on the rise and those out of work going longer without new jobs, we have provided both a boost to our economy and to these workers' well-being by extending the Emergency Unemployment Compensation program through December 2009, increasing weekly UI benefits by $25, and providing financial incentives for States to modernize their UI systems to expand coverage. Beyond this year, the Administration will update the Nation's UI system to better address the challenges and realities of the 21st Century workforce. The Budget proposes changes to make the UI program a more responsive and effective social safety net and economic stabilizer. The Administration will propose to make the permanent Extended Benefit program more responsive to changing economic conditions, making benefits available more quickly and avoiding the delays associated with special, temporary extended unemployment programs. Finally, despite the efforts of States to reduce improper benefit payments, over $3.9 billion in UI benefits were erroneously paid in 2008. The Administration will tackle this problem by increasing funding for program integrity and proposing legislative changes that would have the direct and indirect effect of reducing UI improper payments by $3.9 billion and reducing employer tax evasion by almost $300 million over 10 years.

Reform Asset Tests. The Administration would like to work with the Congress to revisit asset limits for Federal means-tested programs in the wake of new and expanded refundable tax credits. Current asset rules across a variety of programs are antiquated, inconsistent, and present obstacles for low-income individuals who aspire to achieve self-sufficiency. The intersection of the new credits and outdated asset rules may disqualify new and current individuals and families from Federal benefits, including Medicaid and Supplemental Nutrition Assistance Program (formerly Food Stamps).

Creating Jobs and Investing in Long-Term Economic Growth

These tax and benefit provisions of the recovery plan will provide an immediate stimulative effect on the economy. The other part of the stimulus comes from expenditures on projects that will promote medium-term economic activity while also providing some lift to the economy in the near term—as homes are weatherized, and health records are digitized—to name just a few. In addition to immediate hiring and expansion as these projects begin, the American people will reap benefits from these investments for years to come because the economic benefits of modern infrastructure, world-class schools, investments in research and development, health care reform, and clean energy will be enjoyed by generations of Americans. The expenditures in many of these areas then serve a dual role: to revive the economy in the short term and to restore its health for the long term. Through ambitious investments in clean energy, health care, education and other key areas, the plan will address long-ignored national priorities and make a historic down payment on our Nation's economic future. The 2010 Budget will support, and in some cases extend as well as expand the down payments made in the Recovery Act.

Building a 21st Century Infrastructure

A century ago, Theodore Roosevelt called together leaders from business and government to develop a plan for a 20th Century infrastructure. More than 50 years ago, Republican Dwight Eisenhower and Democrat Al Gore, Sr. worked together to launch the Interstate Highway System. Today, however, too many of our Nation's railways, highways, bridges, airports, and neighborhood streets are aging and congested due to lack of investment and strategic long-term planning. In the short term, modernizing our infrastructure will create new jobs and provide a boost to the economy. In the longer term, infrastructure investment will provide our Nation a foundation for long-term economic growth. The Budget will:

Establish a National infrastructure Bank. The Budget proposes to expand and enhance existing Federal infrastructure investments through a National Infrastructure Bank designed to deliver financial resources to priority infrastructure projects of significant national or regional economic benefit. The mission of this entity will be to not only provide direct Federal investment but also to help foster coordination through State, munici pal, and private co-investment in our Nation's most challenging infrastructure needs. These projects will directly and indirectly support jobs and stimulate substantial long-term economic growth.

Invest in Our Nation's Roads, Bridges, and Mass Transit. The President is committed to instituting accountability for the $35.9 billion provided in the Recovery Act and to responsibly reauthorizing the Nation's highway and mass transit programs. The Administration intends to work with the Congress to reform surface transportation programs both to put the system on a sustainable financing path and to make investments in a more sustainable future, enhancing transit options and making our economy more productive and our communities more livable. Further, our surface transportation system must generate the best investments to reduce congestion and improve safety. To do so, the Administration will emphasize the use of economic analysis and performance measurement in transportation planning. This will ensure that taxpayer dollars are better targeted and spent.

Initiate a New federal Commitment to high-Speed Rail. To provide Americans a 21st Century transportation system, the Administration proposes a $1 billion-a-year high-speed rail State grant program, in addition to the $8 billion provided in the Recovery Act. This proposal marks a new Federal commitment to give the traveling public a practical and environmentally sustainable alternative to flying or driving. Directed by the States, this investment will lead to the creation of several high-speed rail corridors across the country linking regional population centers.

Improve and Modernize Air Traffic Control. Because of an outdated air-traffic control system and over-scheduling at airports already operating at full capacity, an ordinary trip to a business meeting or to visit family can become marred by long delays. The Budget provides $800 million for the Next Generation Air Transportation System in the Federal Aviation Administration, a long-term effort to improve the efficiency, safety, and capacity of the air traffic control system. The 2010 Budget supports moving from a ground-based radar surveillance system to a more accurate satellite-based surveillance system; development of more efficient routes through the airspace; and improvements in aviation weather information.

Maintain Rural Access to the Aviation System. The Administration is committed to maintaining small communities' access to the National Airspace System. The Budget provides a $55 million increase over the 2009 level to fulfill current program requirements as demand for subsidized commercial air service increases. However, the program that delivers this subsidy is not efficiently designed. Through the budget process, the Administration intends to work with the Congress to develop a more sustainable program model that will fulfill its commitment while enhancing convenience for travelers and improving cost effectiveness.

Enhance Security at Over 90 Major Ports, to improve Homeland Security, Increase international Trade and Commerce, and Create Jobs. This investment will help make our Nation's ports a vital and secure link to the global economy, not a vulnerable entry point for those who seek to harm us. The Administration is committed to improving the protection of our critical port infrastructure. The Budget continues to provide risk-based funding through the Port Security Grant Program and builds upon the over $1.4 billion provided for port security grants over the past few years. These awards can be used by grantees to purchase a wide variety of security- enhancing investments including watercraft for increased patrolling of facilities, canine, bomb-sniffing units, and updating port vulnerability assessments. Additional funding will be used by Customs and Border Protection to purchase technology enhancements, such as non-intrusive inspection X-ray equipment and radiation portal monitors to detect nuclear materials.

Invest in Clean and Safe Drinking Water. The Budget requests $3.9 billion for the Environmental Protection Agency's Clean Water State Revolving Fund and the Drinking Water State Revolving Fund (SRFs), in addition to the $6 billion provided in the Recovery Act. With this historic increase, the programs will fund over 1,000 clean water and nearly 700 drinking water projects annually based on average project costs. In addition, the Recovery Act will support over 1,300 new wastewater projects and over 700 new drinking water SRF projects. Through Recovery Act funding for the Department of Agriculture's (USDA's) rural water and wastewater grants and loans, the Administration will support a $3.8 billion program level for the repair, upgrade, and construction of 2,000 rural water and sewer systems, providing new or improved service to 3 million people. Together with funding increases for the SRFs, the Administration will pursue SRF program reforms that will put resources for these ongoing needs on a firmer foundation.

Expand Access to Broadband. As a country, we have made significant public investments so that, regardless of economic status, Americans have access to telephone service and electricity. In this day and age, we must do the same for broadband. Like any network, the more people who are a part of it, the stronger we all are. The more communities that have access to high-speed Internet connections, the more businesses can grow and jobs can be created. When that happens, the entire Nation wins. That is why the Recovery Act included $7.2 billion for broadband expansion and the 2010 Budget includes $1.3 billion in USDA loans and grants for the Department of Agriculture to increase broadband capacity and improve telecommunication service as well as education and health opportunities in rural areas.

Invest in the Sciences. Investments in science and technology foster economic growth; create millions of high-tech, high-wage jobs that allow American workers to lead the global economy; improve the quality of life for all Americans; and strengthen our national security. The Recovery Act included a $5 billion investment in key science programs, which is by itself an almost 50-percent increase for these programs over 2008 and represents a significant down-payment toward the President's plan to double the fund-ing for these agencies over 10 years. Under the President's doubling plan, the Budget provides a 16-percent increase over 2008 funding levels for the National Science Foundation and similarly large increases for the Department of Energy's Office of Science and the Department of Commerce's National Institute of Standards and Technology. The Budget also increases support for promising, but exploratory and high-risk research proposals that could fundamentally improve our understanding of climate, revolutionize fields of science, and lead to radically new technologies. In addition, the Budget funds cutting-edge, fundamental research in traditional and emerging disciplines to help transform the Nation's air transportation system and to support future aircraft. The National Aeronautics and Space Administration (NASA) research in aeronautics will focus on how to increase airspace capacity and mobility, enhance aviation safety, and improve aircraft performance while reducing noise, emissions, and fuel consumption.

Creating a Clean Energy Economy

The high gas prices of last summer only underscored what we have known for decades: we cannot afford to depend so heavily on foreign oil and other fossil fuels to power our economy. While the national security implications have been clear for some time, the more we learn about global warming, the more we see that failure to wean ourselves off of fossil fuels also jeopardizes our economy and our entire planet.

Countries and companies around the world recognize this and are working day and night to develop clean energy technologies that will change everything from how we generate our electricity to how we power our cars and trucks. While the challenge is great, the promise of the moment is unparalleled. If we lead the world in the research and development of clean energy technology, we can create a whole new industry with high-paying jobs that cannot be shipped overseas. Some compare the promise of this sector to information technology. The difference is that with clean energy we can bring new jobs to rural areas long left behind in economic growth. Moreover, if we take the time now to start transforming our economy, we will enjoy the benefits of a lower cost and more efficient energy supply for years to come. As a down payment on an energy independent, clean energy economy, in this Budget, the Administration will:

Begin a Comprehensive Approach to Transform Our Energy Supply and Slow Global Warming. The Administration is developing a comprehensive energy and climate change plan to invest in clean energy, end our addiction to oil, address the global climate crisis, and create new American jobs that cannot be outsourced. After enactment of the Budget, the Administration will work expeditiously with key stakeholders and the Congress to develop an economy-wide emissions reduction program to reduce greenhouse gas emissions approximately 14 percent below 2005 levels by 2020, and approximately 83 percent below 2005 levels by 2050. This program will be implemented through a cap-and-trade system, a policy approach that dramatically reduced acid rain at much lower costs than the traditional government regulations and mandates of the past. Through a 100 percent auction to ensure that the biggest polluters do not enjoy windfall profits, this program will fund vital investments in a clean energy future totaling $150 billion over 10 years, starting in FY 2012. The balance of the auction revenues will be returned to the people, especially vulnerable families, communities, and businesses to help the transition to a clean energy economy.

Provide the Capital to double Renewable Energy Generating Capacity. Renewable power has grown dramatically over the past several years. Unfortunately, the current credit crisis has brought this dynamic progress to a halt. The programs in the Recovery Act will help to revive the renewable industry, doubling the amount of renewable energy generated. Collectively, the loan guarantees provided in the recovery plan and in this Budget are expected to leverage tens of billions of dollars in private capital. The Recovery Act also extends the production tax credit (PTC) to 2012 for wind and 2013 for other renewable sources of energy. This extension creates three years of certainty for investors, eliminating the delays historically associated with the PTC. The Act also expands authority for clean renewable energy bonds and creates new manufacturing tax credits to spur domestic manufacturing of clean energy equipment

Develop Low-Carbon Emission Technologies. The Recovery Act provides funding to meet the President's campaign commitment to build five commercial scale coal-fired plants with carbon capture and storage technology through public-private partnerships. The Energy Department will also scale up its demonstration projects for geologic storage for carbon dioxide. Combined, this funding will set the foundation for significant efforts to mitigate greenhouse gas emissions from coal-fired power plants.

Modernize federal Buildings and Slash the federal Government's Energy Bill by 25 Percent. The Federal Government is the largest energy consumer in the world. Making substantial investments to reduce Federal energy consumption can spur job creation while delivering long-term Government savings through lower energy bills. The Budget will build upon the more than $11 billion provided for building moderization in the Recovery Act to achieve the President's 25 percent energy efficiency improvement goal by 2013.

Weatherize Low-income homes, Saving Working families on Average $350 Per year. Across the Nation, families spend a significant portion of their budget running their furnaces and air conditioners as well as keeping the lights on. By upgrading a home's furnace, sealing leaky ducts, and adding insulation, a homeowner can cut their energy bills by 20 to 40 percent, and the substantial savings accrue in summer as well as winter and for years to come. By adding-energy efficient appliances and lighting, the savings are even greater. The Department of Energy's weatherization budget of $227 million in 2008 could only provide benefits for 76,000 U.S. homes. While the Nation has weatherized about six million low-income homes since 1976, more than 28 million remain eligible. The Budget will build upon the $5 billion provided in the Recovery Act for weatherization assistance in order to spur development of an industry that will have the capacity to meet the President's goal of weatherizing one million homes annually.

Use Title Xvii Loan Guarantee to Reduce Greenhouse Gas Emissions. Loan guarantee volume under Title XVII of the Energy and Policy Act of 2005 will support innovative and advanced technologies that avoid, reduce, or sequester anthropogenic greenhouse gas emissions or air pollutants. The Budget will support a wide-range of eligible projects such as renewable energy systems, electric system transmission projects, and carbon capture and sequestration projects that will result in a cleaner environment and potentially, a transformed energy sector.

Help State and Local Governments be More Energy Efficient. After the Federal Government, State and local governments are some of the largest users of energy. Facing budget shortfalls, many States and local governments now lack sufficient financial resources to tap the full potential of clean energy development and deployment. This situation is exacerbated by private sector financing drying up as a result of the recent credit crisis. The Budget will build upon $6.3 billion provided for clean energy and energy efficiency grants to state and local governments in the Recovery Act to help support their efforts to reduce their energy use.

Green Our Nation's farms. The Budget increases funding levels over those provided in previous years for programs, such as the Conservation Stewardship Program and the Environmental Quality Incentives Program that provide incentives for farmers to better conserve their lands and reduce pollution such as from animal feeding operations. In addition, USDA intends to work with farmers to help them take advantage of opportunities to participate in emerging markets for carbon credits, alternative energy and in other environmental services, such as wildlife habitat, clean water, and clean air.

Modernize the Electric Grid. We know that the existing electricity grid today is insufficient and outdated. In order to bring significant amounts of renewable energy online, tens of thousands of miles of new, high-voltage national transmission is necessary. For example, North Dakota—a State with significant wind energy potential—cannot carry the energy to the population centers that need the electricity without a new transmission superhighway. The Budget will build on efforts in the Recovery Act to create this new, smarter electric grid for the integration and use of greater amounts of renewable energy; increased utilization of innovative efficiency technologies; and a reduction in the electric congestion that costs ratepayers billions of dollars each year. The Recovery Act includes funds to complete additional significant work in improving the national grid with regional transmission planning and interconnection based transmission planning. Included is a $100 million workforce training program. To make the grid smarter, millions of Smart Meters—a key first step to a Smart Grid—will be deployed as well as investments in a host of other smart grid technologies.

Preparing Our Children for the 21st Century Economy

America faces few more urgent challenges than preparing our children to compete in a global economy. The decisions our leaders make about education in the coming years will shape our future for generations to come. The Administration is committed to meeting this challenge, and its vision for a 21st Century education begins with demanding more reform and accountability coupled with the resources needed to carry out that reform; asking parents to take responsibility for their children's success; and recruiting, retaining, and rewarding an army of new teachers to teach at new, successful schools that prepare our children for success in college and the workforce. Throughout our history, our Nation's schools from the local elementary school to the large university have been the gateway into the middle class and a better life for millions. That is why it's so important that the investments we make in education are ones that work—that help children learn and pursue their dreams. When it comes to our children's future, we cannot waste dollars on methods, programs, and initiatives that are not effective and efficient. Consequently, in this Budget, the Administration makes significant investments in approaches that have proven to deliver for our children and will reallocate funds away from and terminate programs that do not. To restore the promise of America's public education and to help America's children again lead the world in achievement, creativity, and success, the Budget will:

Make A New investment in Early Childhood Education. We know that a dollar invested in early education will pay off handsomely as these children grow older. That is why the Administration is proposing to help States strengthen their early education programs. The Administration will broaden the reach of these programs and boost their quality—encouraging new investment, a seamless delivery of services, and better information for parents about program options and quality. In addition, through funds from the Recovery Act and this Budget, the President will provide funding to double the number of children served by Early Head Start and expand Head Start, both of which have proven to be successful with younger children. Finally, the Department of Health and Human Services will begin a major effort to ramp up a new Nurse-Home Visitation program. Rigorous research has shown that a well-structured program can have large and measurable impacts in helping at-risk expectant and new parents give their children a healthy start in life.

Support High Standards and Rigorous Assessments Aligned with the Demands of the Global Economy. Students need to meet high standards, and tests need to measure the full range of skills that children must learn. Building on investments made through the Recovery Act, the Administration will help States strengthen their standards so they are rigorous and reflect readiness for success in college and a career. Resources will also be available to improve the quality of assessments, including assessments for students with disabilities and English language learners. Such reforms will lay the ground-work for reauthorizing the Elementary and Secondary Education Act.

Prepare and Reward Effective Teachers and Principals. Almost all successful students can remember a teacher who had an outsized impact on their education. Indeed, the quality of the education workforce is a critical factor in educational success. The Budget builds on the investments funded under the Recovery Act designed to significantly upgrade the skills and effectiveness of the education workforce. The Administration will invest in efforts to strengthen and increase transparency around results for teacher and principal preparation programs, including programs in schools of education, alternative certification programs, and teacher and principal residency programs. The Budget supports additional investments in State and local efforts, developed in consultation with teachers and other stakeholders, to implement systems that reward strong teacher performance and help less effective teachers improve or, if they do not, exit the classroom. Resources are also included to develop better systems and strategies for recruiting, evaluating, and supporting teachers and other educators to provide a better supply and distribution of well-prepared and effective education workforce.

Increase Support for Effective Charter Schools. The President's Budget will promote successful models of school reform by taking the first major step to fulfilling its commitment to double support for charter schools. The Department of Education will help create new, high-quality charter schools, ensure that States properly monitor and support these schools, and, in the case of chronic underperformance, close existing charter schools.

Expand Pell Grants and Put the Program on Sure footing. Because the Administration is committed to making college affordable for all Americans, the 2010 Budget builds on the Recovery Act by supporting a $5,550 Pell Grant maximum award in the 2010-2011 school year. But it's not enough just to make Pell Grants more generous and to put on a short-term patch. Fourteen times since 1973, the maximum Pell Grant has failed to increase even in nominal dollars. To make sure that we have a highly educated workforce and that the opportunity to go to college is not determined by how much money you have, the Budget puts the Pell Grant program on sure footing. The Administration will index Pell grants to the Consumer Price Index plus 1 percent in order to account for inflation in this sector. In addition, the Administration proposes to make the Pell Grant program mandatory to provide a regular stream of funding and eliminate the practice of "backfilling" billions of dollars in Pell shortfalls each year.

Stabilize the Student Loan Program for Students and Save Billions of dollars for Taxpayers. Right now, the subsidies in the Government-guaranteed student loan program are set by the Congress through the political process. That program has not only needlessly cost taxpayers billions of dollars, but has also subjected students to uncertainty because of turmoil in the financial markets. The President's Budget asks Congress to end the entitlements for financial institutions that lend to students, and instead to take advantage of low-cost and stable sources of capital so students are ensured access to loans— while providing high-quality services for students by using competitive, private providers to service loans. The approach in the Budget, originating all new loans in the direct lending program, saves more than $4 billion a year, and reinvests it in aid to students. The Budget also makes campus-based, low-interest loans more widely available through a new modernized Perkins Loan program, overhauling the inefficient and inequitable current Perkins program.

Help At-Risk Students Complete College. It is not enough for our Nation to enroll more students in college; we also need to graduate more students from college. A few States and institutions have begun to experiment with these efforts to accomplish this, but there is much more they can do. The Budget includes a new five-year, $2.5 billion Access and Completion Incentive Fund to support innovative State efforts to help low-income students succeed and complete their college education. The program will include a rigorous evaluation component to ensure that we learn from what works.

Make Permanent the New American Opportunity Tax Credit. If we do not make college more affordable, we run the risk of losing a whole generation of potential and productivity. To help students pay for college, the Administration created a new $2,500 American Opportunity Tax Credit in the Recovery Act. The credit makes college more affordable for millions of middle-class families and for the first time makes college tax incentives partially refundable. The Budget proposes to make this tax cut permanent.

Eliminate or Cut Education Programs with Records of Low Performance. When it comes to educating our children, we cannot afford to waste a dollar. The Administration proposes to eliminate, cut, or place under intensive review Education Department programs that are not helping to improve educational outcomes for students. These are efforts that lack strong evidence to justify taxpayer support and that, in many cases, could be funded in competitive funding streams that require evidence of results.

Invest in innovations and in What Works. While it is important to increase support for education, it is also critical to invest in learning which programs are effective and in growing the ones that are. Through the Innovation Fund, the Administration will invest in school systems and non-profit organizations with demonstrated track records of success in raising student achievement to expand their work or implement new innovative approaches. For instance, the Harlem Children's Zone aims to improve college-going rates by combining a rigorous K-12 education with a full network of supportive services—from early childhood education to after school activities to college counseling—in an entire neighborhood from birth to college. It has yielded encouraging results, and the President's Budget provides funds to expand this concept by supporting "Promise Neighborhoods," a new effort to test innovative strategies to improve academic achievement and life outcomes in high-poverty areas. The Budget also increases funding for rigorous evaluation in a first step toward doubling the Department of Education's support for education research. The Department's Institute of Education Sciences will use this funding to conduct rigorous evaluations of approaches to improve student learning and achievement with a focus on evaluating and scaling up promising innovative practices.

Triple the Number of Graduate Fellowships in Science to Help Spur the Next Generation of Home-Grown Scientific innovation. The industries of tomorrow will begin with ideas dreamed up in the classrooms and laboratories of today. Without investments in human capital today, we will not be able to reap the benefits of scientific innovation. That is why the Administration provided in the Recovery Act funds to be used as a down-payment toward the goal of tripling the number of graduate fellows in science.

Lowering Health Care Costs and Ensuring Broader Health Care Coverage

One of the biggest drains on American pocketbooks is the high cost of health care. Many families are one illness or accident away from financial ruin. Health insurance costs reduce workers' take-home pay to a degree that is both underappreciated and unnecessarily large. At the same time, health care costs are consuming a growing share of Federal and State government budgets. The United States spends over $2.2 trillion on health care each year—almost $8,000 per person. That number represents approximately 16 percent of the total economy and is growing rapidly. By 2017, almost 20 percent of the economy—more than $4 trillion—will be spent on health care.

Across our Nation, health care costs vary substantially, yet the higher-cost areas do not generate better health outcomes than the lower-cost areas. Even among our Nation's leading medical centers, costs vary significantly—with costs at some centers twice as high as others—but the higher-cost centers do not achieve higher quality than the lower-cost centers. Some researchers believe that health care costs could be reduced by a stunning 30 percent—or about $700 billion a year—without harming quality if we moved as a Nation toward the proven and successful practices adopted by the lower-cost areas and hospitals.

Capturing this opportunity would help to boost family take-home pay and put the Nation on a sounder fiscal path. It will require many steps, including expanding the use of health information technology, more aggressively studying what works and what doesn't, experimenting with different payment systems to health care providers, and promoting prevention and healthy living—many of which are advanced dramatically through the Recovery Act.

At the same time that we strive to contain costs, we cannot stand by as tens of millions of American lack health care coverage. An unhealthy workforce leads to an unhealthy economy, and moving to provide all Americans with health insurance is not only a moral imperative, but it is also essential to a more effective and efficient health care system.

The President has already begun the process of reforming health care by:

Instituting Temporary Provisions to Make Health Care Coverage More Affordable for Americans Who Have Lost Their Jobs. As part of the Recovery Act of 2009, the Administration will provide Americans who lose their jobs or have recently lost their jobs a tax credit to keep their health insurance through COBRA. These steps are estimated by the Joint Committee on Taxation to help provide coverage for approximately seven million Americans.

Increasing Health Care Coverage for Children. In one of his first official acts, the President signed into law the reauthorization of the Children's Health Insurance Program (CHIP)— bipartisan legislation vetoed twice by the previous President. It provides the support, options, and incentives for States to provide coverage for an additional four million children on average in CHIP and Medicaid who are now uninsured. The President is committed to implementing this law quickly and aggressively to help families whose children are at risk of losing coverage in this weak economy.

Computerizing America's Health Records in Five years. The current, paper-based medical records system that relies on patients' memory and reporting of their medical history is prone to error, time-consuming, costly, and wasteful. With rigorous privacy standards in place to protect sensitive medical record, we will embark on an effort to computerize all Americans' health records in five years. This effort will help prevent medical errors, and improve health care quality, and is a necessary step in starting to modernize the American health care system and reduce health care costs.

Developing and Disseminating information on Effective Medical interventions. Medicine is changing so rapidly it is almost impossible for any individual physician to keep abreast of all the latest research studies. Without the most recent information on effective treatments, it is increasingly more difficult for a doctor to give a patient the type of individualized treatment he or she deserves. Each month, for instance, nearly 500 articles are published on breast cancer alone. Despite this profusion of research, there are often gaps especially an absence of data that compares how well different diagnostic tests and treatments work for the very same conditions and diseases. To help physicians get the information they need to provide the highest quality care for patients, the Recovery Act of 2009 devotes $1.1 billion to comparative effectiveness research—the reviews of evidence on competing medical interventions and new head-to-head trials. The information from this research will improve the performance of the U.S. health care system.

Investing in Prevention and Wellness. Over a third of all illness is the result of poor diet, lack of exercise, and smoking. Indeed, obesity alone leads to many expensive, chronic conditions including high blood pressure, heart disease, diabetes, and even cancer. Furthermore, there are important vaccines that can prevent diseases, and screening tests that can detect cancer and other diseases at an early stage when they are more curable. Yet many Americans are not getting these effective interventions. For instance, according to the Centers for Disease Control and Prevention fewer than 75 percent of women get mammograms, and fewer than 50 percent of Americans receive any type of colon cancer screening. The President has devoted in the Recovery Act an unprecedented $1 billion for prevention and wellness interventions. This will dramatically expand community-based interventions proven to reduce chronic diseases.

These investments made in the Recovery Act will help, in the long-run, to slow health care cost growth which is the key driver of the Nation's overall long-term fiscal gap. Specifically, the investments in information technology will provide not only higher quality of care and less hassle for patients, but also the data necessary to examine what works and what doesn't—which, in turn, will be the focus of the research on effective medical interventions. The emphasis on prevention and wellness will help reduce the incidence of diseases and chronic conditions and lead to a healthier, more productive America. All in all, these investments will create the underpinnings of a more efficient health care system—one that delivers better care rather than just more care— and will put the Nation on a much sounder longterm fiscal path.

Transforming and Modernizing America's Health Care System

To build on these steps, the Budget sets aside a reserve fund of more than \$630 billion over 10 years that will be dedicated towards financing reforms to our health care system. The President recognizes that while a very large amount of money and a major commitment, \$630 billion is not sufficient to fully fund comprehensive reform. But this is a first crucial step in that effort, and he is committed to working with the Congress to find additional resources to devote to health care reform. The Administration will explore all serious ideas that, in a fiscally responsible manner, achieve the common goals of constraining costs, expanding access, and improving quality. This past year, for instance, the President proposed to use rescission of the high-income tax provisions. Others have proposed different ideas to finance expanded health coverage such as capping the tax exclusion for employer-sponsored health insurance, a value-added tax, or additional offsets in existing health care programs. To achieve these goals and finance reform, the President looks forward to working with the Congress over the coming year, and as he does, the President will adhere to the following set of eight principles:

- *Protect Families' Financial Health.* The plan must reduce the growing premiums and other costs American citizens and businesses pay for health care. People must be protected from bankruptcy due to catastrophic illness.
- *Make Health Coverage Affordable.* The plan must reduce high administrative costs, unnecessary tests and services, waste, and other inefficiencies that consume money with no added health benefits.
- *Aim for Universality.* The plan must put the United States on a clear path to cover all Americans.
- *Provide Portability of Coverage.* People should not be locked into their job just to secure health coverage, and no American should be denied coverage because of pre-existing conditions.
- *Guarantee Choice.* The plan should provide Americans a choice of health plans and physicians. They should have the option of keeping their employer-based health plan.
- *Invest in Prevention and Wellness.* The plan must invest in public health measures proven to reduce cost drivers in our system—such as obesity, sedentary lifestyles, and smoking—as well as guarantee access to proven preventive treatments.
- *'Improve Patient Safety and Quality Care.* The plan must ensure the implementation of proven patient safety measures and provide incentives for changes in the delivery system to reduce unnecessary variability in patient care. It must support the widespread use of health information technology and the development of data on the effectiveness of medical interventions to improve the quality of care delivered.
- *Maintain Long-Term Fiscal Sustainability.* The plan must pay for itself by reducing the level of cost growth, improving productivity, and dedicating additional sources of revenue.

Table 1. Reserve for Health Reform

$ in billions	2010	2011	2012	2013	2014	2010-14	2010-19
Federal Health Savings	-1.8	-5.1	-18.0	-24.5	-34.3	-83.7	-316.0
Aligning incentives toward quality	0.0	-0.4	-1.3	-1.7	-2.1	-5.4	-20.5
Promoting efficiency/accountability	-1.8	-4.3	-16.2	-22.2	-31.5	-75.9	-287.4
Encouraging shared responsibility	0.0	-0.4	-0.6	-0.7	-0.8	-2.4	-8.1
New Revenues		-11.1	-30.8	-33.5	-35.5	-110.8	-317.8
Subtotal: Reserve for Health Reform	-1.8	-16.2	-48.8	-58.0	-69.8	-194.6	-633.8
Additional resources and new benefits, to be determined with Congress							
Net Cost—Reserve Fund	0.0	0.0	0.0	0.0	0.0	0.0	0.0

Financing Health Care Reform. The reserve fund is financed by a combination of rebalancing the tax code so that the wealthiest pay more as well as specific health care savings in three areas: promoting efficiency and accountability, aligning incentives toward quality, and encouraging shared responsibility (see Table 1). Taken together, the health care savings would total $316 billion over 10 years while improving the quality and efficiency of health care, without negatively affecting the care Americans receive. These savings include:

- *Reducing Medicare Overpayments to Private Insurers Through Competitive Payments.* Under current law, Medicare overpays Medicare Advantage plans by 14 percent more on average than what Medicare spends for beneficiaries enrolled in the traditional feefor-service program. The Administration believes it's time to stop this waste and will replace the current mechanism to establish payments with a competitive system in which payments would be based upon an average of plans' bids submitted to Medicare. This would allow the market, not Medicare, to set the reimbursement limits, and save taxpayers more than $175 billion over 10 years, as well as reduce Part B premiums.
- *Reducing Drug Prices.* Prescription drug costs are high and rising, causing too many Americans to skip doses, split pills, or not take needed medication altogether. The Administration will accelerate access to make affordable generic biologic drugs available through the establishment of a workable regulatory, scientific, and legal pathway for generic versions of biologic drugs. In order to retain incentives for research and development for the innovation of breakthrough products, a period of exclusivity would be guaranteed for the original innovator product, which is generally consistent with the principles in the Hatch-Waxman law for traditional products. Additionally, brand biologic manufacturers would be prohibited from reformulating existing products into new products to restart the exclusivity process, a process known as "ever-greening." The Administration will prevent drug companies from blocking generic drugs from consumers by prohibiting anticompetitive agreements and collusion between brand name and generic drug manufacturers intended to keep generic drugs off the market. Finally, the Budget will bring down the drug costs of Medicaid by increasing the Medicaid drug rebate for brand-name drugs from 15.1 percent to 22.1 percent of the Average Manufacturer Price, apply the additional rebate to new drug formulations, and allow States to collect rebates on drugs

provided through Medicaid managed care organizations. All the savings would be devoted to the health care reserve fund.

- *Improving Medicare and Medicaid Payment Accuracy.* The Government Accountability Office (GAO) has labeled Medicare as "high- risk" due to billions of dollars lost to overpayments and fraud each year. The Centers for Medicare and Medicaid Services (CMS) will address vulnerabilities presented by Medicare and Medicaid, including Medicare Advantage and the prescription drug benefit (Part D). CMS will be able to respond more rapidly to emerging program integrity vulnerabilities across these programs through an increased capacity to identify excessive payments and new processes for identifying and correcting problems.
- *Improving Care after Hospitalizations and Reduce Hospital Readmission Rates.* Nearly 18 percent of hospitalization of Medicare beneficiaries resulted in the readmission of patients who had been discharged in the hospital within the last 30 days. Sometimes the readmission could not have been prevented, but many of these readmissions are avoidable. To improve this situation, hospitals will receive bundled payments that cover not just the hospitalization, but care from certain post-acute providers the 30 days after the hospitalization, and hospitals with high rates of readmission will be paid less if patients are re-admitted to the hospital within the same 30-day period. This combination of incentives and penalties should lead to better care after a hospital stay and result in fewer readmissions—saving roughly $26 billion of wasted money over 10 years. The money saved will also be contributed to the reserve fund for health care reform.
- *Expanding the Hospital Quality Improvement Program.* The health care system tends to pay for quantity of services not quality. Experts have recommended that hospitals and doctors be paid based on delivering high quality care, or what is called "pay for performance." The President's Budget will link a portion of Medicare payments for acute in-patient hospital services to hospitals' performance on specific quality measures. This program will improve the quality of care delivered to Medicare beneficiaries, and the higher quality will save over $12 billion over 10 years. Again, the money saved will be contributed to the Reserve Fund for health care reform.
- *Reforming the Physician Payment System to Improve Quality and Efficiency.* The Administration believes that the current physician payment system, while it has served to limit spending to a degree, needs to be reformed to give physicians incentives to improve quality and efficiency. Thus, while the baseline reflects our best estimate of what the Congress has done in recent years, we are not suggesting that should be the future policy. As part of health care reform, the Administration would support comprehensive, but fiscally responsible, reforms to the payment formula. The Administration believes Medicare and the country need to move toward a system in which doctors face better incentives for high-quality care rather than simply more care.
- *Reducing Itemized Deduction Rate for Families With Incomes Over $250,000.* Lowering health care costs and expanding health insurance coverage will require additional revenue. In the health reform policy discussions that have taken place over the past few years, a wide range of revenue options have been discussed—and these options are all worthy of serious discussion as the Administration works with the Congress to enact health care reform. The Administration's Budget includes a

proposal to limit the tax rate at which high-income taxpayers can take itemized deductions to 28 percent—and the initial reserve fund would be funded in part through this provision. This provision would raise $318 billion over 10 years.

Restoring America's Place in the World and Keeping America Safe

Just as a strong economy bolsters our standing in the world and enhances our national security, strong leadership in the world helps us thrive in an interdependent, global economy. The line between economic policy and foreign policy is now very hard to draw. In the past, our greatest threats came from distant countries with armies and navies who engaged us in direct battle. Now, our open, interdependent world that makes it so easy to do business, travel, or communicate with people from all over the globe also makes us vulnerable to new threats and security challenges. As we all learned on September 11th, a small band of terrorists has the ability to kill thousands of civilians who are just going about their lives. Dangerous weapons, including nuclear materials, could fall into the hands of terrorists. Programmers sitting in their local coffee shop could launch cyber-attacks on the Pentagon, the CIA, or key parts of our security infrastructure. A small nation thousands of miles away which slips into chaos and anarchy could become a failed state that incubates terrorists and regional conflict. An outbreak of a deadly infectious disease in a rural, undeveloped corner of the world can quickly make its way to our biggest cities.

America alone cannot defeat these threats, but neither can the world defeat them without America. That is why the Administration will invest in our Armed Forces and our wounded warriors to ease the burdens of two wars and multiple deployments, while also asking more of our allies in Afghanistan and elsewhere. And it is why the Administration will increase investments in other elements of our national power—like diplomacy, economic development, and education—so that we end the reliance on our military alone to defeat emerging threats. In addition, the Administration will make critical investments for America's veterans to make sure that they receive the funding and the care they deserve for defending this country.

Taken together, this will restore America's leadership role in the world after years of disregarding our allies and ignoring the values that have earned America respect the world over. Already, the President has pledged to close the detention facility at Guantanamo Bay, Cuba within a year and has overhauled detention and interrogation practices. He is committed to responsibly redeploying our combat brigades from Iraq while bringing all the elements of American power to bear on the threat posed by extremists from Afghanistan and Pakistan. The President will work with our allies to ensure that Iran lives up to its responsibilities to the world community, and rededicate America to the agreement at the heart of the Nuclear Nonproliferation Treaty to work toward a world without nuclear weapons while working over the next four years to lock down all loose fissile material.

These are big challenges, and while we recognize the perils we face, we must not forget that it is also a time of immense promise. We can rebuild our alliances and rally the world to tackle these truly transnational challenges, replace despair with hope, and keep America secure, prosperous, and free. To achieve these goals, we need to allocate our resources to reflect the reality of the threats we face today and do so in a way that limits waste. The Administration will:

Increase Funding for the Department of Defense (DOD). As we look to the challenges facing our Nation, it's imperative that we invest our defense dollars effectively and wisely. To that end, the President is committed to supporting the men and women who make our military the best in the world. He wants to increase the size of the Army and Marine Corps, improve the pay for our men and women in uniform, and improve the medical treatment of wounded servicemembers. At the same time, the President will pursue a reform of the acquisition process to make sure that funds are not being wasted on expensive and outdated weapon systems. To fund these efforts, the Administration requests for DOD an increase of $20.4 billion, or 4 percent, from the 2009 enacted level of $513.3 billion excluding funding in the Recovery Act. This funding increase allows DOD to address the President's highest priorities. In addition, the Administration will request sufficient funding to enable the Department to carry out the recommendations of the 2005 Defense Base Closure and Realignment Commission and meet the mandated September 2011 implementation deadline, which will help to align DOD's domestic bases and medical facilities with operational needs—and will go a long way to preventing the mistreatment reported at Walter Reed Army Medical Center over the past few years.

Responsibly Remove Combat Forces From Iraq and Focus on the Fight in Afghanistan. The Budget recognizes and funds the President's strategy to increase our resources in Afghanistan while responsibly removing combat brigades from Iraq. To address the costs of military operations in Iraq and Afghanistan, the Administration requests $75.5 billion for the remainder of 2009 and $130 billion for 2010. The Administration will provide the details of the 2009 supplemental appropriations request to the Congress in the next few weeks, and will transmit the detailed 2010 request with the President's 2010 Budget.

Increase the Size of the Army and Marine Corps. While the best technology and up-to-date equipment are important to maintaining the predominance of our military, our Armed Forces ultimately rely on the commitment and skill of the men and women who wear its uniform. Recognizing this, the Budget supports additional permanent forces in the Army and Marine Corps, which will increase to 547,400 and 202,000, respectively, by the end of 2010. This growth is two years ahead of schedule and will reduce stress on servicemembers and their families, while providing heightened readiness for a full spectrum of military operations anywhere in the world.

Increase Pay for Men and Women in uniform. After years of asking more and more from our troops and their families, this Budget reflects the priorities of an Administration that is committed to caring for the servicemembers who protect our security and the families who support them. The Budget includes funding for a 2.9 percent pay raise for men and women in uniform, an amount that will improve their purchasing power.

Improve Mental Health Care for Soldiers and veterans. The Budget funds expanded efforts at DOD to address mental health needs. Post-traumatic stress disorder, traumatic brain injury (TBI) and associated ailments are, and will continue to be, key military medical challenges facing the Armed Forces for years to come. DOD will fully implement a comprehensive TBI registry including a single point of responsibility to track incidents and recovery. The armed services will expand the number of integrated mental health professionals with their deployed units to better channel medical attention to those who need help quickly. In addition, the National Intrepid Center of Excellence for Psychological Health and TBI will be dedicated in the late fall of 2009. This will serve as the clinical research and educational arm of DOD's Center of Excellence for psychological health and TBI. The Budget expands the mental health screening and treatment services offered by the Department of Veterans Affairs (VA) and focuses on reaching veterans in rural areas. The VA also will increase the number of Vet Centers and mobile health clinics to expand access to mental health screening and treatment in rural areas. In addition, new funding ensures that veterans and their families are informed of these resources and are encouraged to pursue needed care.

Reform Defense Department Acquisition. When it comes to the defense of our Nation, it's critical that every dollar is spent in the most effective way possible. Funds need to be allocated in ways that take into the account the needs of today as well as the threats of tomorrow. Moreover, we must make sure that the men and women who serve our Nation in its defense have the training, resources, material, and support they need to do the job. We know that DOD's new weapons programs are among the largest, most expensive, and technically difficult that the Department has ever tried to develop. Consequently, they carry a high risk of performance failure, cost increases, and schedule delays. With this in mind, the Administration is committed to reforming the defense acquisition process so that taxpayer dollars are not wasted. The Administration will set realistic requirements and stick to them and incorporate "best practices" by not allowing programs to proceed from one stage of the acquisition cycle to the next until they have achieved the maturity to significantly lower the risk of cost growth and schedule slippage.

Put the United States on a Path to Double Foreign Assistance. It has become clear over the past decade that all the elements of American power must be developed to protect our people, interests, and values. That is why the Administration is committed to placing the Nation on a path to double foreign assistance to $50 billion. Doing so, the United States will reach out to the global community, lay the groundwork for stability and security at home and abroad, and strengthen its role as a leader in global development and diplomacy. These are important investments that will help bring stability to other parts of the globe and greater security for our Nation. Through increased foreign assistance funding, the United States will embark on several new initiatives that will give children in the poorest countries access to education; foster global food security through sustainable agriculture; expand goodwill and inspire service by increasing the size of the Peace Corps; and help stabilize post- conflict states, creating room for them to plant the seeds of democracy.

Expand the Size of the Foreign Service. To face the threats of the 21st Century, we need to use all the instruments of our power, including diplomacy, to ensure the safety and security of the United States. The 2010 Budget includes funding for the first year of a multi-year effort to significantly increase the size of the Foreign Service at both the Department of State and the U.S. Agency for International Development (USAID). An increased cadre of State and USAID Foreign Service officers will help advance our critical foreign policy goals and deliver on our expanding U.S. foreign assistance commitments.

Increase Funding for Global Health Programs. Boosting the quality of health around the world is not only a moral consideration; it is also in the country's interest as pandemics and poor health care can destabilize whole regions as well as travel around the globe. In the Budget, the United States will continue to build on its commitment to save lives through increasing investments in global health programs, including in areas such as maternal and child health, family planning and other core health programs, while also emphasizing a commitment to HIV/ AIDS, malaria, and tuberculosis through successful programs such as the President's Emergency Plan for AIDS Relief and the Malaria Initiative. In addition, together with our multilateral partners, the Administration will continue to provide global leadership to improve the health status of the world's poorest populations.

Reinvigorate Counter-Proliferation, Anti- Terrorism, and Transnational Crime-Fighting Efforts. The Budget will fund reinvigorated efforts to counter nuclear proliferation, terrorism, and transnational crime. Specifically, the Budget includes first-year funding for a multi-year counterterrorism and law enforcement assistance program that strengthens the capabilities of our international partners in the Western Hemisphere and other critical regions around the world. The Budget also provides additional nonproliferation and counter-proliferation funding to help secure nuclear materials and promote safe civilian uses of nuclear energy.

Meet Our Challenges in Afghanistan, Pakistan, and Iraq. The 2010 Budget refocuses U.S. resources toward addressing the resurgence of al Qaeda and the Taliban in Afghanistan and Pakistan. The Administration increases non-military assistance to both countries, providing additional funding for governance, reconstruction, counter- narcotics, and other development activities that will help counter extremists. It expands the number of civilian personnel in Afghanistan and Pakistan in an effort to stabilize strategic areas of the countries, build government capacity, and successfully manage expanded assistance programs. In Iraq, the Administration strengthens our assistance to those who have been displaced from their homes because of the war, and realigns our assistance efforts in Iraq to ensure that Iraqis can assume more responsibility for their own political and economic future.

Boost Compensation to Disabled Military Retirees. The Budget contains a proposal to expand concurrent receipt of military retired pay and Veterans Disability Compensation to retirees who were medically retired from active service. Under current law, these benefits are offset. Disabled military retirees would receive significantly greater compensation when the offset is removed.

Improve the Quality of Life for Our Armed Forces. The Administration is committed to improving the quality of life for American military personnel. Therefore, the Budget continues to sustain and modernize barracks and dormitories housing service members around the world and works to end all inadequate housing for military families. It provides funds to build or renovate base facilities at a rate sufficient to ensure the safety and functionality of all structures while meeting the needs of users.

Care for Wounded, ill, and injured Servicemembers. DOD will continue its efforts to improve the medical care and housing for wounded, ill, and injured servicemembers. DOD will add 21 more Warrior in Transition Complexes at posts throughout the continental United States, as well as sites in Alaska, Hawaii and Germany. DOD and the VA will expand pilot programs to expedite processing of injured troops through the Disability Evaluation System. The expedited system substantially reduces the time required to determine disability rating and, more importantly, alleviates frustration caused by a needlessly complex process.

Increase Funding for vA by $25 Billion Over the Next Five years. The President's Budget increases funding for VA by $25 billion over the next five years in order to honor our Nation's veterans and expand the services they receive. Some of these funds will be used to transform VA into a 21st Century organization, including investments in information technology that directly benefit veterans in the areas of both health care and benefits. Through improved electronic medical records, VA will more efficiently retrieve active duty health records from DOD and enable all VA care sites to access the records of veterans needing care. The VA will also invest in the development of rules-based electronic processes to increase accuracy, consistency, and timeliness in veterans' receipt of benefits.

Dramatically Increase Funding for VA Health Care. The President's Budget funds VA medical care with the resources it needs to provide 5.5 million veterans with timely and high quality care. This funding also enables VA to create Centers of Excellence for hearing and vision impairment and to provide additional veteran- oriented specialty care in areas including prosthetics, spinal cord injury, aging, and women's health.

Restore Health Care Eligibility for Modest-Income Veterans. For the first time since January 2003, the President's Budget restores eligibility for VA health care to non-disabled veterans earning modest incomes. By 2013, this initiative will bring over 500,000 additional veterans into the VA health care system while maintaining high quality and timely care for the lower-income and disabled veterans who currently rely on VA medical care.

Combat Homelessness by Safeguarding vulnerable veterans. The Administration expands VA's current services to homeless veterans through a collaborative pilot program with non-profit organizations. This pilot will help maintain stable housing for veterans who are at risk of falling into homelessness while helping VA to continue providing them with supportive services.

Facilitate Timely Implementation of the Comprehensive Education Benefits Veterans Earn Through Their Dedicated Service. This Budget supports VA's prompt, accurate, and efficient implementation of the Post-9/11 GI Bill-providing unprecedented levels of educational assistance to the men and women who have served our country through active military duty.

Changing the Way Washington Does Business

Just as important as changing what Washington does is to change how it does it. We cannot begin to tackle the challenges we face in the short term to revive our economy and in the long term to put us on the path to growth without restoring responsibility and accountability to Government. Being entrusted with Americans' tax dollars is a huge responsibility, and for far too long, there has been insufficient regard for how those funds are spent; a high tolerance of waste, fraud, and abuse; and a passive acceptance of inefficiencies and ineffectiveness. Changing this will take time, and in the few weeks that the Administration has been in office, it has started that lengthy process.

Restoring Fiscal Discipline and Planning for the Future

Over the past eight years, fiscal recklessness replaced fiscal responsibility. Huge tax cuts and spending increases were undertaken without being paid for. Large extra-budgetary expenses put a veneer on our fiscal situation. Special interest- driven spending grew out of control. Long-term challenges to our country and our fiscal situation were ignored. Taken together, this has put the Nation in an even more precarious fiscal position as we confront this economic crisis. In light of this inheritance of irresponsibility, the Administration in its first weeks has taken the initial steps to restore fiscal discipline by requesting and signing into law an economic recovery bill that is free of all earmarks and by instituting a system whereby the public will be able to track how and where recovery funds are actually used. To continue this progress in the months and years ahead, the Administration will:

Cut the Deficit in Half by End of the President's First Term. The current economic crisis has resulted in a $1 trillion a year gap between what the economy can produce and what it is actually producing. With all the monetary policy levers already employed, the Government had to step in to stimulate the economy and avoid an economic catastrophe. While the Recovery Act has entailed increasing deficit spending—since that is the fastest and surest way to create jobs in a recession—we cannot see this as a new norm. It is an extraordinary response to an extraordinary crisis. So while this Budget will add to our national deficit in the short-term, the President is committed to cutting in half by the end of his first term in office the deficit he inherited on January 20, 2009.

Review the Budget Line-By-Line for Waste. The President believes that we should be investing taxpayer dollars in efforts and programs with proven records of success and reallocating or cutting programs that do not work or whose benefits are not worth their cost. To this end, the Administration has begun an exhaustive line-by-line review of the Federal Budget, the first stage of which will be partially reflected in the spring release of the full Fy 2010 Budget and will continue in subsequent years. However, already the Administration has identified cuts and savings that include:

- *Increasing Federal Health Savings.* As discussed in detail above, the President is proposing substantial savings in health care by aligning incentives toward quality, promoting efficiency, and encouraging responsibility.
- *Eliminating Cotton Storage Credits.* The President's Budget proposes to eliminate the requirement for the Government to pay the storage costs of cotton that is put under loan with USDA. Cotton is the only commodity for which this assistance is provided without exception. Storage credits for cotton have been found to have a negative impact on the amount of cotton on the market. Because cotton storage is

covered by the Government, producers may store their cotton for longer than necessary. There is no reason the Government should be paying for the storage of cotton, particularly since it does not provide this assistance for most other commodities.

- *Eliminating Mine Clean-Up Payments to States that Have Completed Clean-Up.* Abandoned Mine Lands (AML) payments from the Office of Surface Mining are made to States with abandoned coal mines requiring clean up. These AML payments were originally intended to be used only for clean-up efforts. In 2006, a provision was added that provided payments, available for unrestricted use, for States that have completed clean-up of all of their abandoned coal mines. This proposal would eliminate these unrestricted payments to States that have completed cleanup, saving close to $200 million in 2014.
- *Eliminating the Resource Conservation and Development (RC&D) Program.* The Budget eliminates funding for RC&D. First begun in 1962, the program was intended to build community leadership skills through the establishment of RC&D councils that would access Federal, State and local programs for the community's benefit. After 47 years, this goal has been accomplished. These councils have developed sufficiently strong State and local ties that the Administration believes they are now able to secure funding for their continued operation without Federal assistance.
- *Reforming the Market Access Program (MAP).* The Budget reforms MAP by reducing program funding for overseas brand promotion and minimizes the benefits that large for-profit entities may indirectly gain as members of trade associations who participate in MAP. An annual funding reduction of 20 percent will improve the program by placing greater emphasis on promoting generic American agricultural products overseas and assisting small business entities.
- *Reducing Direct Payments to Farmers.* The President wants to maintain a strong safety net for farm families and beginning farmers while encouraging fiscal responsibility. As part of a broad effort to move farmers from a program of direct payments to a program where agricultural producers earn payments from environmental improvements, the President's Budget phases out direct payments over three years to farmers with sales revenue of more than $500,000 annually. Presently, direct payments are made to even large producers regardless of crop prices, in-come, and profits or whether the land is still farmed.
- *Increasing Collection of Delinquent Tax From Federal Contractors.* Federal contractors owe billions of dollars in unpaid Federal taxes. IRS currently collects some of this debt by levying Federal payments made to these debtors. In some cases, administrative procedures prevent IRS from collecting this debt. In fact, IRS loses the opportunity to collect approximately $114 million per year in tax debt because of administrative delays. The Budget proposes to address this problem by streamlining administrative processes in order to make it easier for IRS to collect tax debt owed by Federal contractors.
- *Eliminating or Reforming Small, Ineffective Housing and Urban Development Programs.* Programs that are either ineffective or duplicative divert us from achieving their ultimate policy goals and are a waste of taxpayer dollars. The Administration proposes eliminating a list of programs that includes: the American Dream Downpayment Initiative, which is too small to operate effectively and the Community

Development Loan Guarantee program, which is not structured effectively to encourage communities to finance large-scale development; plus reform the Rural Housing and Economic Development program so that it is not duplicative of similar USDA programs.

- *Eliminating Education Programs With Records of Low Performance.* When it comes to educating our children, we cannot afford to waste a dollar. The Administration proposes to immediately terminate, or intensively review with an expectation of overhauling or terminating, a series of small Education Department programs. Many of these programs have long provided funding for narrowly focused curricula, staffing choices, or school types. None has strong evidence to justify this support; the programs either have never been seriously evaluated or have received weak evaluations; and the programs often could be funded in competitive funding streams that could require evidence of results.

Return to Honest Budgeting. Too often in the past several years, budget tricks were used to make the Government's books seem stronger than they actually were. If this Budget used the gimmicks employed in recent budgets, it would show in excess of another $250 billion annually in available funds each year, and a bottom line that would appear approximately $2.6 trillion better over 10 years. Pretending that the Budget has this money available may be gratifying, but it's an accounting sleight-of-hand, not reality. We should not tolerate these kinds of tricks when it comes to accounting for the public's tax dollars. This Budget, therefore, provides a projected cost for the wars in Iraq and Afghanistan; does not assume that all of the 2001 and 2003 tax legislation magically disappears at the end of 2010; does not allow the alternative minimum tax to take over the tax code, which almost every observer agrees is unrealistic; recognizes the statistical likelihood of natural disasters instead of assuming that there will be no disasters over the next decade; includes a contingent reserve as a placeholder in case further legislative action becomes necessary to stabilize the financial system; and provides a 10- year rather than a 5-year look into our fiscal situation.

Account for future Emergencies. One can never know what kind of disaster or unexpected emergency may occur that will require the help of the Federal Government. If we do not account for these costs as we project the Federal Government's future fiscal health, we run the risk of allowing these unforeseen events to cause even more economic pain and derail our long-term growth. In the past, budgets assumed that there would not be any natural disasters in our Nation that would necessitate Federal help—no major earthquakes, hurricanes, floods, or man-made disasters. This omission is irresponsible, and has permitted past Administrations to project deficits that were lower than were likely to occur. Breaking with past practice, the President's Budget puts more than $20 billion annually (the statistical probability of the costs of dealing with these emergencies) in its budget projections.

Return to Pay-As-you-Go Budgeting. While the economic crisis we have inherited is a once-in-a-generation meltdown, it should not be seen as an opportunity to abandon the fiscal discipline that we owe each and every taxpayer in spending their money. This discipline is critical to keeping the United States strong in a global, interdependent economy. Moving forward, we need to return to pay-as-you-go budgeting that we had in the 1990s for all non-emergency measures. The President and his economic team look forward to working with the

Congress to develop budget enforcement rules that are based on the tools that helped create the surpluses of a decade ago, including statutory pay-as-you-go rules.

Create a Reserve for financial Stabilization Efforts. The Nation has inherited deep problems in its financial system. Additional action is likely to be necessary to stabilize the financial system and thereby facilitate economic growth. Although the Administration is not requesting additional funds from the Congress at this point and although it is not yet possible to provide a precise estimate of how much additional Federal action may be involved should the Administration need to request such funds, the President's Budget nonetheless includes a $250 billion contingent reserve for further efforts to stabilize the financial system. The approach for this financial stabilization reserve is similar in spirit to the one adopted with regard to future war costs; the Budget includes a placeholder for future war costs even though such costs if any are difficult to predict. Estimates of the value of the financial assets acquired by the Federal Government to date suggest that the Government will get back approximately two-thirds of the money spent purchasing such assets—so the net cost to the Government is roughly 33 cents on the dollar. These transactions are typically reflected in the budget at this net cost, since that budgetary approach best reflects their impact on the Government's underlying fiscal position. The figure recorded in this Budget as a placeholder similarly reflects this net cost concept. The $250 billion reserve would support $750 billion in asset purchases.

The existence of this reserve in the Budget does not represent a specific request. Rather as events warrant, the Administration will work with the Congress to determine the appropriate size and shape of such efforts, and as more information becomes available the Administration will define an estimate of potential costs. In addition, should a request become necessary, the Administration is committed to working with the Congress so that to the maximum extent possible, taxpayers are paid back over time for any additional emergency assistance provided to the financial system. The compensation to taxpayers could include requiring dividend payments, warrants, equity and other forms of upside opportunities from those firms receiving assistance. The compensation could also include a fee or assessment on financial institutions or financial activity, which would have to commence only when the financial system had stabilized and which would be designed to minimize adverse effects on the long-term recovery of our financial system.

Limit Pay increases in the Federal Workforce. As families are tightening their belts in this economic crisis across the country, the President ordered a freeze of White House senior staff pay. In this Budget, Federal employees also will be asked to do their part: the 2010 pay increase for Federal civilian employees, 2.0 percent, is responsive to the current economic climate, bringing Federal pay and benefit practices more in line with the private sector.

Making Saving for Retirement Easier as the Economy Recovers. Over the long-term families need personal savings, in addition to Social Security, to prepare for retirement and to fall back on during tough economic times like these. However, 75 million working Americans— roughly half the workforce—currently lack access to employer-based retirement plans. In addition, the existing incentives to save for retirement are weak or non-existent for the majority of middle- and low-income households. The President's 2010 Budget lays the groundwork for the future establishment of a system of automatic workplace pensions, on top of and clearly outside Social Security, that is expected to dramatically increase both the number of Americans who save for retirement and the overall amount of personal savings for individuals. Research has shown that the key to saving is to make it automatic and simple. Under this proposal, employees will be automatically enrolled in workplace pension plans—and will be allowed to opt out if they choose. Employers who do not currently offer a retirement plan will be required to enroll their employees in a direct-deposit IRA account that is compatible with existing direct-deposit payroll systems. The result will be that workers will be automatically enrolled in some form of savings vehicle when they go to work—making it easy for them to save while also allowing them to opt out if their family or individual circumstances make it particularly difficult or unwise to save. Experts estimate that this program will dramatically increase the savings participation rate for low and middle-income workers to around 80 percent.

Creating a More Ethical and Transparent Government and Improving Oversight

Washington cannot be responsive to the American people if the doors of Government are shut to everyone except those with lobbyists and influence. An unresponsive Government not only offends our democratic sensibilities; it also leads to disastrous policy outcomes—initiatives and programs that are constructed to serve a select few and not the public interest.

That is why in his first days in office, the President signed an executive order that: prohibits executive branch employees from accepting gifts from lobbyists; closes the revolving door that allows Government officials to move to and from private sector jobs in ways that give that sector undue influence over Government; and requires that Government hiring be based upon qualifications, competence, and experience—not political connections. The President has ordered every one of his appointees to sign a pledge abiding by these tough new rules as a down payment on the change he has promised to bring to Washington. In three separate Presidential Memoranda, the President instructed all members of his Administration to operate under principles of openness, transparency, and of engaging citizens with their Government; and ended the practice of having others besides the President assert executive privilege for records after an administration ends.

Building on his career working for a more ethical and transparent Government, the President will:

Shine a Bright Light on Washington Lobbying. The Administration will take steps to make sure that the public has specific, useful, and meaningful information about how lobbyists are trying to influence Federal spending and tax policy. A centralized, online database will contain lobbying reports, disclose how much money Federal contractors are spending on lobbying, and provide other relevant information.

Let Americans Track How Their Tax Dollars Are Spent. Americans have a right to know how the Government spends their tax dollars, but that information is usually hard to find and often not made available at all. The President is committed to changing that by making this data easy to find and review. He will:

- Maintain Recovery.gov, an unprecedented effort to bring transparency and accountability to the money spent in the American Recovery and Reinvestment Act.

This site will allow taxpayers learn where recovery funds are going, for what purpose, and to what result.

- Give the public five days to review all non- emergency bills before they are signed into law.
- Disclose each earmark and the name of the legislator who asked for each earmark, and make this information available on a searchable public website.
- Clean up military contracting by establishing the reporting requirements, accounting, and accountability needed for good gover-nance and cost savings, and by scrutinizing no-bid contracting.

Increase Transparency in Earmarks. From 1994 until 2006, the cost and number of Congressional earmarks expanded dramatically, raising concerns that lawmakers were funneling Federal money home to projects that may not be the best use of taxpayer dollars. In 2007 and 2008, the Congress took important steps to shine light on the allocation of congressional earmarks by requiring members' names to be listed next to requests funded in appropriations bills and reports, while also reducing the total funding for earmarks. However, more work needs to be done. The Administration will continue to work with the Congress to provide greater transparency and accountability of earmarks, and to ensure that the American people are made well aware of how and where Federal money is spent.

Bolster Oversight of the Financial Markets. Robust markets depend on clear rules of the road enforced by strong, impartial regulators. This past year, the consequences of poor market oversight became abundantly clear. The Budget, therefore, will increase resources for the Securities and Exchange Commission (SEC) by over 13 percent and the Commodity Futures Trading Commission (CFTC) by over 44 percent relative to 2008 levels. In 2010, the SEC will build its staff and technology resources and pursue a risk-based, efficient regulatory structure that will better detect fraud and strengthen markets. The CFTC will implement new program responsibilities promulgated in the Farm Bill—filling gaps in regulatory oversight of energy and over- the-counter derivatives trading, as well as foreign exchange.

Making Government More Effective

For decades, the argument in Washington has been between those who say that government is the cause of every problem and those who say that it's the answer. What has become clear over the past eight years, especially in light of the Federal Government's response to Hurricane Katrina, is that what bothers Americans is bad government—government that does not to do its job effectively and efficiently. To make Government more effective, the Administration will:

Eliminate Wasteful Redundancy. Too often, Federal departments take on functions or services that are already being done or could be done elsewhere within the Federal Government more effectively. The result is unnecessary redundancy and the inability of the Government to benefit from economies of scale and integrated, streamlined operations. The Administration will conduct an immediate and periodic public inventory of administrative offices and functions and require agency leaders to work together to root out redundancy.

Where consolidation is not the right strategy to improve efficiency, the Administration will improve information-sharing and use of common assets to minimize wasteful duplication.

Streamline Government Procurement. The President will implement the GAO's recommendations to reduce erroneous Federal payments, reduce procurement costs with purchase cards, and implement better management of surplus Federal property.

Reform Federal Contracting and Acquisition. The Administration will take several steps to make sure that taxpayers get the best deal possible for Government expenditures. We will review the use of sole source, cost-type contracts; improve the quality of the acquisition workforce; and use technology to create transparency around contracting. We will review acquisition programs that are on the GAO high-risk list for being over- budget and prone to abuse. The Administration also will clarify what is inherently a governmental function and what is a commercial one; critical Government functions will not be performed by the private sector for purely ideological reasons.

Put Performance First. The President is creating a focused team within the White House that will work with agency leaders and the Office of Management and Budget (OMB) to improve results and outcomes for Federal Government programs while eliminating waste and inefficiency. This unit will be composed of top-performing and highly-trained Government professionals and will be headed by a new Chief Performance Officer (CPO). The CPO will work with Federal agencies to set tough performance targets and hold managers responsible for progress. The President will meet regularly with cabinet officers to review the progress their agencies are making toward meeting performance improvement targets.

Enforce Standards in Addition to Measuring Performance. The Administration will fundamentally reconfigure the Program Assessment Rating Tool. We will open up the insular performance measurement process to the public, the Congress and outside experts. The Administration will eliminate ideological performance goals and replace them with goals Americans care about and that are based on congressional intent and feedback from the people served by Government programs. Programs will not be measured in isolation, but assessed in the context of other programs that are serving the same population or meeting the same goals.

Table 2. Program Integrity Savings from Increased Investment in Years 2010 through 2014

(in billions of dollars)	2011	2012	2013	2014	2010-2014	2010-2019
SSA	–1.7	–2.5	–3.4	–4.4	–12.1	–27.9
HHS	–0.5	–0.5	–0.6	–0.6	–2.7	–2.7
UI	–0.2	–0.2	–0.3	–0.3	–1.1	–1.2
IRS	–1.1	–2.3	–3.9	–5.7	–13.3	–16.6
Total Savings	**–3.5**	**–5.6**	**–8.1**	**–11.0**	**–29.2**	**–48.5**

Increased revenue due to IRS enforcement funding is shown as a negative for consistency. Numbers may not add to totals due to rounding.

Increase Use of Technology. Meeting 21st Century challenges will require a Government that leverages 21st Century technologies and keeps up with the private sector. The President will appoint the Nation's first Chief Technology Officer (CTO) to ensure that our Government and all its agencies have the right infrastructure, policies and services for the 21st Century. The CTO will work with each of the Federal agencies, to ensure that they use best-in-class technologies and share best practices.

Make Sure that Taxpayer Dollars Are Spent Wisely in Our Large Entitlement Programs. With billions of dollars being spent in programs such as Social Security, Medicare, and Medicaid upon which so many Americans rely, it is important that they are run efficiently and effectively. The Administration will make significant investments in activities to ensure that taxpayer dollars will be spent correctly, expanding oversight activities in the largest benefit programs and increasing investments in tax compliance and enforcement activities.

The Administration proposes a significant increase in program integrity activities at the Social Security Administration (SSA), the Department of Health and Human Services (HHS), the Department of Labor (DOL), and the Internal Revenue Service (IRS). The Administration proposes a multi-year strategy, which will permit the agencies to pay closer attention to the risk of improper payments, commensurate with the large and growing costs of the programs administered by these agencies, including Social Security, Medicare, Medicaid, and Unemployment Insurance (UI). As an example, the funding provided for SSA will enable the agency to work down a backlog of Continuing Disability Reviews, which determine whether an individual continues to qualify for Disability Insurance or Supplemental Security Income. The number of these reviews has fallen in recent years even as the Disability Insurance program has grown.

There is solid and rigorous evidence that these investments can significantly decrease the rate of improper payments and recoup many times their initial investment. For every $1 spent by SSA on a disability review, $11 is saved in erroneous payments. Similarly, for every $1 spent by HHS to fight health care fraud, approximately $1.60 is saved or averted, and the IrS activities recoup $5 for every $1 spent. As shown in Table 2, the initial five-year investment of $13.5 billion for 2010 through 2014 is estimated to result in nearly $50 billion in lower spending and additional tax revenue over the next 10 years, with additional savings accruing after the 10-year period.

In addition to the initiatives described above, the Administration will launch a new Federal-State partnership to reduce error and improper payments in Federal means-tested programs administered by States. Many State- administered programs—such as Medicaid and the Supplemental Nutrition Assistance Program (formerly Food Stamps)—operate independently of each other yet serve similar low-income populations. Integrating and modernizing processes will provide opportunities to improve services to beneficiaries, improve eligibility determination, and reduce errors. Through this initiative, the Federal Government will collaborate with States to identify the most promising approaches and fund development and rigorous testing to determine which ones have a high return on investment that could be replicated on a broader scale. OMB will oversee the development of rigorous methodologies for measuring the potential savings from these investments, including both administrative efficiency gains and reductions in erroneous payments. No projects would be funded unless they demonstrate their potential to result in more than one dollar in administrative and program savings for each dollar invested once the project is fully in effect. The results of the pilots will be reported to the Congress and used to inform administrative and legislative policies for achieving programmatic savings in future years.

Budget Mechanism for Improving Program Integrity

The Administration proposes to protect the dollars requested for these activities in the appropriations process through allocation adjustments, a mechanism that has been used by past administrations and Congresses. Allocation adjustments are increases in the ceiling or allocation for annual appropriations, but these increases are granted only if appropriations bills increase funding for the specified programs integrity purposes above specified base levels. This budget mechanism will ensure that this funding will not supplant other Federal spending on these activities or be diverted to other purposes. The base level of funding assumed in each appropriations request and the allocation adjustment for each agency is listed in the table.

Table 3. Program Integrity Allocation Adjustment Requests (budget authority in millions of dollars)

		2010	2011	2012	2013	2014	2010-2014
SSA Program Integrity	Base	273					
	Allocation adjustment	485	722	837	1,020	1,225	4,289
HHS Health Care Fraud and Abuse Control Program	Base (mandatory)	1,179					
	Allocation adjustment	311	327	343	361	381	1,723
DOL Unemployment Insurance Improper Payments	Base	10					
	Allocation adjustment	50	55	60	65	70	300
IRS Enforcement	Base	7,100*					
	Allocation adjustment	890	1,115	1,357	1,724	2,105	7,191
Federal-State Partnership	Allocation adjustment	175					175
Total Allocation Adjustment Request		1,911	2,219	2,597	3,170	3,781	13,678

* The IRS enforcement base total should be considered a placeholder pending final approval and will be updated in subsequent Budget documents.

CONCLUSION

At this moment of economic crisis and uncertainty, our country is being tested. We can continue the irresponsible ways of the past and pretend that our problems are not there. We can put off for tomorrow what must be done today. And we can just concern ourselves with ourselves—pursuing profits without any regard for principles. Or we can take a new path, usher in a new era of responsibility, and renew America's promise. We can jumpstart our economy and create or save millions of jobs. We can invest now to address the long-term drags on our economic competitiveness. And we can create a government that is open and responsive to the people it serves.

Especially now, this may seem like a difficult course to take. But it is precisely in these tough times that America has always come through. Through Depressions and disasters, world wars and the Cold War, our Nation has turned moments of adversity into opportunities of great progress. Once again, we face such a moment, and it is up to each of us to roll up our sleeves and show, once again, that we are equal to the task at hand; that we are committed to the hard work of getting America moving again.

This Budget lays out a plan for our Nation to get back on its feet and restore our competitiveness in this new century. It details how we are going to steer the United States out of this deep recession, and begins laying the groundwork for long-term growth. It makes overdue investments in improving our schools and opening up opportunities to learn for all our children. It explains how we are going to build the infrastructure upon which our entrepreneurs and inventors will build the industries and create the jobs of tomorrow. The Budget includes a bold commitment to improving our health care system and reforming it so that it no longer is a weight on our economy. recognizing how critical it is to tackle climate change as well as the immense opportunity that investments in clean energy technology present to our economy, the Budget invests in this promising sector. Finally, the Budget reflects how important it is that we keep our people safe and keep America leading in the world, with investments in our armed services and international capabilities.

This Budget also reflects the belief that Americans deserve a government that is open, honest, and accountable. New transparency and program integrity initiatives will be started that will open the doors of the Government to the public and help make sure that taxpayer dollars are spent wisely and carefully. Moreover, the Budget itself does not use budget gimmicks or accounting sleights-of-hand to hide our plans or the status of our economy. It is forthright in the challenges we face and the sacrifices we must make. It is honest in evaluating what programs work and which do not; shifting resources from the latter to the former.

Overcoming the problems we have inherited will not be completed in one budget, in one month, or in one year. It will take months and years of ingenuity and innovation, courage and commitment. It will take all Americans, including those in Washington and beyond living up to the responsibilities we have to each other as neighbors and citizens. But if we come together and pull together, there is little doubt that America will be growing, innovating, and creating jobs for generations to come.

DEPARTMENT OF AGRICULTURE

Funding Highlights

- Provides over $20 billion in loans and grants to support and expand rural development activities, including small businesses, renewable energy, and telecommunications.
- Includes a $50 million increase to address deferred maintenance on the most critical health and safety infrastructure within our national forests.
- Supports the implementation of a $250,000[1] commodity program payment limit. The payment limit will help ensure that payments are made to those who most need them.
- Reflects the President's commitment to wildfire management and community protection by fully funding suppression costs at the 10-year average, establishing a discretionary contingent reserve for wildfires, and including program reforms to ensure fire management resources are focused where they will do the most good.
- Fully funds the Special Supplemental Nutrition Program for Women, Infants, and Children (WIC) to serve all eligible individuals.
- Includes $1 billion per year for the Child Nutrition reauthorization.
- Supports a pilot program to help increase senior participation in the Supplemental Nutrition Assistance Program.
- Reflects the President's commitment to supporting independent producers through improved enforcement of the Packers and Stockyards Act and investing in the full diversity of agricultural production, including organic farming and local food systems.
- Reflects the President's commitment to fiscal responsibility by reducing direct payments to the largest farmers, reducing crop insurance subsidies, eliminating cotton storage credits, eliminating funding for the Resource Conservation and Development program, and reducing program funding for overseas brand promotion.

[1] This page corrects an amount erroneously included in the printed version of *A New Era of Responsibility*.

The United States Department of Agriculture (USDA) provides leadership on food, agriculture, natural resources, and related issues based on sound public policy, the best available science, and efficient management. USDA focuses on further developing alternative markets for agricultural products and activities, providing financing needed to help expand job opportunities and improve housing, utilities and infrastructure in rural America, enhancing food safety by taking steps to reduce the prevalence of foodborne hazards from farm to table, improving nutrition and health by providing food assistance and nutrition education and promotion, supporting international agricultural and economic development, and managing and protecting America's public and private lands working cooperatively with other levels of government and the private sector. This Budget provides $26 billion in discretionary budget authority to support this mission.

Supports Strong Farm and Rural Economic Development. The president's Budget targets farm programs to family farmers and provides the stability and predictability they need. The Budget will also provide American farmers with protection from market disruptions and weather disasters. At the same time, program effectiveness will be improved through restrictions on commodity payments to wealthy farmers. The president supports the implementation of a $250,000[1] commodity program payment limit, which will help ensure that payments are made only to those that most need them. To spur the development of small business and value-added agriculture in rural America, the president's Budget provides $61 million for five Rural Development programs: the rural microentrepreneur assistance program, rural cooperative development grants, value-added producer grants, grants to minority producers, and cooperative research agreements.

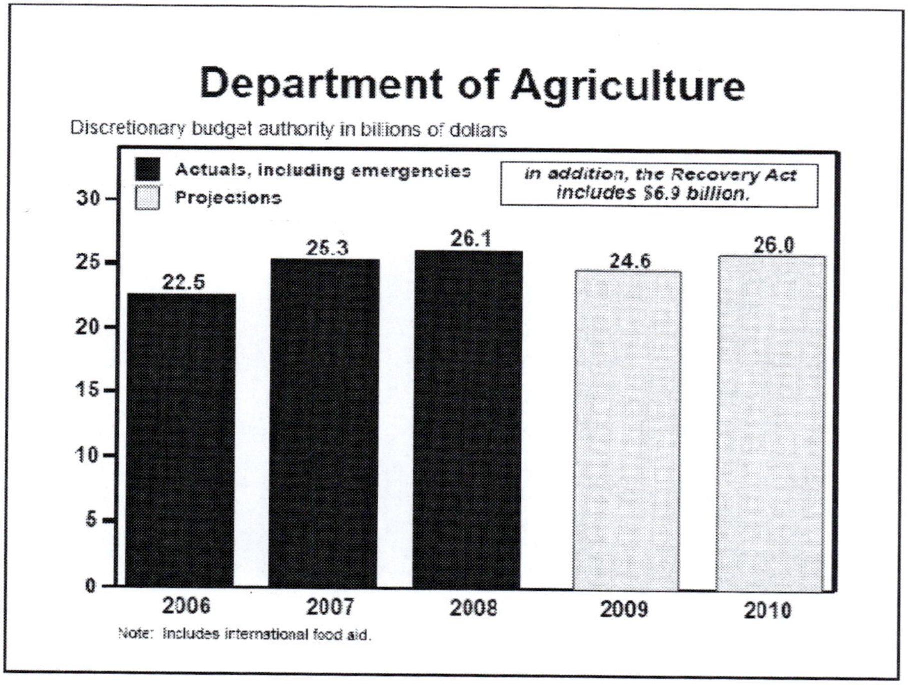

Develops Rural Broadband Services. Modern technology is critical to the expansion of business, education, and health care opportunities in rural areas and the competitiveness of the Nation's small towns and rural communities. The Budget provides $1.3 billion in loans and grants to increase broadband capacity and improve telecommunication service and education and health opportunities in rural areas.

Promotes Rural America's Leadership in Developing Renewable Energy. America's farmers have been on the forefront of the renewable fuels movement. The president has been a strong proponent for increasing the national supply of home-grown American renewable fuels. This Budget ensures that the Nation's rural areas continue their leadership in this arena by supporting an additional $250 million in loans and grants. Rural America is poised to produce and refine more American biofuels; provide more wind power than ever before; and create millions of new jobs across the country.

Supports Rural Revitalization, Education, and Land Grant programs. The Budget includes an additional $70 million for rural areas, for competitive research grants that provide incentives for teachers working in rural areas to pursue professional development, and to enhance existing rural research and extension programs at land grant and minority-serving institutions.

Protects the Nation's Forests. The Budget reflects the President's commitment to protecting and restoring our national forests as a cornerstone of a healthy, sustainable environment. The Budget provides a $50 million increase (plus inflation) for national forest operations to protect natural resources and maintain facilities, including those that are restored with 2009 American Recovery and Reinvestment Act investments.

Responsibly Budgets for Wildfires. The Budget fully funds the 10-year average suppression costs, establishes a discretionary funding reserve, and ensures fire management resources are used in a cost-effective manner in high-priority areas. The $282 million discretionary contingent reserve provides funding for firefighting when the $1.1 billion appropriated 10-year average is exhausted. This proposal will ensure that fire management resources are sufficient to allow for other critical Forest Service activities.

Conserves New Lands. The Budget includes $119 million, a $34 million increase, in Forest Service funding through the Land and Water Conservation Fund to acquire easements on forested lands under significant development pressures. These conservation easements will protect air and water quality, provide access to national forests, and provide habitat for threatened or endangered wildlife and fish.

Supports Conservation. The Administration fully supports partnering with landowners to conserve land, protect wetlands, improve wildlife habitat, expand hunting and fishing opportunities, and promote other conservation initiatives. In this vein, the Administration funds several vital conservation programs including the Conservation Stewardship Program, the Conservation Reserve Program, and the Environmental Quality Incentives Program and conservation tax incentives that were provided in the 2008 Farm Bill.

Strengthens Nutrition Assistance. The President's Budget supports a strong Child Nutrition and WIC reauthorization package that will ensure that low-income children receive the nutrition assistance they need and help fulfill the President's pledge to end childhood hunger by 2015. The Budget provides an increase of $1 billion annually for program reforms aimed at improving program access, enhancing the nutritional quality of school meals, expanding nutrition research and evaluation, and improving program oversight. Funding is also provided to support over 9.8 million participants in the WIC program, which is critical to the health of pregnant women, new mothers, and their infants.

Responds to the Needs of Low-income Americans. The President supports the nutrition provisions incorporated in the American Recovery and Reinvestment Act, including a temporary increase in the Supplemental Nutrition Assistance Program (SNAP), formerly Food Stamps, to help strengthen the food purchasing power of low-income families during these tough economic times. The President also supports additional resources for food banks and community-based food providers, which help many families put food on the table. Additionally, the Budget provides funding for an innovative pilot initiative to increase participation among low-income seniors, who are among the most vulnerable and hardest-to-reach populations in SNAP, to ensure they receive the benefits for which they qualify.

Enhances Food Safety. The President's Budget takes steps to improve the safety of the Nation's supply of meat, poultry and processed egg products and to ensure that these products are wholesome, and accurately labeled and packaged. The Budget provides additional resources to improve food safety inspection and assessment and the ability to determine food safety risks. This will lead to a reduction in foodborne illness and improve public health and safety.

Supports independent Producers. Protecting producers against unfair, deceptive, and fraudulent practices is essential to a fair and efficient marketing system. Additional resources are provided to improve the enforcement of the Packers and Stockyards Act to help accomplish this. The Budget also proposes increased funding to enhance the National Organic Program through additional education and outreach, as well as enforcement to maintain labeling credibility.

Pursues fiscal Responsibility. As part of the President's commitment to fiscal responsibility, the Budget includes several significant offsets. The proposals include programmatic changes that:

- **Reduce Direct Payments**. As part of an effort to transition large farms from direct payments provided to owners of base acres to increased income from revenue derived from emerging markets for environmental services, the President's Budget phases out direct payments over three years to farmers with sales revenue of more than $500,000 annually. Presently, direct payments are made to even large producers regardless of crop prices, losses, or whether the land is still under production. The program was introduced in the 1996 Farm Bill as a temporary payment scheduled to expire, but was included in the 2002 and 2008 Farm Bills. The President wants to maintain a strong safety net for farm families and beginning farmers while encouraging fiscal responsibility. Large farmers are well positioned to replace those payments with alternate sources of income from emerging markets for environmental services, such as carbon sequestration, renewable energy production, and providing clean air, clean water, and wildlife habitat. USDA will increase its research and analytical capabilities and conduct Government-wide coordination activities to encourage the establishment of markets for these ecosystem services.

- **Reduce Crop Insurance Premium Subsidies and Underwriting Gains.** This proposal would reduce the Federal subsidy to both insurance companies and farmers. Over the last several years, subsidies for crop insurance companies have grown rapidly without improving program coverage or customer service for farmers. Current subsidy levels exceed what is necessary to encourage farmer participation and they do not constitute a sound value to taxpayers.
- **Eliminate Cotton Storage Credits.** The President's Budget proposes to eliminate the requirement for the Government to pay the storage costs of cotton that is put under loan with USDA. Cotton is the only commodity for which this assistance is provided. Storage credits for cotton have been found to have a negative impact on the amount of cotton on the market. Because cotton storage is covered by the Government, producers may store their cotton for longer than necessary.
- **Eliminate the Resource Conservation and Development (RC&D) Program.** The Budget eliminates funding for the RC&D program. First begun in 1962, the program was intended to build community leadership skills through the establishment of RC&D councils that would access Federal, State and local programs for the community's benefit. After 47 years, this goal has been accomplished. These councils have developed sufficiently strong State and local ties that the Administration believes they are now able to secure funding for their continued operation without Federal assistance.
- **Reform the Market Access Program (MAP).** The Budget reforms MAP by reducing program funding for overseas brand promotion and minimizes the benefits that large for-profit entities indirectly gain as members of trade associations who also participate in MAP. An annual funding reduction of 20 percent will reduce Federal spending and place a greater emphasis on promoting generic American products overseas.

Support Economic Recovery. The Recovery Act provides USDA with a total of $27.6 billion, most of which will fund increased benefits to low income families through the Supplemental Nutrition Assistance Program ($20 billion). In addition, the Act provides $6.9 billion in discretionary appropriations for rural development activities such as construction and renovation of rural water and wastewater systems, low income housing loans, broadband infrastructure in rural areas, rural business programs, and construction of Forest Service facilities. Finally, the Act provides $700 million in mandatory farm disaster assistance.

Conducts the Decennial Census. The President's Budget ensures the Census Bureau will have the resources it needs to complete the 2010 Decennial Census effectively, efficiently, and on- time by providing over $4 billion of additional funding. These funds are in addition to the $1 billion recently provided by the American recovery and reinvestment Act. The decennial census is the Nation's largest peacetime mobilization, and will entail the hiring of approximately half of a million temporary workers, as well as extensive advertising and partnership activities to encourage participation by hard-to-reach populations and completion of an accurate count.

DEPARTMENT OF COMMERCE

Funding Highlights

- Mobilizes resources to conduct the 2010 Decennial Census.
- Improves prediction and monitoring of the planet's weather and climate and sustainable management of marine fisheries and ocean resources.
- Invests in America's economic competitiveness by promoting innovation in U.S. manufacturing, deploying broadband, and advancing measurement science, standards, and technology.
- Expands economic development through the promotion of regional innovation clusters and the creation of a national network of public-private business incubators.
- Promotes opportunities for U.S. exporters in new markets and eliminates barriers to U.S. sales abroad.
- Protects intellectual property rights created through patents and trademarks.

Improves Weather Forecasting, Climate Monitoring, Fisheries Management and Ocean Programs. The Budget helps ensure continuity of National Oceanic and Atmospheric Administration (NOAA) satellite coverage needed for weather forecasting and climate data records by providing over $1.3 billion to fund the development and acquisition of vital weather satellites and climate sensors. Funding is also provided to advance climate and ocean research, including efforts to understand and monitor ocean acidification. In addition, the Budget fully supports implementation of the Magnuson-Stevens Act and its requirement to eliminate overfishing by 2011. All of these activities build upon the recently enacted recovery Act, which provides $600 million for the construction and maintenance of NOAA research facilities, vessels, and satellites, as well as $230 million for habitat restoration, hydrographic services, research, and management operations.

Invests in America's Competitiveness. The Budget supports the Nation's technology infrastructure by funding advanced measurement and standards development at the National Institute of Standards and Technology (NIST).

These activities will build upon the Recovery Act, which includes $240 million for NIST's scientific research activities and lab equipment and $180 million for construction of NIST facilities. The 2010 Budget also provides $70 million for the Technology Innovation Program, which invests in high-impact research that will address critical national needs and advance innovation. The Hollings Manufacturing Extension Partnership will receive $125 million to enhance the competitiveness of the Nation's manufacturers by facilitating the adoption of more efficient manufacturing processes. In addition, Commerce's National Telecommunications and Information Administration will be focused on administering the $4.7 billion provided by the Recovery Act for programs to expand broadband deployment, adoption, and data collection.

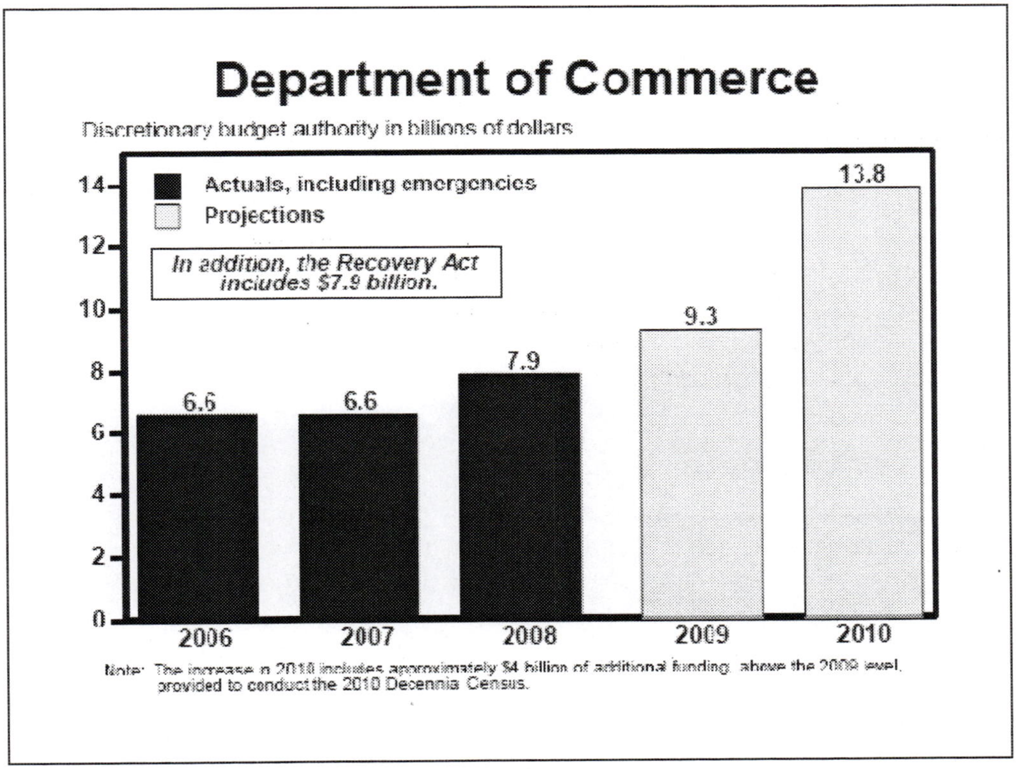

Spurs Regional Economic Development and Creation of New Businesses. The Budget provides $50 million in regional planning and matching grants within the Economic Development Administration (EDA) to support the creation of regional innovation clusters that leverage regions' existing competitive strengths to boost job creation and economic growth. The Budget also launches a $50 million initiative in EDA that will create a nationwide network of public-private business incubators to encourage entrepreneurial activity in economically distressed areas. The Recovery Act provides EDA $150 million to distribute as economic adjustment assistance and infrastructure funding, with priority for areas experiencing severe job losses.

Promotes Opportunities for American Exporters in New Markets. The Budget fully supports the International Trade Administration's efforts to promote exports from small businesses and eliminate barriers to sales of U.S. products.

Promotes Innovation. The President's Budget gives the U.S. Patent and Trademark Office full access to its fee collections, which will provide resources to strengthen the Office's ability to encourage innovation and safeguard the value of intellectual property through more efficient and higher quality patent and trademark examinations.

DEPARTMENT OF DEFENSE

Funding Highlights

- Provides $533.7 billion for the Department of Defense base budget in 2010, a four-percent increase over 2009.
- Includes $75.5 billion in supplemental appropriations for 2009 and $130.0 billion for 2010 to support ongoing overseas contingency operations, while increasing efforts in Afghanistan and drawing down troops from Iraq responsibly.
- Supports a transparent budget process, which simultaneously and separately requests estimated base budget and overseas contingency operations costs.
- Expands concurrent receipt of military retired pay and Veterans Disability Compensation for those disabled upon retirement from active duty.
- Improves efforts to care for wounded servicemembers and to treat mental health needs.

The U.S. military, the strongest and most capable in the world, faces a host of external and internal challenges. Meeting these challenges requires evaluating the country's strategic priorities and aligning scarce resources to accomplish the highest of those priorities efficiently and effectively.

External challenges include undertaking a responsible drawdown of troops from Iraq, and focusing the appropriate resources on achieving U.S. objectives in Afghanistan. In addition, we must leverage allied support to help struggling states such as Pakistan, which are the keystone for regional stability. The military must also vigilantly anticipate and meet threats from asymmetrical and non-conventional attacks, such as those posed by cyber, biological, radiological, and nuclear warfare, whether instigated by nation- states or non-state aggressors.

The military's internal challenges focus on three general areas: continuing to restructure the Nation's forces to better address long-term warfare challenges; continuing to support, care for, and compensate military professionals commensurate with their service while seeking reforms that will improve service and protect a benefit package that is sustainable and affordable; and reforming the costly and inefficient weapon development and acquisition process.

How the country should meet its strategic goals will be addressed in an upcoming Defense review, which will identify and prioritize goals and assess how best to achieve them within available resources.

Finally, this Budget will transparently present the full costs of providing national security. The Budget will clearly show the costs of the base defense budget and the incremental costs of ongoing military operations in Iraq and Afghanistan for 2010. For the years beyond, the Budget includes placeholder numbers with the understanding that these should be considered subject to change as policy decisions are made.

Department of Defense

Discretionary budget authority in billions of dollars

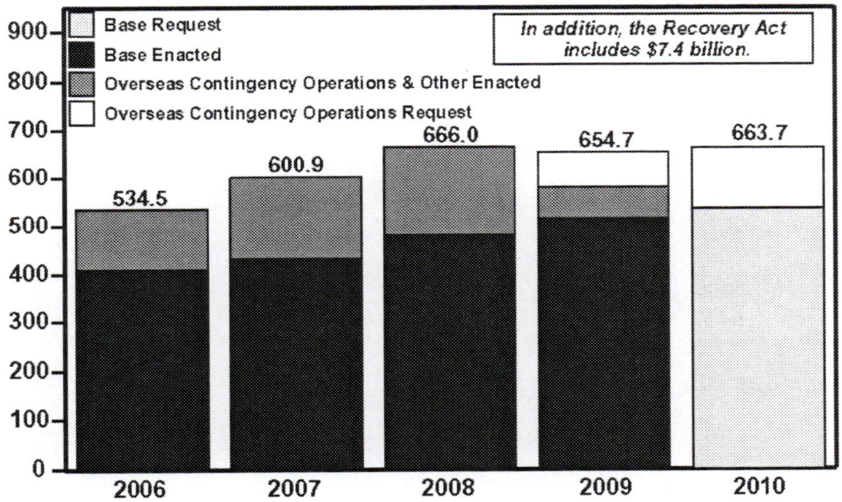

Note: Overseas contingency operations includes costs in support of operations in Iraq and Afghanistan. Other funding includes supplemental appropriations that supported responses to hurricanes and the 2004 Tsunami and that funded base activities such as Base Realignment and Closure implementation. Also, 2009 includes amounts transferred to the Coast Guard.

2010 Base Funding

The 2010 Budget for the Department of Defense (DOD) requests $533.7 billion, or an increase of four percent from the 2009 enacted level of $513.3 billion (excluding funding from the American Recovery and Reinvestment Act of 2009). This funding increase allows DOD to address its highest priorities, such as the President's commitment to meet the military's goal to increase the size of the Army and Marine Corps, to continue to improve the medical treatment of wounded servicemembers, and to reform the acquisition process. In addition, the Budget will incorporate into the base those items previously funded in emergency supplementals that should be considered base or ongoing activities, including certain medical services, family support initiatives, security assistance to foreign governments, and enhancements to intelligence, surveillance, and reconnaissance.

Increases the Size of the Army and Marine Corps. The 2010 Budget supports additional permanent forces in the Army and Marine Corps, which will increase to 547,400 and 202,000, respectively, by the end of 2009. This growth is two to three years ahead of schedule and will reduce stress on servicemembers and their families, while ensuring heightened readiness for a full spectrum of military operations.

Cares for Men and Women in uniform. The Administration is committed to caring for the servicemembers who protect American freedom and the families who support them. To that end, the Budget proposes pay and benefits that keep pace with or exceed those of the private sector. The 2010 Budget includes funding for a 2.9 percent pay raise for men and women in uniform, an amount that will improve their purchasing power.

The Budget also contains a proposal to expand concurrent receipt of military retired pay and Veterans Disability Compensation to all retirees receiving disability retired pay. Under current law, the prohibition on concurrent receipt means that these benefits offset each other so that disabled military retirees cannot receive full DOD retirement and Veterans disability payments. When the offset is removed, disabled military retirees would receive additional monthly compensation.

Reforms Acquisition. DOD's new weapons programs are among the largest, most expensive and technically difficult that the Department has ever tried to develop. As a consequence, they carry a high risk of performance failure, cost increases, and schedule delays. The Administration will set realistic requirements and stick to them and incorporate "best practices" by not allowing programs to proceed from one stage of the acquisition cycle to the next until they have achieved the maturity to clearly lower the risk of cost growth and schedule slippage.

Improves Facilities. The Administration is committed to improving the quality of life for American Soldiers, Sailors, Airmen and Marines. Therefore, the Budget continues to sustain and modernize barracks and dormitories housing servicemembers around the world and works to end all inadequate housing for military families. In addition, it builds or renovates base facilities at a level sufficient for safe operation of all structures while meeting the needs of users.

The Administration will request sufficient funding to enable the Department to continue its efforts to meet the requirements of the Base Realignment and Closure 2005 Commission, which will help to align DOD's domestic bases with meeting operational needs.

Cares for Wounded, Ill, and Injured Servicemembers (WII). The Department will continue its efforts to improve the medical care and housing for WII. DOD will complete additional Army wounded warrior complexes at posts throughout the continental United States, as well as sites in Alaska, Hawaii, and Germany. DOD and the Department of Veterans Affairs will expand pilot programs to expedite processing of injured troops through the Disability Evaluation System. The expedited system substantially reduces the time required to determine disability rating and, more importantly, to alleviate frustration caused by a needlessly complex process.

Addresses Mental Health Issues. The Department is also doing more to address mental health needs. Post-traumatic stress disorder, traumatic brain injury (TBI) and associated ailments are, and will continue to be, the signature military medical challenges facing the Department for years to come. DOD will fully implement a comprehensive TBI registry including a single point of responsibility to track incidents and recovery. The Services will expand the number of integrated mental health professionals with their deployed units to better channel medical attention to those who need help quickly. The National Intrepid Center of Excellence for psychological health and traumatic brain injury will be dedicated in the late fall of 2009. This will serve as the clinical research and educational arm of DOD's Center of Excellence for psychological health and TBI.

Funding for Overseas Contingency Operations

The President is working with his military commanders to increase the number of U.S. troops in Afghanistan while responsibly removing combat forces from Iraq. To address the costs of military operations in Iraq and Afghanistan, the Administration requests $75.5 billion for the remainder of 2009 and $130.0 billion for 2010. The Administration will provide the details of the 2009 supplemental appropriations request to the Congress in the next few weeks, and will transmit the detailed 2010 request with the President's 2010 Budget.

The Budget includes placeholder estimates of $50 billion per year for 2011 and beyond. These estimates do not reflect any policy decisions about specific military or intelligence operations.

National Intelligence Program

Funding Highlights

- Strengthens the capabilities of the Nation's intelligence agencies to furnish timely, accurate, and insightful intelligence on the capabilities and intentions of foreign powers, including international terrorist groups.
- Enhances Federal cybersecurity capabilities.
- Prioritizes resources to support a U.S. Government-wide counterterrorism action plan.
- Improves the sharing of terrorist-related information with Federal, State, local, tribal and foreign partners.
- Increases collection capabilities and continues transforming intelligence analysis.

The National Intelligence Program (NIP) funds intelligence activities in several Departments and the Central Intelligence Agency (CIA). NIP's budget is classified, so the 2010 Budget does not publicly disclose funding requests for intelligence activities. However, since NIP supports key elements of America's national security, this chapter highlights some NIP-funded activities without detailing funding information.

To protect America's national security, the Intelligence Community (IC) provides effective intelligence collection, the analysis of that intelligence, and the production of finished intelligence products. IC is responsible for ensuring timely and effective dissemination of intelligence to those who need it, ranging from the President, to heads of Executive Departments, military forces, and law enforcement agencies. To meet this country's national security challenges, IC is strengthening its components' abilities to collect intelligence, increasing the security of Federal cyber networks, and protecting against the threat of international terrorism in the United States.

The 2010 budget for NIP will support the Administration's national security objectives. The Director of National Intelligence, the Director of the CIA, and Department Secretaries with intelligence organizations will use 2010 NIP funds to defeat terrorist networks, prevent the spread of weapons of mass destruction, penetrate and analyze the most difficult targets of U.S. foreign policy, and anticipate developments of strategic concern.

The Administration will request funding for IC for the remainder of 2009 and for 2010 to cover the costs of global intelligence operations. The details of the 2009 supplemental appropriations request will be provided to the Congress in the next few weeks while the detailed 2010 request will be transmitted with the President's 2010 Budget request.

Increases Funding for Cybersecurity. The threat to Federal information technology networks is real, serious, and growing. To address this threat, the President's 2010 Budget includes substantial funding for cybersecurity efforts; such activities will take an integrated and holistic approach to address current cybersecurity threats, anticipate future threats, and continue innovative public-private partnerships. These efforts encompass the homeland security, intelligence, law enforcement, military and diplomatic mission areas of the U.S. Government.

Implements Counterterrorism Plan. The National Counterterrorism Center (NCTC) has developed a U.S. Government-wide counterterrorism action plan. This plan lays out broad strategic objectives aligned with policy objectives to guide the overall implementation of this national strategy on counterterrorism. The Administration will work with NCTC, IC, and relevant Departments such as Defense, State, and Homeland Security to direct resources in support of counterterrorism implementation objectives.

Facilitates Information Sharing. The President's 2010 Budget will support initiatives to improve the sharing of intelligence, including terrorist-related information, with Federal, State, local, tribal and foreign partners. These efforts include advancing the National Suspicious Activity Reporting Initiative; establishing agency-based, outcome-oriented performance targets for information sharing; and institutionalizing the use of effective business practices.

Improves Collection and Analysis Capabilities. The 2010 Budget provides funding to improve mission performance by increasing intelligence collection capabilities and continuing to transform intelligence analysis in IC.

DEPARTMENT OF EDUCATION

Funding Highlights

- Creates incentives and supports for States to build comprehensive, coordinated, high-quality early childhood "Zero to Five" systems, building on the early childhood investments in the American Recovery and Reinvestment Act of 2009.
- Strengthens and reforms public schools to meet the needs of all students, by helping States to develop high quality, rigorous standards and assessments, vigorously supporting and rewarding effective teaching, and investing in and widely disseminating effective approaches to improving student achievement to help all students make progress toward high standards.
- Expands opportunities for students to go to college and graduate by expanding student aid, shifting resources from banks and middlemen toward students, creating new incentives for colleges to focus on student completion, and expanding access to low-cost Federal student loans.

Expands Access to High-Quality Early Childhood Education. Decades of rigorous research demonstrates that high-quality early childhood education programs help children succeed in school and throughout their lives. Building on strong investments in the Recovery Act, the President's Budget also includes new initiatives aimed at ensuring that early childhood programs yield strong results for children. The Budget invests additional resources to encourage State and local investment in early childhood education; support coordination among local, State, and Federal partners and a seamless delivery of services; and provide better information to parents about program options and quality.

Supports High Standards and Rigorous Assessments Aligned with the Demands of the Global Economy. Students must achieve to high standards in order to be successful in the global economy. Assessments must accurately measure students' knowledge and skills, including critical thinking skills. Building on the Recovery Act, the new Administration will help States increase the rigor of their standards so they prepare students for success in college and a career. Resources will also be available to improve the quality of assessments, including assessments for students with disabilities and English language learners. Such reforms will lay the groundwork for reauthorizing the Elementary and Secondary Education Act.

Prepares and Rewards Effective Teachers and Principals. The Budget builds on the investments funded under the Recovery Act designed to significantly upgrade the skills and effectiveness of the education workforce. The Administration will invest in efforts to strengthen and increase transparency around results for teacher and principal preparation programs, including programs in schools of education, alternative certification programs, and teacher and principal residency programs. The Budget supports additional investments in State and local efforts, developed in consultation with teachers and other stakeholders, to implement systems that reward strong teacher performance and help less effective teachers improve or, if they do not improve, exit the classroom. Resources are also included to develop better systems and strategies for recruiting, evaluating, and supporting teachers and other educators to provide a better supply and distribution of well-prepared and effective education workforce.

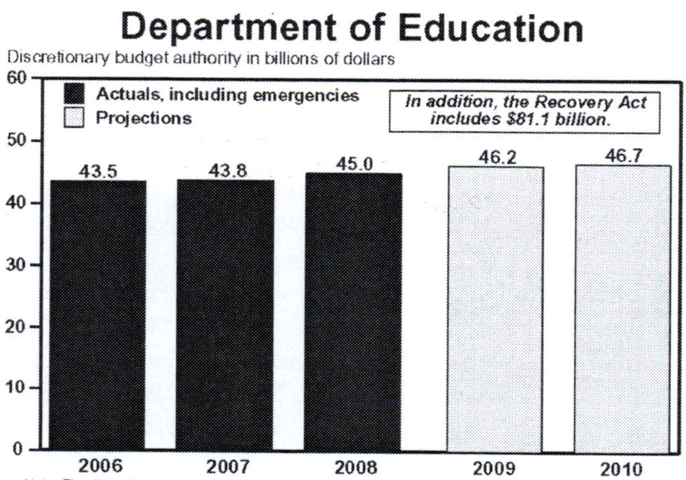

Note: The discretionary budget authority amounts are adjusted for comparability to account for increases in advance appropriations in prior years, and to exclude discretionary funding for Pell Grants in accordance with the Budget's policy to make the program mandatory. The Recovery Act total includes $53.6 billion for State Stabilization Grants and excludes $15.6 billion for Pell Grants.

Supports Innovative and Effective Strategies to Improve Achievement. Through the Innovation Fund, the Administration will invest in school systems and non-profit organizations with demonstrated track records of success in raising student achievement to expand their work or implement new innovative approaches. The President's Budget also provides funds to support Promise Neighborhoods, a new effort to test innovative strategies to improve academic achievement and life outcomes in high-poverty areas. The program will be modeled after the Harlem Children's Zone, which aims to improve college-going rates by combining a rigorous K-12 education with a full network of supportive services—from early childhood education to after-school activities to college counseling—in an entire neighborhood from birth to college.

Funds Education Research to Ensure that Teachers and School Leaders Have the Tools and Information They Need to Prepare Students for the Global Economy. The Budget includes funds to carefully study, improve, and scale up promising educational innovations that focus on improving student learning and achievement. The additional funds will also be used to rigorously evaluate Federal education programs so that Federal investments are preparing students for success in college and the workforce.

Promotes Successful Models for Turning Around Low-Achieving Schools. The Budget builds on the Recovery Act's focus on strategic investments in scaling up educational practices that show results and cultivating promising new practices. The President's Budget commits resources to turn around high-need, low-performing schools with strong supports, not just sanctions. The Administration's new strategy will support State efforts to diagnose and address the root causes of schools' low performance. In addition, the Budget increases funding for the Charter School program to support the expansion of successful charter school models, while increasing State oversight to monitor and shut down low-performing charter schools.

Expands Pell Grants and Puts the Program on Sure Footing. Because the Administration is committed to making college affordable for all Americans, the 2010 Budget builds on the Recovery Act by supporting a $5,550 Pell Grant maximum award in the 2010-2011 school year. But it is not enough just to make Pell Grants more generous and to put on a short-term patch. Fourteen times since 1973, the maximum Pell Grant has failed to increase even in nominal dollars. To make sure that we have a highly-educated workforce and that the opportunity to go to college is not determined by how much money you have, we need to put the Pell Grant program on sure footing. The Administration will index Pell grants to the Consumer Price Index plus 1 percent in order to address inflation. In addition, the Administration proposes to make the Pell Grant program mandatory to ensure a regular stream of funding and eliminate the practice of "backfilling" billions of dollars in Pell shortfalls each year. Finally, while expanding student aid, the Administration will also simplify the student aid application process.

Stabilizes the Student Loan Program for Students and Saves Billions of Dollars for Taxpayers. Right now, the subsidies in the Government-guaranteed student loan program are set by the Congress through the political process. That program has not only needlessly cost taxpayers billions of dollars, but has also subjected students to uncertainty because of turmoil in the financial markets. The President's Budget asks the Congress to end the entitlements for financial institutions that lend to students. The Administration will instead take advantage of low-cost and stable sources of capital so students are ensured access to loans, while providing high-quality services for students by using competitive, private providers to service loans. The approach in the Budget, originating all new loans in the direct lending program, saves more than $4 billion a year that is reinvested in aid to students. The Budget also makes campus-based, low-interest loans more widely available through a new modernized Perkins Loan program, overhauling the inefficient and inequitable current Perkins program.

Focuses on College Completion. It is not enough for the Nation to enroll more students in college; we also need to graduate more students from college. A few States and institutions have begun to experiment with these approaches, but there is much more they can do. The Budget includes a new five-year, $2.5 billion Access and Completion Incentive Fund to support innovative State efforts to help low-income students succeed and complete their college education. The program will include a rigorous evaluation component to ensure that we learn from what works.

DEPARTMENT OF ENERGY

Invests in the Sciences. As part of the President's plan to double Federal investment in the basic sciences, the 2010 Budget, along with the $1.6 billion provided in the recovery Act for the Department of Energy's basic science programs, provides substantially increased support for the Office of Science. The Budget increases funding for improving our understanding of climate science and continues the United States' commitment to international science and energy experiments. The Budget also expands graduate fellowship programs that will train students in critical energy-related fields.

Funding Highlights

- Begins to build a new economy that is powered by clean and secure energy through funding provided in the 2010 Budget and the $39 billion provided for energy programs in the American Recovery and Reinvestment Act of 2009.
- Provides significant increases in funding for basic research and world-leading scientific user facilities to support transformational discoveries and accelerate solutions to our Nation's most pressing problems – including the development of clean energy.
- Supports economic investment and positions the United States as the world leader in climate change technology.
- Accelerates the transition to a low-carbon economythrough increased support of the development and deployment of clean energy technologies such as solar, biomass, geothermal, wind, and low-carbon emission coal power.
- Builds on the $1 1 billion provided in the Recovery Act for smart grid technologies, transmission system expansion and upgrades, and other investments to modernize and enhance the electric transmission infrastructure to improve energy efficiency and reliability.
- Supports and encourages the early commercial deployment of innovative, clean energy technologies through loan guarantees.
- Reduces security risks through the detection, elimination, and securing of nuclear material and radiological sources worldwide while maintaining the safety, security, and reliability of the nuclear weapons stockpile.
- Continues the Nation's efforts to reduce environmental risks and safely manage nuclear materials.

Department of Energy

Discretionary budget authority in billions of dollars

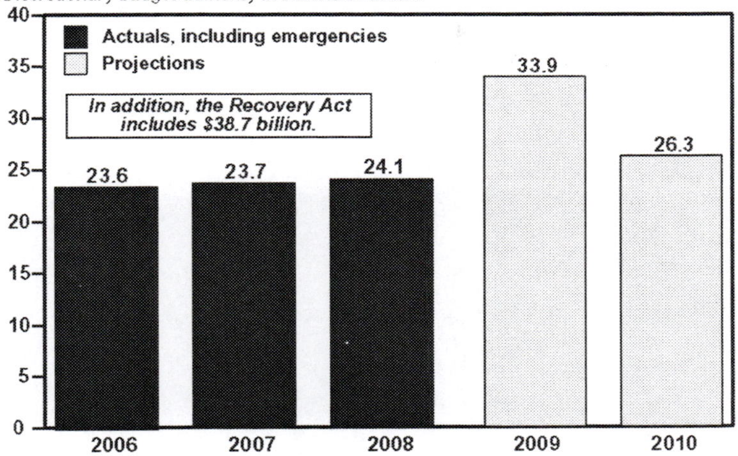

Note: Included in 2009 is emergency funding for Advanced Technology Vehicles Manufacturing Loan Program, $7.5 billion, and $250 million for Weatherization.

Encourages the Early Commercial use of New, Innovative Energy Technologies that Will Reduce Greenhouse Gas Emissions. The Budget supports loan guarantees for innovative energy technologies including renewable energy projects, transmission projects, and carbon sequestration projects that avoid, reduce, or sequester air pollutants and greenhouse gases while simultaneously creating green jobs and contributing to long-term economic growth and international competitiveness.

Advances the development of Low-Carbon Coal Technologies. The Budget supports Carbon Capture and Storage technology, and along with the $3.4 billion provided in the Recovery Act for low-carbon emission coal power and industrial projects, these funds will help allow the use of our extensive domestic coal resource while reducing the impacts on climate change.

Invests in Smart, Energy Efficient, Reliable Electricity Delivery Infrastructures. The Budget provides support for the Office of Electricity Delivery and Energy Reliability as part of the President's investment plan to modernize the Nation's electric grid. It includes: energy storage; cyber-security and investments in research, the development and demonstration of smart grid technologies that will accelerate the transformation of the Nation's energy transmission and distribution system; enhancement of security and reliability of energy infrastructure; and facilitat-ing recovery from disruptions to the energy supply.

Invests in Clean Energy Technologies to Reduce dependence on Foreign Oil and Accelerate the Transition to a Low-Carbon Economy. The Budget provides support for accelerating research, development, demonstration, deployment, and commercialization of clean energy technologies, including biofuels, renewable energy, and energy efficiency projects. These investments will reduce dependence on foreign oil and create long-term, sustainable economic growth in the green industries of the future.

Reduces Proliferation Risks and Ensures the Safety, Security, and Reliability of the Nuclear Weapons Stockpile Without Nuclear Testing. The Budget supports increased efforts to secure and dispose of nuclear material and invests in innovative science and technology to detect and deter nuclear smuggling and the development of weapons of mass destruction programs. Development work on the Reliable Replacement Warhead will cease, while continued work to improve the nuclear stockpile's safety, security, and reliability is enhanced with more expansive life extension programs.

DEPARTMENT OF HEALTH AND HUMAN SERVICES

Funding Highlights

- Accelerates the adoption of health information technology and utilization of electronic health records.
- Expands research comparing the effectiveness of medical treatments to give patients and physicians better information on what works best.
- Invests over $6 billion for cancer research at the National Institutes of Health as part of the Administration's multi-year commitment to double cancer research funding.
- Strengthens the Indian health system with sustained investments in health care services for American Indians and Alaska Natives to address persistent health disparities and foster healthy Indian communities.
- Invests $330 million to increase the number of doctors, nurses, and dentists practicing in areas of the country experiencing shortages of health professionals.
- Supports families by providing additional funding for affordable, high-quality child care, expanding Early Head Start and Head Start, and creating the Nurse Home Visitation program to support first-time mothers.
- Strengthens the Medicare program by encouraging high quality and efficient care, and improving program integrity.
- Invests over $1 billion for Food and Drug Administration food safety efforts to increase and improve inspections, domestic surveillance, laboratory capacity and domestic response to prevent and control foodborne illness.

Focuses on the Cleanup and Management of Radioactive Waste and Nuclear Materials. The Budget focuses on improved performance and accountability for the environmental legacy of the Nation's nuclear weapons program by addressing health and safety risks across the country. The Yucca Mountain program will be scaled back to those costs necessary to answer inquiries from the Nuclear Regulatory Commission, while the Administration devises a new strategy toward nuclear waste disposal.

The Department of Health and Human Services (HHS) is the Federal Government's principal agency for protecting the health of all Americans and for providing essential human services. This Budget provides $76.8 billion in support of HHS' mission.

Makes a Down Payment on Health Care Reform. The Budget establishes a reserve fund of more than $630 billion over 10 years to finance fundamental reform of our health care system that will bring down costs and expand coverage. The reserve is funded half by new revenue and half by savings proposals that promote efficiency and accountability, align incentives toward quality, and encourage shared responsibility. In addition, the Budget calls for an effort beyond this down payment, to put the Nation on a path to health insurance coverage for all Americans. However, additional funding will be needed. This effort must be open, and must consider all kinds of approaches as part of this process. Some major strides have already been made in the American Recovery and Reinvestment Act of 2009, including $19 billion for health information technology, $1 billion for comparative effectiveness research, and subsidies for the newly unemployed to maintain their health insurance. These initiatives put the Nation on the path toward fundamental health reform.

Begin the Doubling of Funding for Cancer Research. The Budget includes over $6 billion within the National Institutes of Health (NIH) to support cancer research. This funding is central to the President's sustained, multi-year plan to double cancer research. These resources will be committed strategically to have the greatest impact on developing innovative diagnostics, treatments, and cures for cancer. This initiative will build upon the unprecedented $10 billion provided in the Recovery Act, which will support new NIH research in 2009 and 2010.

Accelerates the Adoption of Health Information Technology (IT). Building on the historic $19 billion investment in the Recovery Act, the Administration will continue efforts to further the adoption and implementation of health IT—an essential tool to modernize the health care system. The Recovery Act offers physicians and hospitals participating in the Medicare program temporary incentive payments starting in 2011 for using a certified electronic health record (EHR), followed by financial penalties starting in 2015 for failure to use such a system. It also offers incentive payments to Medicaid providers, including physicians and children's hospitals, to assist with the purchase, implementation, and use of certified EHR technology. These incentives, coupled with other activities authorized in the Recovery Act, are expected to result in a dramatic increase in the percentage of health care providers using health IT within five years. Computerizing health records—while protecting the privacy and security of personal health information—is expected to facilitate improvements in the quality of health care, prevention of unnecessary health care spending, and a reduction in medical errors.

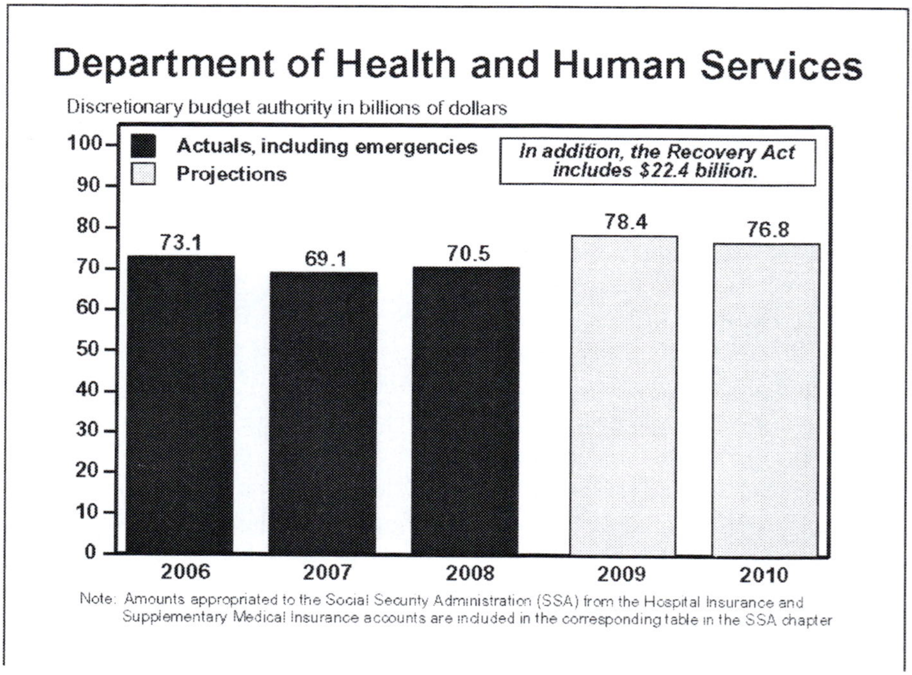

Lowers Drug Costs and Improves Food and Medical Product Safety. The Budget supports the Food and Drug Administration's (FDA's) new efforts to allow Americans to buy safe and effective drugs from other countries and to establish a new regulatory pathway to approve generic biologics. The Budget also includes a substantial increase to strengthen FDA's efforts to make food and medical products safer.

Strengthens Program Integrity. Reducing fraud, waste, and abuse is an important part of restraining spending growth and providing quality health care service delivery to beneficiaries. The Budget proposes to dedicate additional resources that will initially be targeted to improving oversight and program integrity activities for the Medicare Prescription Drug Program (Part D), Medicare Advantage, and the Medicaid Program. These resources will enable the Centers for Medicare and Medicaid Services to more rapidly respond to emerging program integrity vulnerabilities, identify excessive payments, and establish new processes for correcting problems. As a result, the Administration will be better able to minimize inappropriate payments, close loopholes, and provide greater value for program expenditures to beneficiaries and taxpayers.

Improves Medicare's Sustainability. The Administration is committed to strengthening Medicare's long-term sustainability so that beneficiaries can continue to rely on this critical program. The Budget strengthens the Medicare program by encouraging high quality and efficient care, and reducing excessive Medicare payments.

Expands the Medicare and Medicaid Research Agenda. The Budget includes new funding to broaden the Medicare and Medicaid research agenda. The expanded agenda will take advantage of the robust data available for these programs. New Medicare and Medicaid demonstration and pilot projects will evaluate payment reforms, ways to provide higher quality care at lower costs, improve beneficiary education and understanding of benefits offered, and better align provider payments with costs.

Provides Health Care Coverage to Low-Income Individuals. Medicaid is a means-tested health care entitlement program financed by States and the Federal Government. On average, the Federal Government pays 57 percent of Medicaid costs. The Recovery Act protects health care coverage for millions of Americans during the recession by temporarily increasing Federal Medicaid funding to help States facing budget shortfalls maintain their current programs.

In addition, the Children's Health Insurance Program Reauthorization Act of 2009, signed by the President on February 4, 2009, extends the program through 2013 by providing an additional $44 billion in allotments above baseline funding levels of $25 billion. This funding provides access to nearly four million newly insured children by 2013.

Enhances HIV/AIDS Prevention and Treatment. The Budget increases resources to detect, prevent, and treat HIV/AIDS domestically, especially in underserved populations.

Strengthens the Health Professions Workforce. The Budget invests $330 million to address the shortage of health care providers in certain areas. The Budget expands loan repayment programs for physicians, nurses, and dentists who agree to practice in medically underserved areas. This funding will enhance the capacity of nursing schools to increase the number of nurses. It will also allow States to increase access to oral health care through dental workforce development grants. The Budget's new resources will sustain the expansion of the health care workforce funded in the Recovery Act.

Expands Access to Health Care for American Indians and Alaska Natives (AI/ANs). The Budget includes over $4 billion for the Indian Health Service (IHS) to support and expand the provision of health care services and public health programs for AI/ANs. Investments in the Indian health system will focus on improving the health outcomes of AI/ANs and promoting healthy Indian communities. The President's Budget builds upon resources provided in the Recovery Act for IHS.

Supports Americans with Autism Spectrum Disorders (ASD). The President is committed to expanding support for individuals, families, and communities affected by ASD. The Budget includes $211 million in HHS for research into the causes of and treatments for ASD, screenings, public awareness, and support services.

Improves Rural Health. The Budget includes $73 million to improve both access to and quality of health care in rural areas. This funding will strengthen regional and local partnerships among rural health care providers, expand community-based prevention interventions, and promote the modernization of the health care infrastructure in rural areas.

Compares the Effectiveness of Treatments. Building on the unprecedented $1.1 billion included in the Recovery Act for comparative effectiveness research, the Administration will continue efforts to produce state-of-the-science information on what medical treatments work best for a given condition. When coupled with electronic health records, these findings can form the basis for clinical decision support tools— distilling all available evidence on the outcomes of different treatment options into user-friendly pop-up alerts for physicians at the point of care. These findings can thereby enhance medical decision-making by patients and their physicians.

Makes a Down Payment on the President's "Zero to Five" Plan. The Recovery Act makes a down payment on the President's comprehensive Zero to Five plan, providing $1.1 billion to double the number of children served by Early Head Start over two years, an additional $1 billion to expand and improve Head Start, and an additional $2 billion in funding for the Child Care and Development Block Grant. The Budget sustains critical support for young children and their families by building on these investments.

The Budget also creates the Nurse Home Visitation program, which will provide funds to States to provide home visits by trained nurses to first-time low-income mothers and mothers-tobe. The program has been rigorously evaluated over time and proven to have long-term effects including substantial reductions in child abuse and neglect, preterm births, and arrests for both parents and adolescents who participated in the program as children, putting estimates of its return-on-investment between 3 to 6 dollars per dollar invested. This Budget builds the foundation for a program that could ultimately serve all eligible mothers who seek services.

Provides Energy Assistance to Low-Income Families. The Budget provides $3.2 billion for the Low-Income Home Energy Assistance Program (LIHEAP) to help low-income families with their home heating and cooling expenses. That is the highest level of LIHEAP funding for any year except for the most recent, when the Nation was threatened with an unprecedented increase in energy costs. In addition, the Administration proposes creating a new trigger mechanism to provide automatic increases in energy assistance whenever there is a spike in energy costs. The normal appropriations process cannot always respond to the volatile energy market on a timely basis; the trigger will ensure a prompt and potentially significant increase in funds in response to a rapid future rise in costs.

Prevents Teen Pregnancy. The Budget supports State, community-based, and faith-based efforts to reduce teen pregnancy using evidence- based models. The program will fund models that stress the importance of abstinence while providing medically-accurate and age-appropriate information to youth who have already become sexually active.

Provides Support for Other Presidential Initiatives. The Budget includes funding to reduce domestic violence and enhance emergency care systems. It also expands the treatment capacity of drug courts including services to protect methamphetamine's youngest victims. Substance addiction is a preventable and treatable chronic condition and this initiative helps address the most urgent needs. The Budget also provides resources to reduce health disparities, which the President has identified as an important goal of his Administration.

DEPARTMENT OF HOMELAND SECURITY

Funding Highlights

- Safeguards the Nation's transportation systems through additional resources to bolster critical transportation sectors and by leveraging a user fee to minimize overall costs.
- Enhances cybersecurity and technology research and development by supporting partnerships with government, industry, and academia to strengthen the Nation's cyber infrastructure and increase research and development in key homeland security technologies.
- Strengthens border security and immigration services.
- Supports State homeland security activities by increasing funding provided to States and localities to protect Americans from terrorist attacks and natural disasters, through effective emergency response plans, and improved information sharing and analysis.

Safeguards our Nation's Transportation Systems. The Budget funds key investments to reinforce public transportation, enhance maritime transportation, and accelerate airline security. Funding of $50 million will provide 15 new Visual Intermodal Protection response teams at the Transportation Security Administration to increase additional random force protection capability by deploying to transit hubs unannounced. Another $25 million in new resources will support integrated planning at the Department of Homeland Security and the Department of Transportation to inform development and modernization of intermodal freight infrastructure linking coastal and inland ports to highway and rail networks. Additional funding supports critical investments to strengthen the security of U.S. airports and adds 55 Bomb Appraisal Officers who specialize in explosives and improvised explosive device recognition and response. The Budget also includes $64 million to modernize the infrastructure used to vet travelers and workers. These funds will strengthen screening in order to reduce the risk of potential terrorism or other unlawful activities that threaten the Nation's transportation system.

To minimize overall costs to taxpayers, the Budget proposes to increase the existing Aviation Passenger Security Fee beginning in 2012. Increasing this fee will offset costs associated with Transportation Security Administration screening of aviation passengers as the current fee only captures 36 percent of the cost of aviation security. By increasing the fee, offsetting collections from all aviation security fees would cover a majority of the estimated costs of passenger and baggage screening.

Department of Homeland Security

Discretionary budget authority in billions of dollars

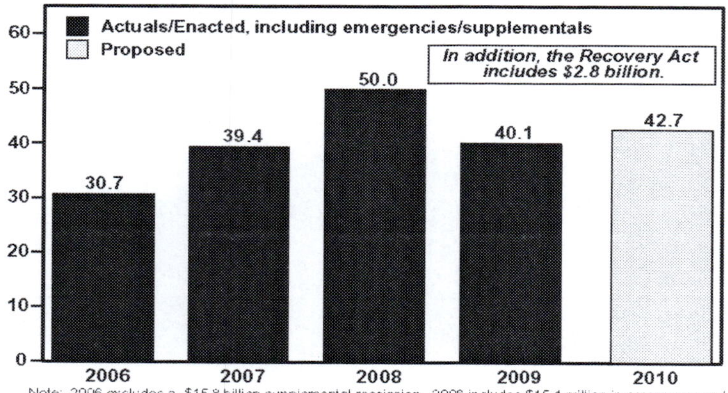

Note: 2006 excludes a -$15.8 billion supplemental rescission. 2008 includes $15.1 million in emergency and supplemental funds appropriated under Public Laws 110-116, 110-161, 110-252, and 110-329. 2009 excludes the one-time advance appropriation for Bioshield funding, $2.175 billion and includes a $112 million transfer from DOD to Coast Guard.

Enhances Cybersecurity and Technology Research and Development. Funding of $355 million is targeted to make private and public sector cyber infrastructure more resilient and secure. These funds will support the base operations of the National Cyber Security Division, as well as initiatives under the Comprehensive National Cybersecurity Initiative to protect our information networks. Funding of $36 million will support ongoing projects to improve surveillance technologies to detect enhanced, emerging and advanced biological threats. Efforts to develop next-generation BioWatch sensors will continue in order to detect bio-attacks at the earliest possible instant. The Budget also supports the termination of outdated systems such as the terrestrial-based, long-range radionavigation (LORAN-C) operated by the U.S. Coast Guard resulting in an offset of $36 million in 2010 and $190 million over five years.

Strengthens Border Security and Immigration Services. The Budget funds $45 million for the expansion of an exit pilot at key land ports of entry and other border security priorities. Funding of $368 million within existing Customs and Border Protection funds support 20,000 Border Patrol agents protecting nearly 6,000 miles of U.S. borders. The Budget provides over $1.4 billion for Immigration and Customs Enforcement programs to ensure that illegal aliens who commit crimes are expeditiously identified and removed from the United States. Funding of $110 million is provided to continue expansion of E-Verify, an electronic employment eligibility verification system. E-Verify helps U.S. employers comply with immigration law and ensures that U.S. jobs are available to U.S. citizens and those authorized to work in the United States. The Budget also supports strengthening the delivery of immigration services by streamlining and modernizing immigration application processes.

Supports State Homeland Security Activities. Making the Federal Government a better partner to States and localities on key homeland security initiatives is an Administration priority. Additional funding is provided to improve coordination between all levels of government, support our first responders, and create more effective emergency response plans. Risk-based exercise assistance grants will assist State, local, and tribal partners in offsetting costs of critical homeland security activities and will expand their Medical Surge Capacity with the stockpiling and storing of essential supplies. Funding of $260 million within the existing Homeland Security Grant program will fortify the Nation's intelligence system by improving information sharing and analysis by adding thousands more State and local level intelligence analysts.

DEPARTMENT OF HOUSING AND URBAN DEVELOPMENT

Funding Highlights

- Provides full funding for the Community Development Block Grant program at $4.5 billion. In addition, the Budget reforms the program's formula to better target economically distressed communities. The program will also stimulate innovations in metropolitan sustainability, university partnerships, and rural housing and economic development.
- Provides $1 billion to capitalize and launch an Affordable Housing Trust Fund that will develop, rehabilitate, and preserve affordable housing targeted to very-low income households. The Fund will help to prevent homelessness and strengthen families.
- Increases funding for the Housing Choice Voucher program, which likewise makes housing affordable to very low-income households. The Department of Housing and Urban Development will also introduce legislative reforms to address the program's costly inefficiencies.
- Enables the Department to preserve approximately 1 .3 million affordable rental units through increased funding for the Department's assisted multifamily properties.
- Combats mortgage fraud and predatory loans. The Budget funds enhanced enforcement of fair housing, mortgage disclosure, and settlement requirements.
- Creates a new Energy Innovation Fund to catalyze private sector investment in the energy efficiency of the Nation's housing stock.
- Creates a new Choice Neighborhoods Initiative to make a range of transformative investments in high-poverty neighborhoods where public and assisted housing is concentrated.
- Eliminates funding for ineffective and duplicative programs, including the Section 108 Community Development Loan Guarantees program and the American Dream Downpayment Initiative.

The Department of Housing and Urban Development (HUD) is committed to fulfilling its mission of increasing homeownership, supporting innovative and sustainable community development, and increasing access to affordable housing free from discrimination. The President's Budget restores and increases funding for many HUD programs to achieve these important goals while reforming or eliminating duplicative and inefficient programs.

Provides Full Funding for the Community Development Block Grant (CDBG) Program. The President is fulfilling his pledge to fully fund CDBG. The Budget provides $4.5 billion for 2010 to ensure that communities continue to invest in and expand economic opportunities for low-income families. In addition to the significant funding increase, the Budget will modernize the program through statutory reforms. Through a more effective formula, appropriate incentives and accountability measures, and a new Sustainable Communities Initiative, the Administration will revamp the CDBG program to better target funds to distressed communities and promote sustainable and economically viable communities.

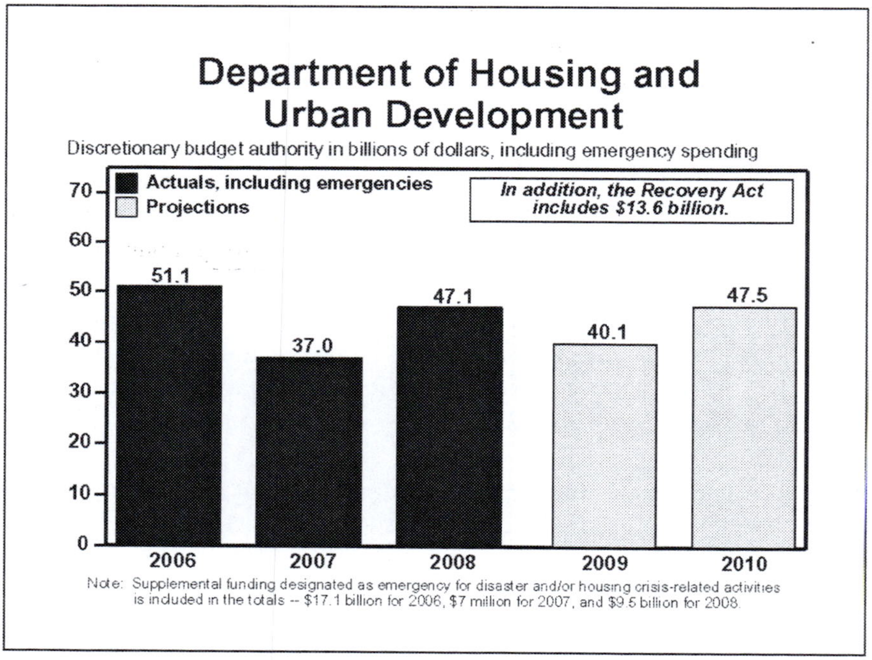

Provides Funding for an Affordable Housing Trust Fund for the First Time. The Housing Trust Fund was originally authorized in the Housing and Economic Recovery Act of 2008, with a dedicated funding stream from assessments on Fannie Mae and Freddie Mac. However, given their financial difficulties, the Federal Housing Finance Agency has indefinitely suspended these assessments. The Budget restores funding for the Housing Trust Fund by requesting $1 billion to finance the development, rehabilitation, and preservation of affordable housing for very low income residents.

Increases Funding for the Housing Choice Voucher Program. A robust Housing Choice Voucher program will help more than two million extremely low- to low-income families with rental assistance to live in decent housing in neighborhoods of their choice. To address the program's costly inefficiencies, the Administration will introduce legislative reforms to help fully utilize available funding, alleviate the administrative burdens on the Public Housing Authorities, and establish a funding mechanism that is transparent and predictable in order to serve more needy families.

Increases Funding for the Project-Based Rental Assistance Program. The Project-Based Rental Assistance program will preserve approximately 1.3 million affordable rental units through increased funding for contracts with owners of multifamily properties. This critical investment will assist low- and very low-income households in obtaining decent, safe and sanitary housing in private accommodations.

Combats Mortgage Fraud and Precautionary Practices. The Budget provides funds for HUD to combat mortgage fraud and predatory practices and includes increased funding for fair housing enforcement. These resources will allow HUD to increase enforcement of mortgage and home purchase settlement requirements. This involves proper disclosure of mortgage terms and permissible business practices and charges. Enhanced enforcement will create an environment in which home-buyers will be served with mortgage terms that are more easily understood and reliably honored by lenders.

Creates a New Energy Innovation Fund. The Budget includes funds for HUD to drive the creation of an energy-efficient housing market—including "retrofitting" of older, inefficient housing—and catalyze private sector lending for this purpose in the residential sector. Partnering with the Department of Energy on this initiative, HUD will contribute to the Administration's broader effort to combat global warming, jump- start the creation of a green economy, and reduce utility bills.

Creates a New Choice Neighborhoods Initiative. The Budget includes funds for HUD to support a range of transformative interventions in neighborhoods of concentrated poverty. This new initiative would challenge public, private and nonprofit partners to identify neighborhood interventions that would have the largest return on Federal investments.

Eliminates Funding for Ineffective and Duplicative Programs. The President's Budget proposes to eliminate funding for two HUD programs totaling $16 million. The Section 108 Community Development Loan Guarantees Program and the American Dream Downpayment Initiative are duplicative of larger programs that achieve similar results. By eliminating separate funding for these programs, HUD will streamline its resources and focus its efforts on programs that are more successful. Section 108 Community Development activities will continue to be eligible under CDBG.

The President's 2010 Budget includes $12 billion for the Department of the Interior (DOI) to undertake initiatives to protect and preserve America's national parks and public lands, conserve wetlands and wildlife habitat, strengthen Native American communities, enhance outdoor opportunities for young people, and promote energy security with a focus on clean renewable sources and strategies to address climate change.

DEPARTMENT OF THE INTERIOR

Funding Highlights

- Protects national parks with $100 million in additional funds to operate and maintain park facilities and resources and $25 million to leverage private donations for park projects.
- Conserves new Federal and State lands and protects endangered species with appropriations of about $420 million from the Land and Water Conservation Fund, with annual increases to reach full funding of $900 million by 2014.
- Assists State and Federal land management agencies with over $130 million in additional funding to monitor, adaptively manage and assess the impacts of climate change on the Nation's lands, fish and wildlife.
- Creates educational and job opportunities for young people through expanded environmental education activities and new programs to encourage them to hunt and fish responsibly.
- Strengthens Native American communities through an increase of over $100 million for enhanced law enforcement and education.
- Anticipates future costs for catastrophic wildfires with a new contingent funding reserve of $75 million for the Department of the Interior.
- Invests over $50 million to promote renewable energy projects on Federal lands and waters.
- Encourages responsible development of oil and gas resources and closes loopholes that have given oil companies excessive royalty relief for offshore leases.

Protects National Parks. The President is committed to preserving the Nation's national parks, with a $100 million increase in park operations (plus inflation) to protect the investments made through the American Recovery and Reinvestment Act of 2009, and maintain facilities and natural resources. An additional $25 million will provide matching funds to leverage private donations in preparation for the 100th anniversary of the National Park Service.

Conserves New Lands. While Americans can take great pride in our existing national parks and other public lands, there are many landscapes and ecosystems that do not have adequate protection. One way to protect these landscapes is to increase funding through the

Land and Water Conservation Fund (LWCF) to acquire and conserve new parks and public lands, with a focus on ecosystems that do not yet have the protection they deserve. The Budget increases LWCF funding for DOI by over $80 million, bringing the total request for the Departments of Agriculture and the Interior to approximately $420 million in 2010. This will put the Administration on track to fully fund LWCF programs at $900 million by 2014.

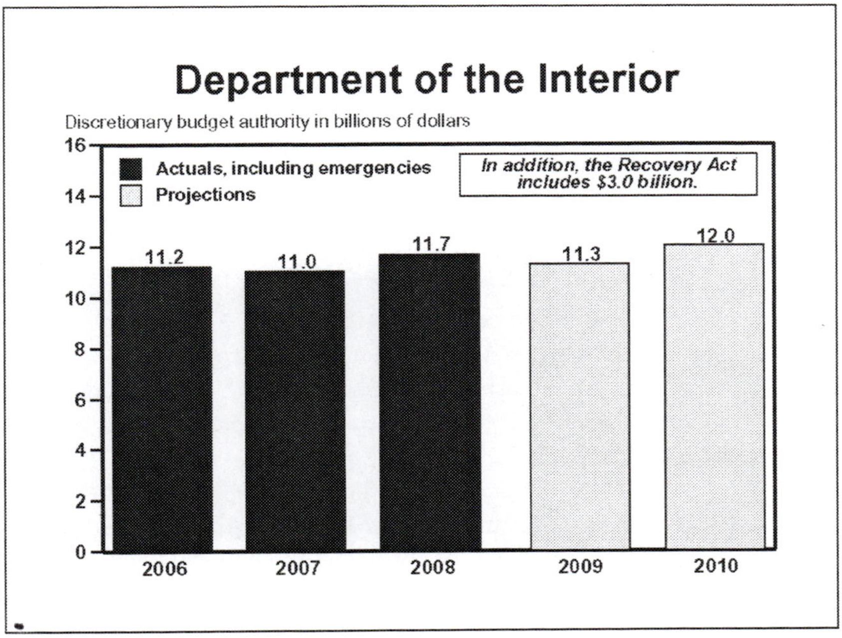

Assesses and Responds to the impact of Climate Change on Wildlife. Climate change poses a threat to America's fish and wildlife, as natural habitats are modified more rapidly than plants and animals can adjust. Scientific analyses are needed to understand the breadth of these changes. Federal land management agencies, States, and Tribes all need to update land management and species recovery plans to reflect the impacts of climate change on wildlife. They also need to monitor how wildlife is adapting and accelerate projects, such as protecting migration corridors, to help wildlife adjust. The Budget includes increases of more than $130 million, of which $40 million is shared with the States for wildlife adaptation. Additionally, the Budget increases funds by $10 million for North American Wetlands Conservation Act (NAWCA) activities to acquire, restore, or protect wetlands used by migratory waterfowl and other birds. This is the first step in fully funding NAWCA at $75 million by 2012.

Encourages youth Education and Involvement. The President is keenly aware of the important role that hunters and anglers play in the conservation of the Nation's wildlife and natural habitats. The Administration seeks to forge a broad coalition to address great conservation challenges, and America's hunters and anglers play an important part. To help preserve the national traditions of hunting and fishing shared by families across the country, the Budget provides funding to help States establish creative programs and strategies to encourage young people and minority populations to responsibly hunt and fish. The Budget also expands opportunities for youth education including internships to instill environmental awareness. These programs will receive increases of over $50 million.

Strengthens Native American Communities. The Administration supports the principle of tribal self-determination and will work to improve tribal law enforcement and education. The Budget includes over $100 million in increased funding to the Bureau of Indian Affairs for law enforcement and education. Additional funding is also available through the Departments of Justice and Education. These funds will strengthen tribal courts, detention centers, and police programs to help Native Americans protect their communities. The Budget also increases funding for tribal colleges and scholarships and provides funding earlier in the academic year, giving the colleges greater financial security.

Establishes a Dedicated Fund to Fight Wildfires. The Budget establishes a dedicated fund for catastrophic wildfires and fully funds the 10-year average suppression costs, coupled with program reforms that ensure fire management resources are focused where they will do the most good. This $75 million discretionary contingent reserve provides funding that is only available for fighting catastrophic wildfires after the appropriated 10-year average is exhausted. This funding and the associated reforms provided in the Budget will improve wildfire operations and promote safe, cost-effective and accountable results from investments made in managing fire on landscapes.

Invests in a Clean Energy Future. DOI will play a central role in achieving the President's vision for a clean energy future advancing our national security, environmental security, and economic opportunity. The Department will help lead the way when it comes to enhancing the Nation's domestic energy supply and moving toward a clean energy economy. Our public lands, and the offshore resources that we control already provide close to one-third of our entire domestic supply of oil and gas resources. The Budget includes over $50 million in increases to conduct the environmental evaluations and technical studies needed to spur development of renewable energy projects, assess available alternative resources, and mitigate the impacts of development.

Ensures Responsible Production of Energy on Federal Lands. DOI will take steps to ensure that oil and gas companies diligently develop their oil and gas leases or risk losing them ("use or lose"). One step is to charge a new fee on non-producing leases in the Gulf of Mexico. This provides an added incentive for oil companies to either start producing or relinquish the leases so that others may bid on them.

Provides a Better Return to Taxpayers from Mineral Development. The public receives over $12 billion annually from fees, royalties, and other Federal payments related to oil, gas, coal, and other mineral development. yet, that return could be improved by closing loopholes, charging appropriate fees, and reforming how royalties are set. The Budget proposes a number of actions to ensure that Federal taxpayers receive their fair share, such as:

- Using a new excise tax on offshore oil and gas production in the Gulf of Mexico to close loopholes that have given oil companies excessive royalty relief. This new tax will begin in 2011, after the economy has had time to recover.

- Terminating payments to coal-producing States that no longer need funds to clean up abandoned coal mines.
- Charging user fees to oil companies for processing oil and gas drilling permits on Federal lands.
- Increasing the return from oil and gas production on Federal lands through administrative actions, such as reforming royalties and adjusting rates.

Conserves Western Water. The Bureau of Reclamation and the Bureau of Indian Affairs support the development, management and restoration of water and related natural resources in 17 Western States and tribal lands while balancing competing uses of water. Consistent with this objective, the Budget provides funding in 2010 for a western water conservation initiative, which includes the Bureau of Reclamation's water reuse and recycling (Title XVI) program. The goal of this effort is to assist local communities' availability of water by encouraging voluntary water banks, wastewater treatment, and other market- based conservation measures.

DEPARTMENT OF JUSTICE

Funding Highlights

- Provides significant increases to address the National Security and Intelligence challenges confronting the FBI and other Department of Justice components.
- Begins funding 50,000 additional police officers through the Community Oriented Policing Services program.
- Provides funding to combat financial fraud and protect the public interest.
- Reinvigorates Federal Civil Rights Enforcement.
- Provides the enforcement, confinement and prosecutorial resources necessary to help ensure the Nation's borders are secure.
- Addresses Federal detention and incarceration programs and ensures that returning Federal prisoners have the support needed to successfully reintegrate into communities.

The President's Budget for the Department of Justice (DOJ) is $26.5 billion. The Budget addresses the key priorities of the President and the Attorney General, including those for National Security and crime fighting programs in the FBI and other DOJ components, to include resources for combating financial fraud and protecting the public interest. The Budget funds the Community Oriented Policing Services (COPS) hiring program, ensures that prison and detention programs are adequately funded, to include prisoner reentry programs, reinvigorates Federal civil rights enforcement, and increases border security.

Counters the Threat of Terrorism and Strengthens National Security. The Budget provides $8 billion for the FBI, including $425 million in enhancements, and $88 million for the National Security Division to address the President's highest priority to protect the American people from terrorist acts. Funding supports the detection and disruption of terrorists, counterintelligence, cyber security, and other threats against our National Security.

Provides Funding to Begin to Put 50,000 More Cops on the Beat. Expanding COPS Hiring Grants, the Budget includes funding to begin hiring 50,000 additional police officers. Supporting the hiring of police nationwide will help States and communities prevent the growth of crime during the economic downturn.

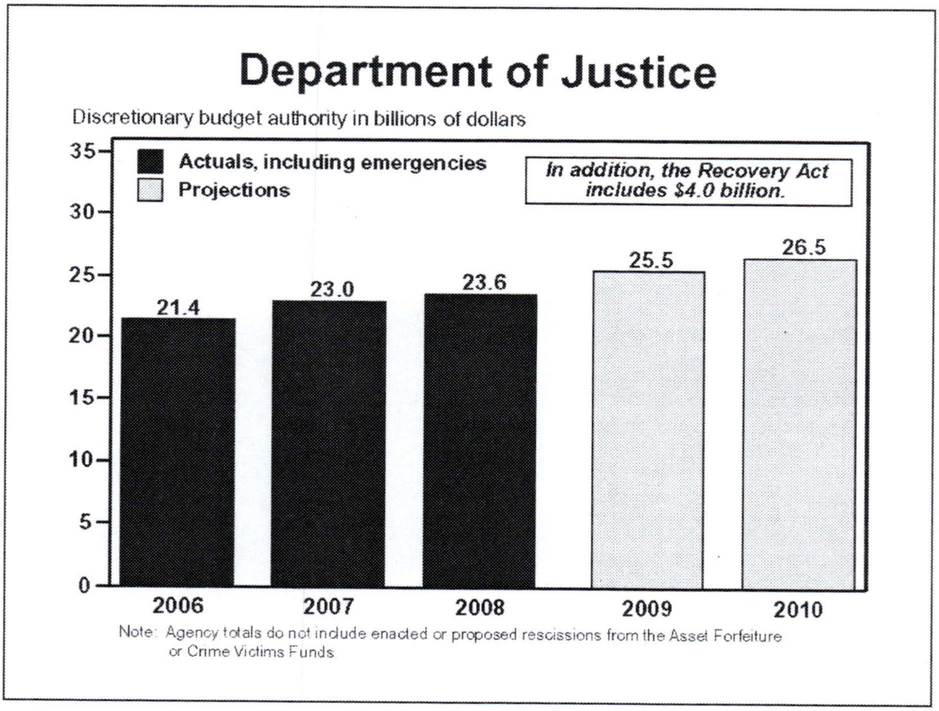

Combats Financial Fraud. The Budget provides resources for additional FBI agents to investigate mortgage fraud and white collar crime and for additional Federal prosecutors, civil litigators and bankruptcy attorneys to protect investors, the market, the Federal Government's investment of resources in the financial crisis, and the American public.

Reinvigorates Federal Civil Rights Enforcement. The Budget includes $145 million for the Civil Rights Division to strengthen civil rights enforcement against racial, ethnic, sexual preference, religious and gender discrimination.

Strengthens immigration Enforcement and Border Security. The Budget includes additional funding for a comprehensive approach to enforcement along the Nation's borders that combines law enforcement and prosecutorial component efforts to investigate, arrest, detain, and prosecute illegal immigrants and other criminals. The initiative also enhances the Department's ability to track fugitives from justice and combat gunrunners and illegal drug traffickers.

Supports Federal Detention and Incarceration Programs. The Budget provides $6 billion for the Bureau of Prisons and $1.4 billion for the Office of the Detention Trustee to ensure that sentenced criminals and detainees are housed in facilities that are safe, humane, cost-efficient, and appropriately secure.

Expands Prisoner Reentry Programs. The Budget includes $109 million for prisoner reentry programs, including an additional $75 million for the Office of Justice Programs to expand grant programs authorized by the Second Chance Act that provide counseling, job training, drug treatment, and other transitional assistance to former prisoners.

DEPARTMENT OF LABOR

Funding Highlights

- Builds on Unemployment Insurance modernization in the American Recovery and Reinvestment Act to make the program a more effective social safety net and economic stabilizer.
- Provides strong support for Federal workforce training programs, and increases their focus on green technologies training.
- Strengthens enforcement of labor standards, including workplace safety and benefit security, reversing years of erosion in funding for labor law enforcement agencies.
- Establishes automatic workplace pensions.

Reforms the Unemployment Insurance System. The Administration seeks to fundamentally reform the Nation's unemployment insurance (UI) system to better address the challenges and realities of the 21st Century workforce. Building on modernization reforms included in the American recovery and reinvestment Act of 2009, the 2010 Budget will focus on making the UI program more accessible to unemployed workers, especially in recessions, and ensuring the financial integrity of the system so that employers' taxes are well used. It will:

- **Improve UI as an automatic stabilizer.** The 2010 Budget will propose changes to make the UI program a more responsive and effective social safety net and economic stabilizer. While the regular State-funded UI program responds readily to rising unemployment, the same cannot be said of the permanent Extended Benefits (EB) program, which provides additional weeks of benefits when unemployment in a State is high and rising. The Budget will propose legislation to make the EB program more responsive to changing economic conditions. These changes will make benefits available more quickly to long-term unemployed workers and avoid the delays associated with enactment of legislation to create special, temporary extended unemployment programs.
- **Improve UI financial integrity.** Despite the efforts of States to reduce improper benefit payments, over $3.9 billion in UI benefits were erroneously paid in 2008. The Administration will tackle this problem by increasing funding for program integrity and proposing legislative changes that would reduce UI improper payments by $3.9 billion and employer tax evasion by almost $300 million over 10 years. The proposal would, among other things, collect benefit overpayments through garnishment of Federal income tax refunds and boost States' resources to go after benefit overpayments and UI tax evasion by allowing them to use a portion of recovered funds on fraud and error reduction.

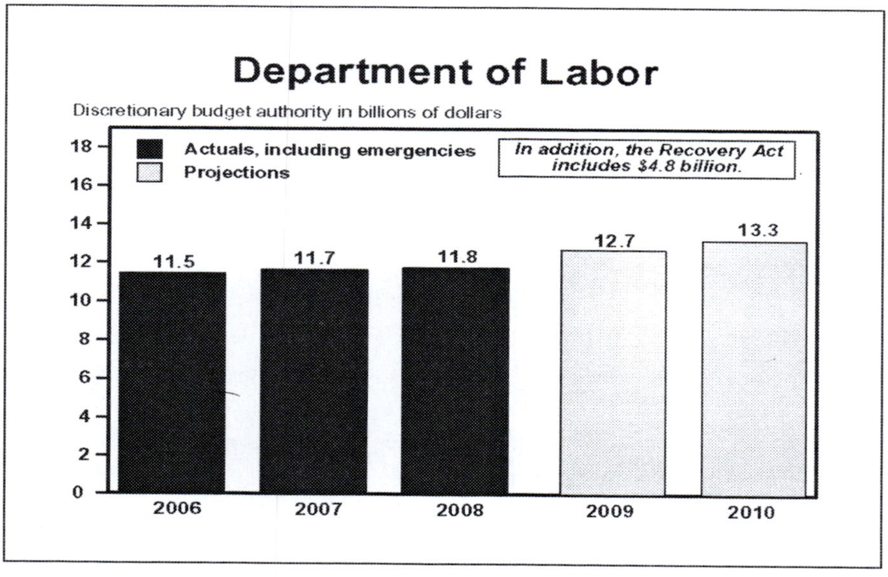

Trains and Prepares the Nation's Workforce for Jobs in Emerging Industries. The President's Budget provides strong support for Federal workforce training programs to help Americans prepare for, find, and retain stable, high-paying jobs. Building on the significant support in the Recovery Act for training in "green jobs," the Administration will direct existing programs to find ways to prepare workers for jobs associated with products and services that use renewable energy resources, reduce pollution, and conserve natural resources. The President's Budget will support new transitional jobs and career pathway programs, testing innovative approaches to helping low-income Americans grab hold of and climb the career ladder. It will add to the Recovery Act investments in youthBuild, expanding opportunities for disadvantaged young people to complete their high school education, learn valuable skills, and build affordable housing in their communities. The Budget provides additional resources to support job training for ex-offenders returning to their communities. The Budget also honors the commitment to return ing servicemembers by supporting training and placement services to ease their transition to civilian employment.

Restores Labor Standards. For the past eight years, the Department's labor law enforcement agencies have struggled with growing workloads and shrinking staff. The President's Budget seeks to reverse this trend, restoring the Department's ability to meets its responsibilities to working Americans under the more than 180 worker protection laws it enforces. The Budget will: increase funding for the Occupational Safety and Health Administration, enabling it to vigorously enforce workplace safety laws and whistleblower protections, and ensure the safety and health of American workers; increase enforcement resources for the Wage and Hour Division to ensure that workers are paid the wages that are due them; and boost funding for the Office of Federal Contract Compliance Programs, which is charged with pursuing equal employment opportunity and a fair and diverse Federal contract workforce.

Establishes Automatic Workplace Pensions and Makes the Saver's Credit Refundable. Currently, 75 million working Americans—roughly half the workforce—lack employer-based retirement plans. The President's 2010 Budget lays the groundwork for future establishment of a system of automatic workplace pensions, to operate along side Social Security, that is expected to dramatically increase both the number of Americans who save for retirement and the overall amount of personal savings for individuals. Under this proposal, employees will be automatically enrolled in workplace pension plans. Employers who do not currently offer a retirement plan will be required to enroll their employees in a direct-deposit IRA account that is compatible with existing direct-deposit payroll systems. Employees may opt-out if they choose. Experts estimate that this program will increase the savings participation rate for low and middle- income workers from its current 15 percent level to around 80 percent.

In addition, the Budget proposes to expand retirement savings incentives for working families by modifying the existing Saver's Credit to provide a 50-percent match on the first $1,000 of retirement savings for families that earn less than $65,000. The credit would be fully refundable to ensure that savings incentives are fair to all workers.

DEPARTMENT OF STATE AND OTHER INTERNATIONAL PROGRAMS

Funding Highlights

- Reflects the Administration's commitment to strengthen diplomatic and assistance tools to address current and future challenges that impact the security of the United States.
- Puts the United States on a path to double U.S. foreign assistance. This funding will help the world's weakest states reduce poverty, combat global health threats, develop markets, govern peacefully, and expand democracy worldwide.
- Supports the worldwide operations of the Department of State and U.S. Agency for International Development, provides new resources to hire additional Foreign Service officers, and builds civilian capacity to meet the challenges of today's world.
- Increases non-military aid to Afghanistan and Pakistan to revitalize economic development and confront the resurgence of the Taliban. Realigns U.S. assistance to Iraq to help responsibly end the war and enable Iraqis to assume more control of their country.
- Provides additional funding for key programs that advance U.S. foreign policy goals, including significantly increasing funding for energy initiatives, programs addressing global climate change, agriculture investments, and the Peace Corps.
- Provides full funding of all 2010 scheduled payments to the Multilateral Development Banks and a portion of the outstanding arrears to reinforce the U.S. commitment to play a leadership role in these institutions. Increases the U.S. quota subscription to the International Monetary Fund as part of the 2008 agreement on the Fund's reform, which will promote a strong international economy and maintain the U.S. voting share at the International Monetary Fund.
- Meets U.S. financial commitments to the United Nations and other international organizations that support a wide range of U.S. national security, foreign policy, and economic goals.
- Supports United Nations peacekeeping activities that help restore and maintain peace around the world.

- Responds to global security threats by increasing counterterrorism and law enforcement aid to critical partner nations including those in the Western Hemisphere, as well as increasing funding for nonproliferation activities to secure nuclear material at vulnerable sites.
- Ensures that the United States continues to be the world's leader in providing food aid and life- sustaining support for refugees and other conflict and disaster victims.
- Improves fiscal discipline and transparency by shifting funding for recurring programs, previously funded in supplemental appropriations, into the 2010 Budget.

Puts the United States on a Path to Double Foreign Assistance. By increasing foreign assistance, the United States will reach out to the global community and renew its role as a leader in global development and diplomacy. Through increased foreign assistance funding, the United States will embark on several new initiatives that will give children in the poorest countries access to education ensuring they can participate in the global marketplace; foster global food security through sustainable agriculture; expand goodwill and inspire service by increasing the size of the Peace Corps; and stabilize post-conflict states, creating room for them to plant the seeds of democracy.

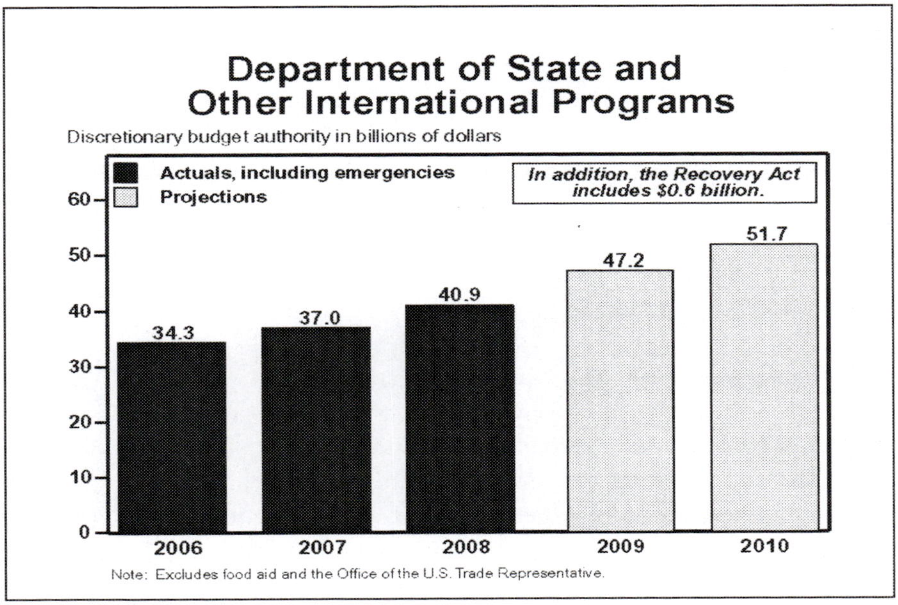

Increases Funding for Global Health Programs. The Administration will continue to build on its commitment to save lives through increasing investments in global health programs, including areas such as maternal and child health, family planning and other core health programs, while also emphasizing a commitment to HIV/AIDS, malaria, and tuberculosis through successful programs, such as the President's Emergency Plan for AIDS Relief and the Malaria Initiative. Together with our multilateral partners, the United States will continue to provide global leadership to improve the health status of the world's poorest populations.

Reinvigorates Counter-Proliferation, Anti- Terrorism, and Transnational Crime-Fighting Efforts. The Budget will fund reinvigorated efforts to counter proliferation, terrorism, and transnational crime. By fostering opportunity and security worldwide, this initiative will make the American people safer at home. This Budget includes first- year funding for a multi-year counterterrorism and law enforcement assistance program that strengthens the capabilities of our international partners in the Western Hemisphere and other critical regions around the world. The Budget also provides additional nonproliferation and counter-proliferation funding that will be used to help secure nuclear materials and promote safe civilian uses of nuclear energy.

Expands Diplomatic and Development Operations. This initiative will strengthen the U.S. Government's diplomatic and development operations to support our national security. The 2010 Budget includes funding for the first year of a multi-year effort to significantly increase the size of the Foreign Service at both the Department of State and the U.S. Agency for International Development (USAID). An increased cadre of State and USAID Foreign Service officers will help advance our critical foreign policy goals and deliver on our expanding U.S. foreign assistance commitments.

Refocuses Resources to Priorities in Afghanistan, Pakistan, and Iraq. The 2010 Budget refocuses U.S. resources toward addressing the resurgence of al Qaeda and the Taliban in Afghanistan and Pakistan. The Budget increases non-military assistance to both countries, providing additional funding for governance, reconstruction, counter-narcotics, and other development activities that will help counter extremists. The Budget expands the number of civilian personnel in Afghanistan and Pakistan in an effort to stabilize these countries, build government capacity, and successfully manage expanded assistance programs. The Budget strengthens our assistance to Iraqis who have been displaced from their homes because of the war. The Budget also realigns our assistance efforts in Iraq to ensure that Iraqis can assume more responsibility for their own political and economic future.

Imposes Transparency on the Budget. The Budget reduces reliance on emergency supplemental appropriations by increasing key accounts and programs for which funding is predictable and recurring. For example, the Budget includes increased funding for humanitarian assistance accounts and U.N. Peacekeeping Missions that reflect ongoing costs. While emergency supplementals may be required in the future, they should focus on truly unanticipated events and not be used to fund regular programs.

Commits to Developing Sustainable Solutions for Surface Transportation Programs and to Improving Program Performance. Surface transportation programs are at a cross-roads. The current framework for financing and allocating surface transportation investments is not financially sustainable; nor does it effectively allocate resources to meet our critical national needs. The Administration intends to work with the Congress to reform surface transportation programs both to put the system on a sustainable financing path and to make investments in a more sustainable future, enhancing transit options and making our economy more productive and our communities more livable. Further, the Nation's surface transportation system must generate the best investments to reduce congestion and improve safety. To do so, the Administration will emphasize the use of economic analysis and performance measurement in transportation planning. This will ensure that taxpayer dollars are better targeted and spent.

DEPARTMENT OF TRANSPORTATION

Funding Highlights

- Commits to better target surface transportation spending and explores options to make the Nation's communities more livable and less congested, such as through road pricing.
- Increases funding for public transit to support commuters, improve air quality, and reduce greenhouse gases.
- Supports development of high speed rail networks across the country to link regional population centers.
- Supports the Next Generation Air Transportation System to modernize the air traffic control system.

Initiates a New Federal Commitment to High Speed Rail To provide Americans a 21st Century transportation system, the Administration proposes a five-year $5 billion high-speed rail State grant program. Building on the $8 billion down payment in the American recovery and reinvestment Act of 2009, the President's proposal marks a new Federal commitment to give the traveling public a practical and environmentally sustainable alternative to flying or driving. Directed by the States, this investment will lead to the creation of several high-speed rail corridors across the country linking regional population centers.

Modernizes the Air Traf~c Control System The Budget provides approximately $800 million for the Next Generation Air Transportation System, a long-term effort to improve the efficiency, safety, and capacity of the air traffic control system. The 2010 Budget supports moving from a ground-based radar surveillance system to a more accurate satellite-based surveillance system; development of more efficient routes through the airspace; and improvements in aviation weather information.

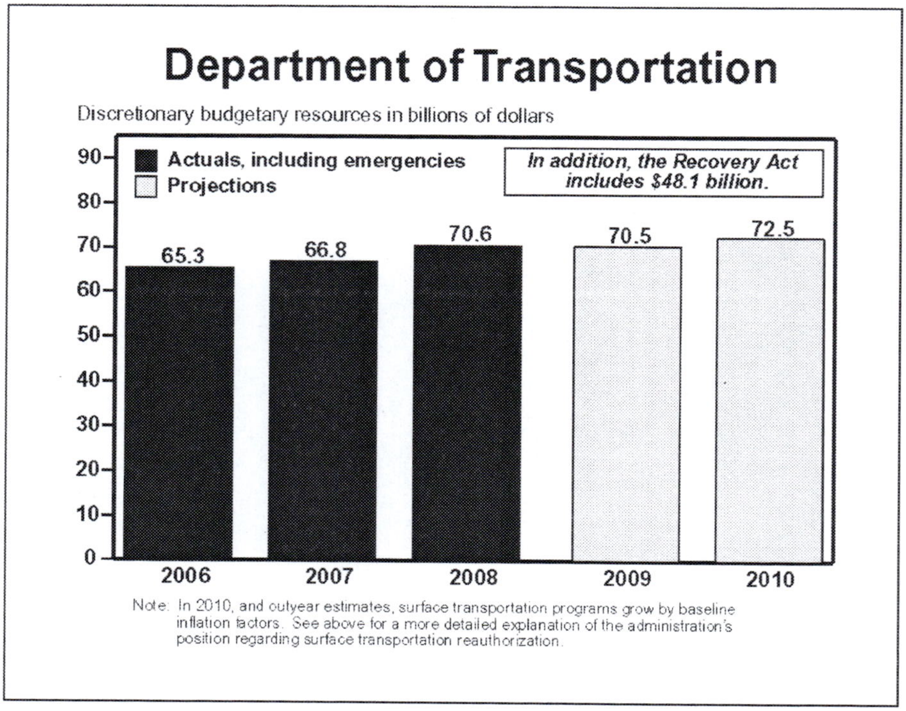

Improves Rural Access to the Aviation System The Administration is committed to maintaining small communities' access to the National Airspace System. The Budget provides a $55 million increase over the 2009 level to the Department of Transportation (DOT) to fulfill current program requirements as demand for subsidized commercial air service increases. However, the program that delivers this subsidy is not efficiently designed. Through the budget process, the Administration intends to work with the Congress to develop a more sustainable program model that will fulfill its commitment while enhancing convenience for travelers and improving cost effectiveness.

Makes Budgetary Treatment of Transportation Programs More Transparent. Budget authority for highway, transit, highway safety, and airport improvement programs usually has been defined as mandatory contract authority provided in authorizing legislation. However, the levels of contract authority have been, for the most part, controlled by obligation limitations in appropriations acts. Outlays from the obligation limitations have always been scored as discretionary. To more transparently display program resources, the Administration proposes changing the budgetary treatment of transportation programs to show both budget authority and outlays as discretionary. For 2009, the discretionary budget authority top line would be increased by approximately $53 billion, increasing DOT budget authority total from $17 billion under the typical presentation to $70 billion. Similar budget authority adjustments would be made for each outyear. The change would not affect outlays or the deficit or surplus—just more transparently convey to the taxpayer the real costs of supporting the transportation infrastructure our Nation needs.

DEPARTMENT OF THE TREASURY

Funding Highlights

- Supports the Administration's new Financial Stability Plan, as well as financial regulatory reform efforts and the effective, transparent governance of the Troubled Assets Relief Program and its successors.
- Expands funding for effective Internal Revenue Service (IRS) enforcement and invests in high return-on-investment activities that generate improved compliance and fairness in the application of tax laws.
- Improves the responsiveness and efficiency of taxpayer services to improve the accuracy of taxpayer filing and the quality of taxpayers' experience when they interact with the IRS.
- Expands job-creating investments and access to credit in disadvantaged communities by doubling funding for the Community Development Financial Institutions Fund.

The Department of the Treasury promotes the economic prosperity and financial security of the United States. Treasury operates 13 bureaus with a vast array of activities that are critical to the core functions of government, including collecting revenue and disbursing payments, managing Federal finances, and protecting the financial system from threats. Treasury also plays a key role in modernizing the American financial regulatory system and ensuring effective, transparent administration of programs designed to revive and strengthen the economy.

Supports the New Financial Stability Plan and the Administration of the Troubled Assets Relief Program (TARP). The Budget supports the Administration's new Financial Stability Plan as well as the management of the TARP, emphasizing effective, transparent, and accountable program management.

In addition, as discussed in the main text of this document, the President's Budget includes a \$250 billion contingent reserve for further efforts to stabilize the financial system. (The reserve, which reflects a net cost to the Government, would support \$750 billion in asset purchases.) The existence of this reserve in the Budget does not represent a specific request. Rather as events warrant, the Administration will work with the Congress to determine the appropriate size and shape of such efforts, and as more information becomes available the Administration will define an estimate of potential costs.

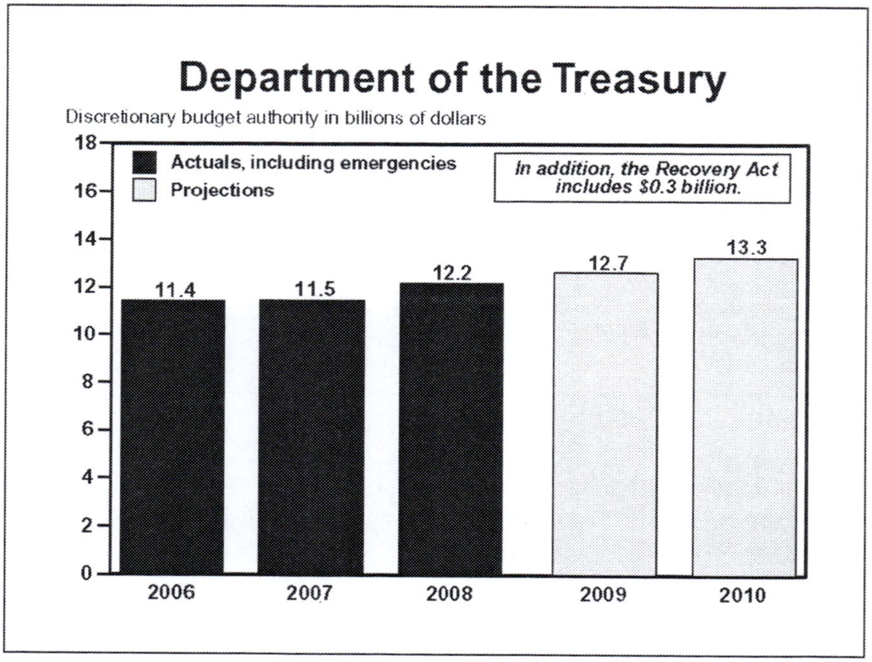

Collects Taxes Owed Here and Abroad. The scope, complexity, and sheer magnitude of the international financial system pose significant enforcement challenges for the IRS in carrying out its tax administration responsibilities. The 2010 Budget includes funding for a robust portfolio of IRS international tax compliance initiatives, and sustains and improves IRS efforts to narrow the annual tax gap of over $300 billion.

Enhances IRS Services to Taxpayers. The Administration will pursue plans to improve the quality of taxpayers' experience when they interact with the IRS. This strategy includes improving relationships with critical third-party stakeholders, such as tax preparers, volunteers and practitioners, as well as enhancing electronic filing capabilities. The end goal envisions an IRS that correctly answers a tax payer's question the first time asked, through the most efficient and taxpayer-friendly means.

Expands Lending in Disadvantaged Communities. The Budget expands lending in underserved neighborhoods by doubling funding for the Community Development Financial Institutions (CDFI) Fund. Through merit-based grant programs, the CDFI Fund helps locally based financial institutions offer small business, consumer and home loans in communities and populations that lack access to affordable credit.

Increases Funding for the Department of Veterans Affairs (VA) by $25 Billion above Baseline Over the Next Five years. The President's Budget takes the first step toward increasing funding for VA by $25 billion over the next five years in order to honor our Nation's veterans and expand the services they receive.

DEPARTMENT OF VETERANS AFFAIRS

Funding Highlights

- Increases funding for the Department of Veterans Affairs by $25 billion above baseline over the next five years.
- Dramatically increases funding for veterans health care.
- Expands eligibility for veterans health care to over 500,000 veterans by 2013.
- Enhances outreach and services related to mental health care and cognitive injuries, including post-traumatic stress disorder and traumatic brain injury, with a focus on access for veterans in rural areas.
- Invests in better technology to deliver services and benefits to veterans with the quality and efficiency they deserve.
- Provides greater benefits to veterans who are medically retired from service.
- Combats homelessness by safeguarding vulnerable veterans.
- Facilitates timely implementation of the comprehensive education benefits that veterans earn through their dedicated military service.

Dramatically Increases Funding for VA Health Care. This increase will provide adequate resources to give 5.5 million veteran patients timely and high quality care. This funding also enables VA to create Centers of Excellence and provides additional veteran-oriented specialty care in areas including prosthetics, vision and spinal cord injury, aging, and women's health.

Restores Health Care Eligibility for Modest-Income Veterans. For the first time since January 2003, the President's Budget expands eligibility for VA health care to non- disabled veterans earning modest incomes. This expansion will bring over 500,000 eligible veterans into the VA health care system by 2013 while maintaining high quality and timely care for the lower-income and disabled veterans who currently rely on VA medical care.

Enhances Outreach and Services Related to Mental Health Care and Cognitive Injuries with a Focus on Access for veterans in Rural Areas. Conditions such as post-traumatic stress disorder and traumatic brain injury present challenges in caring for veterans of current conflicts. The President's Budget expands the mental health screening and treatment services offered by VA and focuses on reaching veterans in rural areas. VA will increase the number of Vet Centers and mobile health clinics to expand access to mental health screening and treatment in rural areas. In addition, new funding will help veterans and their families stay informed of these resources and encourage them to pursue needed care.

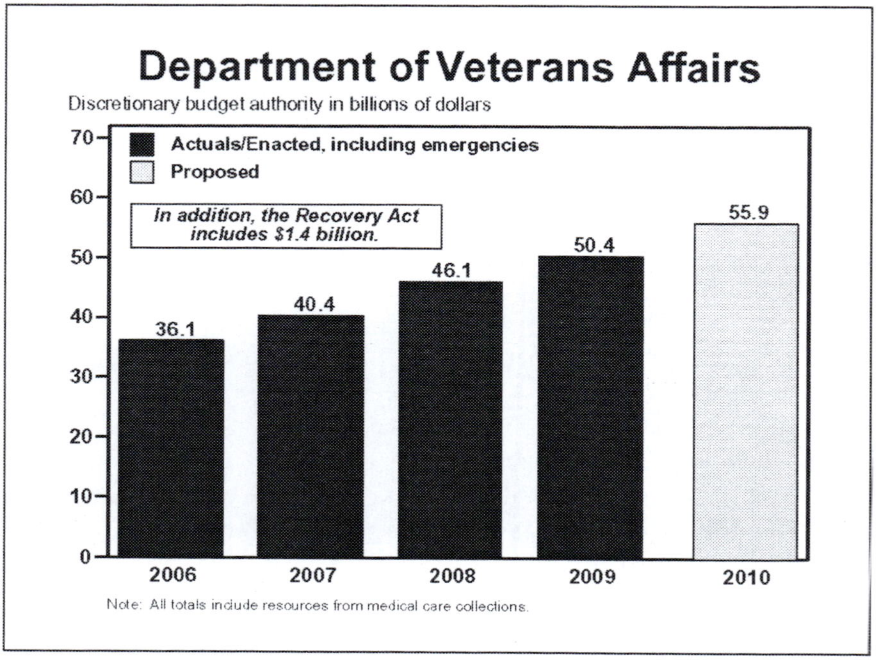

Invests in Better Technology to Deliver Services and Benefits to Veterans with the Quality and Efficiency They Deserve. To transform VA into a 21st Century organization, the President's Budget invests in information technology that directly benefits veterans in the areas of both health care and benefits. Through improved electronic medical records, VA will more efficiently retrieve active duty health records from the Department of Defense and enable all VA care sites to access the records of veterans needing care. VA will also invest in the development of rules-based electronic processes to increase accuracy, consistency, and timeliness in veterans' receipt of benefits.

Provides Greater Benefits for Veterans Who Are Medically Retired from Service. For the first time, highly disabled veterans who are medically retired from service will be eligible for concurrent receipt of disability benefits from VA in addition to Department of Defense retirement benefits.

Combats Homelessness by Safeguarding Vulnerable Veterans. The President's Budget expands VA's current services to homeless veterans through a collaborative pilot program with non-profit organizations. This pilot will help maintain stable housing for veterans who are at risk of falling into homelessness while helping VA to continue providing them with supportive services.

Facilitates Timely Implementation of the Comprehensive Education Benefits veterans Earn Through Their dedicated Service. The Budget provides the resources for effective implementation of the post-9/11 GI Bill—providing unprecedented levels of educational support to the men and women who have served our country through active military duty.

CORPS OF ENGINEERS-CIVIL WORKS

Funding Highlights

- Focuses construction funds on those investments that provide the best return from a national perspective in achieving economic, environmental and public safety objectives.
- Supports the safe and reliable operation and maintenance of key existing water resources infrastructure.
- Improves Corps project planning and program performance.
- Advances aquatic ecosystem restoration efforts, including restoration of Florida's Everglades and Louisiana's coastal wetlands.

The Budget proposes $5.1 billion in discretionary budget authority in 2010 for the Army Corps of Engineers civil works (Corps) program. The Budget will be transparent and based on performance information for projects and activities. The funding for the Corps in the 2010 Budget, together with the $4.6 billion provided for Corps programs in the American recovery and reinvestment Act of 2009, will significantly improve and strengthen the Nation's water resources infrastructure.

Focuses Construction on High-Return Investments. The construction program supports high-return investments in the three main mission areas of the Corps: 1) facilitating commercial navigation; 2) reducing the risk of damage from floods and storms; and 3) restoring significant aquatic ecosystems. To assure that investments in these missions provide the Nation with both high economic and environmental benefits, the Budget supports activities that complement multiple-project purposes and integrate environmental principles into traditional infrastructure efforts.

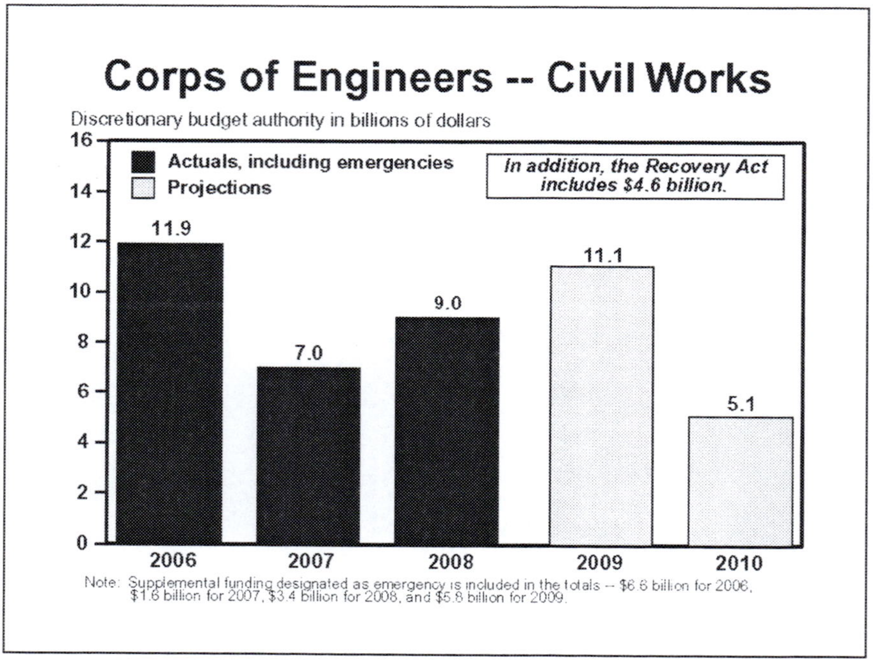

The Budget also will propose to phase out the current excise tax on diesel fuel for the inland waterways and replace it with a lock usage fee, designed to improve economic efficiency and preserve the landmark cost-sharing reform established by the Congress in 1986, while supporting investments in construction, expansion, replacement, and rehabilitation work.

Maintains Key Infrastructure. The Budget will emphasize funding to support maintenance and safe and reliable operation of those facilities that are of central importance to the Nation, and will address deferred maintenance to maintain or improve the performance of aging Corps infrastructure. The Corps will continue to develop and implement an objective risk-based decision-making system for allocating resources to these activities.

Honors the President's Commitments to the Gulf Coast. The Budget will fund continued work to restore coastal Louisiana wetlands, including a study to identify the best ways to restore wetlands affected by the Mississippi River Gulf Outlet, and the science needed to support these efforts. The Budget will also fund continued work on planning sustainable methods to reduce the risk of damage from hurricane storm surges to Gulf coastal areas.

Improves Program Performance. The Corps will focus efforts on developing new strategies, along with other Federal agencies and non-Federal project partners, to better manage, protect, and restore the Nation's water and related land resources, including floodplain and flood-prone coastal areas. The Corps will also pursue management reforms that improve project cost and schedule performance to ensure the greatest value from invested resources, while strengthening the accountability and transparency of the way in which taxpayer dollars are being spent.

ENVIRONMENTAL PROTECTION AGENCY

Funding Highlights

- Provides $10.5 billion in total for the Environmental Protection Agency, a 34-percent increase over the 2009 likely enacted level.
- Provides $3.9 billion for the Clean Water and Drinking Water State Revolving Funds, an unprecedented Federal commitment to water infrastructure investment in the United States.
- Provides $475 million for a new Environmental Protection Agency-led, interagency Great Lakes restoration initiative, which will target the most significant problems in the region, including invasive aquatic species, non-point source pollution, and contaminated sediment.
- Funds the Agency's operating budget, which comprises its core regulatory, research, and enforcement activities, at $3.9 billion, the highest level ever.
- Provides over $1.1 billion in grants for States and Tribes to administer environmental programs.

The Environmental Protection Agency (EPA) is responsible for the abatement and control of pollution, which involves the proper integration of research, monitoring, standard setting, and enforcement. The 2010 Budget requests a substantial increase over the budget requests of the last eight years—$10.5 billion, a 34-percent increase over the 2009 likely enacted budget. This includes $3.9 billion for EPA's operating budget, which is the heart of EPA's environmental protection function and includes funds for research, regulation, and enforcement. EPA's budget also provides State program implementation grants, capitalization grants to State revolving funds to help municipalities pay for the cost of pollution controls, and the clean up of contaminated sites.

Invests in Clean Water. The 2010 Budget requests $3.9 billion for the Clean Water State revolving Fund and the Drinking Water State revolving Fund (SRFs). With this historic increase, the program will fund over 1,000 Clean Water and nearly 700 Drinking Water projects annually in the Nation's States, Tribes, and territories, based on average project costs. The SrF programs provide grants to States to capitalize their own revolving funds, which finance wastewater and drinking water treatment systems. The SRFs use the Federal capitalization, State matches (20 percent), State leveraging, interest, and loan repayments to make low-interest loans to communities. Because repayments and interest are recycled back into the program, SRFs generate funding for loans (revolve) even without Federal capitalization. EPA estimates that for every Federal dollar invested, at least two dollars in financing is provided to municipalities. In conjunction with the dramatic increase in Federal funding for local water infrastructure needs, the Administration will pursue program reforms that will put resources for these ongoing needs on a firmer foundation. EPA will work with State and local partners to develop a sustainability policy including management and pricing for future infrastructure funded through SRFs to encourage conservation and to provide adequate long-term funding for future capital needs. The 2010 Budget also proposes to work with State and local governments to address Federal drinking water policy in order to provide equitable consideration of small system customers.

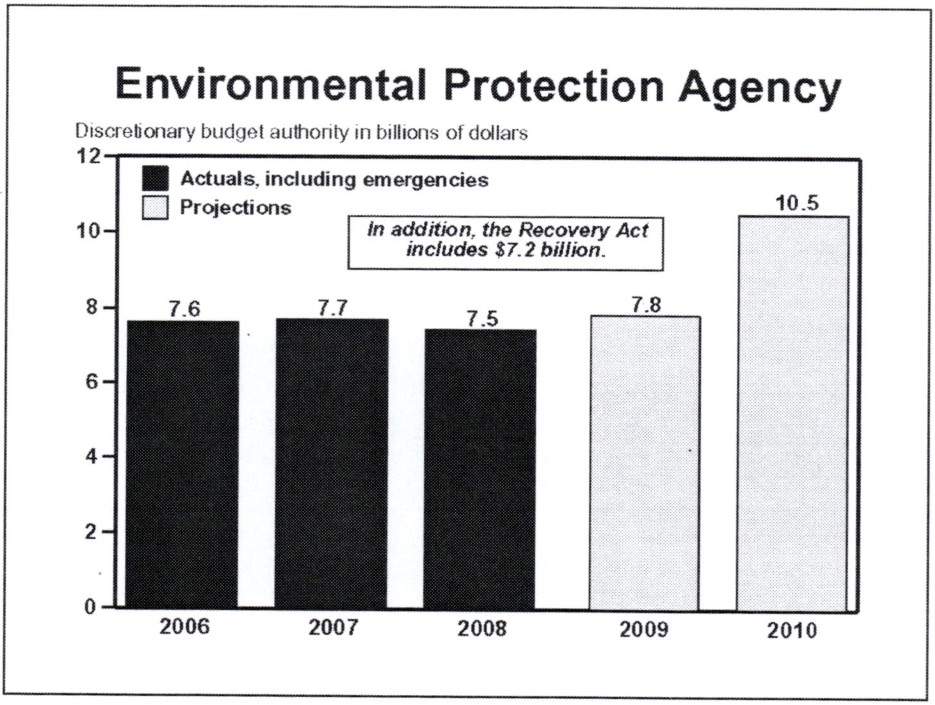

Accelerates the Restoration of the Great Lakes. The 2010 Budget includes a new $475 million inter-agency initiative to address regional issues that affect the Great Lakes, such as invasive species, non-point source pollution, and contaminated sediment. This initiative will use outcome-oriented performance goals and measures to target the most significant problems and track progress in addressing them. EPA and its Federal partners will coordinate State, tribal, local, and industry actions to protect, maintain, and restore the chemical, biological, and physical integrity of the Great Lakes.

Begins a Comprehensive Approach to Transform Our Energy Supply and Slow Global Warming. The Administration is developing a comprehensive energy and climate change plan to invest in clean energy, end our addiction to oil, address the global climate crisis, and create new American jobs that cannot be outsourced. After enactment of the Budget, the Administration will work expeditiously with key stakeholders and Congress to develop an economy-wide emissions reduction program to reduce greenhouse gas emissions approximately 14 percent below 2005 levels by 2020, and approximately 83 percent below 2005 levels by 2050. This program will be implemented through a cap-and-trade system, a policy approach that dramatically reduced acid rain at much lower costs than the traditional Government regulations and mandates of the past. Through a 100 percent auction to ensure that the biggest polluters do not enjoy windfall profits, this program will fund vital investments in a clean energy future totaling $150 billion over 10 years, starting in fiscal year 2012. The balance of the auction revenues will be returned to the people, especially vulnerable families, communities, and businesses to help the transition to a clean energy economy. The Budget includes a $19 million increase for EPA work on a Greenhouse Gas (GHG) emission inventory and to work with affected industry sectors to report high-quality GHG emission data. This will also allow for work on the necessary steps toward implementing a comprehensive climate bill.

Secures the Nation's Water Supply. The 2010 Budget provides $24 million to fully fund all five Water Security Initiative (WSI) pilot cooperative agreements and Water Alliance for Threat Reduction activities begun in response to the Bioterrorism Act of 2002. EPA launched its WSI in 2006 to demonstrate, test, and evaluate a design for a contamination warning system at drinking water utilities. Following completion of these pilots, EPA will issue guidance and promote adoption of effective drinking water contamination warning systems.

Strengthens Superfund. The 2010 Budget proposes to reinstate excise taxes that expired in 1995 and will collect over $1 billion to clean up the Nation's most toxic, contaminated sites within the Superfund program. The reinstated taxes will not begin until 2011 after the economy recovers.

Advances Global Climate Change Research and Monitoring. The National Aeronautics and Space Administration's (NASA's) investment in Earth science research satellites, airborne sensors, computer models, and analysis has revolutionized scientific knowledge and prediction of climate change and its effects. Using the National research Council's recommended priorities for space-based Earth science research as its guide, NASA will develop new space-based research sensors in support of the Administration's goal to deploy a global climate research and monitoring system. NASA will work to deploy these new sensors expeditiously while coordinating with other Federal agencies to ensure continuity of measurements that have long-term research and applications benefits.

Funds a Robust Program of Space Exploration Involving Humans and Robots. NASA's astronauts and robotic spacecraft have been exploring our solar system and the universe for more than 50 years. The Agency will create a new chapter of this legacy as it works to return Americans to the Moon by 2020 as part of a robust human and robotic space exploration program. NASA also will send a broad suite of robotic missions to destinations throughout the solar system and develop a bold new set of astronomical observatories to probe the mysteries of the universe, increasing investment in research, data analysis, and technology development in support of these goals.

Completes the International Space Station and Advances the Development of New Space Transportation Systems. NASA will fly the Space Shuttle to complete the International Space Station and then retire the Shuttle in 2010; an additional flight may be conducted if it can safely and affordably be flown by the end of 2010. Funds freed from the Shuttle's retirement will enable the Agency to support development of systems to deliver people and cargo to the International Space Station and the Moon. As part of this effort, NASA will stimulate private-sector development and demonstration of vehicles that may support the Agency's human crew and cargo space flight requirements.

National Aeronautics and Space Administration

NASA

Funding Highlights

- Provides $18.7 billion for the National Aeronautics and Space Administration. Combined with the $1 billion provided to the agency in the American Recovery and Reinvestment Act of 2009, this represents a total increase of more than $2.4 billion over the 2008 level.
- Funds a program of space-based research that supports the Administration's commitment to deploy a global climate change research and monitoring system.
- Funds a robust program of space exploration involving humans and robots. The National Aeronautics and Space Administration will return humans to the Moon while also supporting a vigorous program of robotic exploration of the solar system and universe.
- Funds the safe flight of the Space Shuttle through the vehicle's retirement at the end of 2010. An additional flight will be conducted if it can be completed safely before the end of 2010.
- Funds the development of new space flight systems for carrying American crews and supplies to space.
- Funds continued use of the International Space Station to support the agency and other Federal, commercial, and academic research and technology testing needs.
- Funds aeronautics research to address aviation safety, air traffic control, noise and emissions reduction, and fuel efficiency.

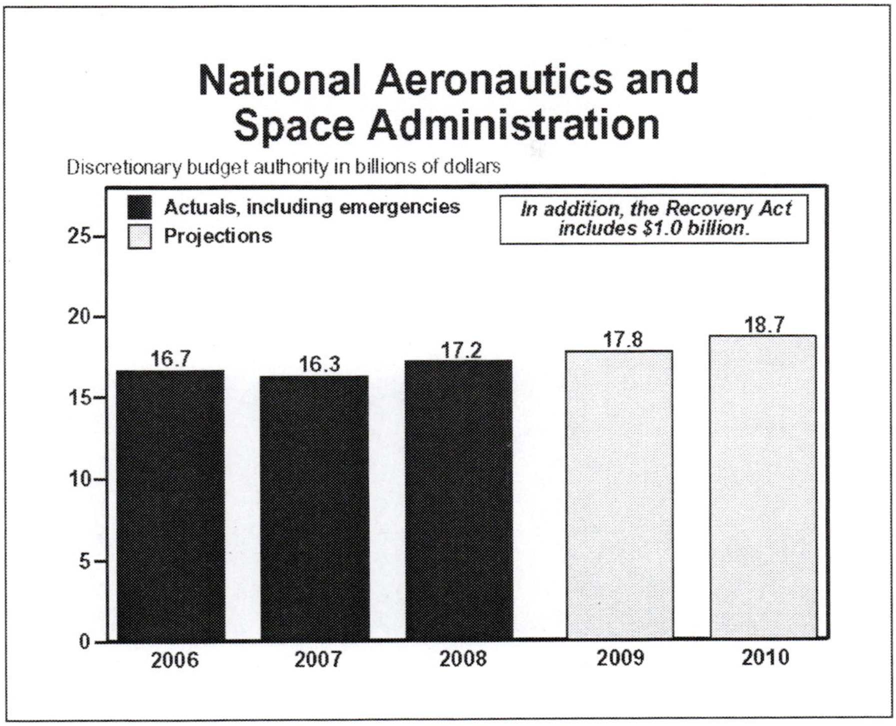

Continues Support of the international Space Station. NASA will continue to assemble and utilize the International Space Station, the permanently crewed facility orbiting Earth that enables the Agency to develop, test, and validate critical space exploration technologies and processes. NASA also will continue to coordinate with international partners to make this platform available for other government entities, commercial industry, and academic institutions to conduct research.

Renews NASA's Commitment to Aeronautics Research. A strong national program of aeronautics research and technology contributes to the economic well-being and quality of life of American citizens. NASA will renew its commitment to cutting-edge, fundamental research in traditional and emerging disciplines to help transform the Nation's air transportation system and to support future aircraft. NASA research will increase airspace capacity and mobility, enhance aviation safety, and improve aircraft performance while reducing noise, emissions, and fuel consumption.

Invests in the Sciences. Investments in science and technology foster economic growth, create millions of high-tech, high-wage jobs that allow American workers to lead the global economy, improve the quality of life for all Americans, and strengthen our national security. For these reasons, the Budget doubles funding for basic research over 10 years, beginning with $3 billion for the National Science Foundation (NSF) in the American recovery and reinvestment Act of 2009 and a 2010 Budget that increases NSF funding by $950 million over 2008.

NATIONAL SCIENCE FOUNDATION

Funding Highlights

- Provides $7 billion for the National Science Foundation, a 16-percent increase over the 2008 level, as part of the President's Plan for Science and Innovation.
- Increases support for graduate research fellowships and for early-career researchers.
- Increases support for the education of technicians in the high-technology fields that drive the Nation's economy.
- Encourages more novel high-risk, high-reward research proposals.
- Increases support for critical research priorities in global climate change.

Supports Researchers at the Beginning of Their Careers. Ensuring America's economic competitiveness requires that we develop the future scientific and technical workforce for our universities, national labs, and companies. To help accomplish these goals, the Budget provides substantial increases for NSF's prestigious Graduate research Fellowship and Faculty Early Career Development programs.

Strengthens the Education of Technicians in High-Technology Fields. The Budget increases support for the Advanced Technological Education program, which focuses on two-year colleges and supports partnerships between academic institutions and employers to promote improvement in the education of science and engineering technicians.

Encourages Promising High-Risk Research. The Budget increases support for promising, but exploratory and high-risk research proposals that could fundamentally alter our understanding of nature, revolutionize fields of science, and lead to radically new technologies.

Makes Climate Change Research and Education a Priority. The Budget supports research to improve our ability to predict future environmental conditions and to develop strategies for responding to global environmental change. The Budget establishes a climate change education program to

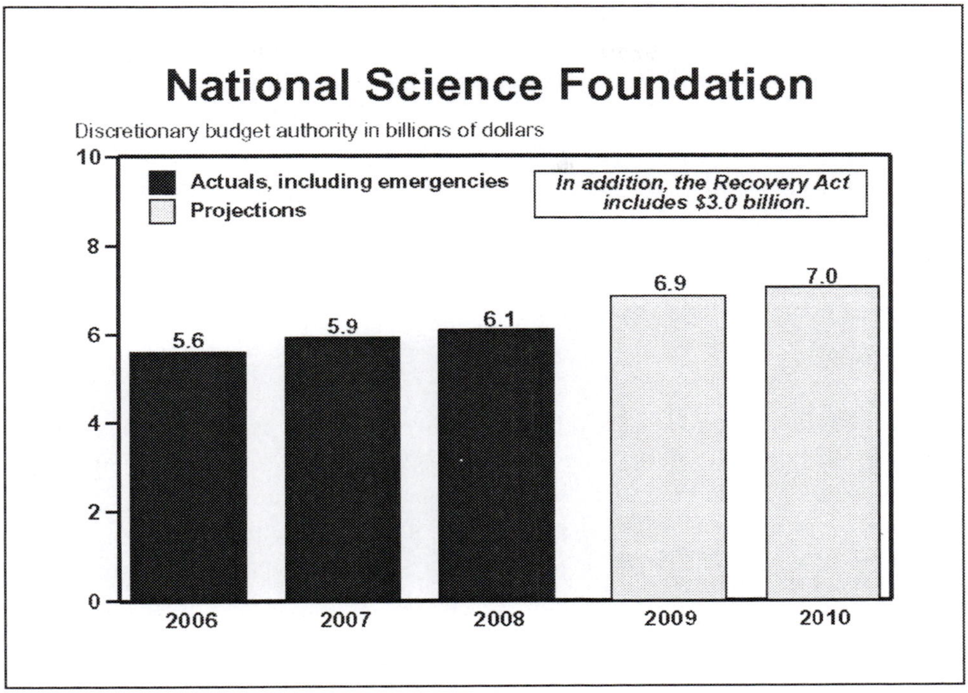

help develop the next generation of environmentally engaged scientists and engineers.

SMALL BUSINESS ADMINISTRATION

Funding Highlights

- Provides $28 billion in loan guarantees to expand credit availability for small businesses.
- Supports disaster recovery for homeowners, renters, and businesses.
- Sustains funding for technical assistance programs.
- Improves targeting of Federal contracting opportunities for small business.
- Modernizes core Agency information systems, streamlines loan processes, and enhances human capital resources.

Helps Small Businesses Weather the Credit Crisis The Budget supports: $17.5 billion in guarantees under the Section 7(a) Guaranteed Loan program, an important source of credit for small businesses; $7.5 billion in guaranteed debentures in the Section 504 Guaranteed Loan Program, providing Certified Development Companies financing to support commercial real estate development; $3 billion in authority for the Small Business Investment Company debenture program; and $25 million in Microloan volume, allowing intermediaries to provide small loans and technical assistance to entrepreneurs and other start-up businesses. In addition, the Administration's Small Business and Community Bank Lending Initiative will expand small business credit availability and affordability by unfreezing the secondary markets for small business loans—as part of the larger plan to revive the flow of credit in the Nation's economy.

Strengthens Tools to Make Government More Effective as a Partner for America's Small Businesses. SBA will leverage existing networks to reinvigorate small business lending by deploying capital through guaranteed loans and investment products. This includes technological improvements to SBA's core operations, as outlined below, so that SBA becomes more transparent, accountable and in touch with entrepreneurs and other partners on "Main Street."

These activities will build on the substantial funding for small business credit programs recently provided by the American recovery and reinvestment Act. The recovery Act provides SBA authority to increase guarantee percentages on new 7(a) loans to 90 percent, to help encourage lenders to make these loans. The recovery Act also provides funding to enable SBA to temporarily lower fees on both 7(a) and 504 loans, expand funding for the Microloan program, and increase the size of bonds available under SBA's surety bond program. In addition, the recovery Act includes a variety of other provisions intended to promote credit availability to small businesses.

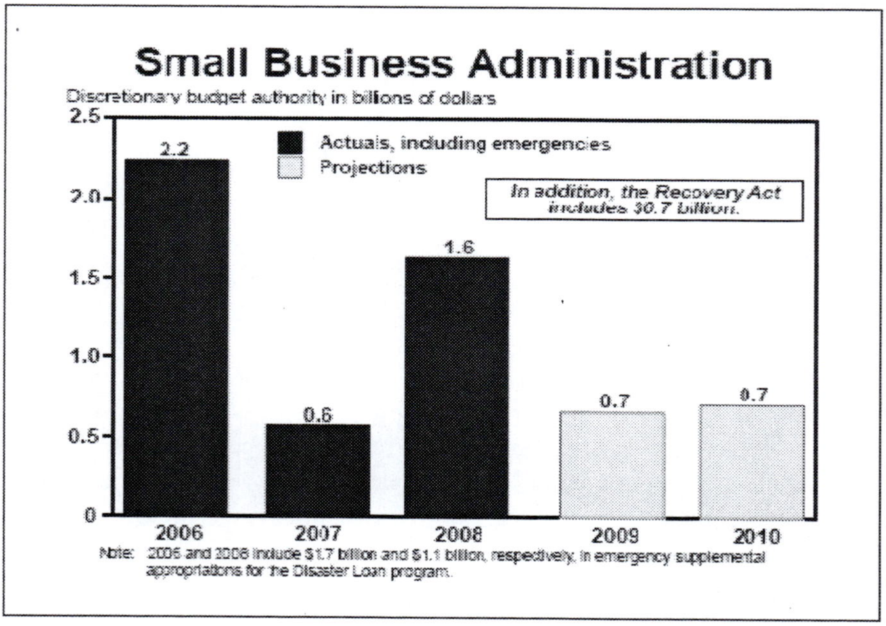

Prepares for Disaster Assistance. The Budget supports $1.1 billion in direct disaster loans, the normalized 10-year average. In addition, $101 million in new budget authority for disaster lending administrative expenses is provided; and disaster loan subsidy funding is available through estimated unobligated balances. Furthermore, in 2010 the Agency will implement a pilot program to test the Guaranteed Disaster Loan programs outlined in Public Law 110–234, the Food, Conservation, and Energy Act of 2008.

Improves Technical and Contracting Assistance Capabilities to Advise Small Businesses. The Budget supports resources for non-credit technical assistance programs, providing entrepreneurs access to counseling and business development expertise. This includes improvements to existing programs such as Small Business Development Centers, Women's Business Centers, SCORE, and microloan technical assistance, as well as incorporating new strategies. The Budget also supports small business access to Federal prime and subcontracting opportunities, improvements to small business procurement data, and continued reviews of small business size standards.

Modernizes the Agency for Better Performance. The Budget provides increased funding for core Agency systems and human capital improvements. This includes continued procurement of a more effective loan accounting system, and a focus on streamlining and automating lender and contracting systems.

SOCIAL SECURITY ADMINISTRATION

Funding Highlights

- Provides $11.6 billion for the Social Security Administration, a 10-percent increase targeted at completing crucial workloads and providing the American public with better service.
- Enables processing of a rising number of retirement and disability claims.
- Provides funding for increasing program integrity efforts to ensure payments are made to the right person and in the correct amount.
- Modernizes rules for evaluating disability.
- Looks forward to working in a bipartisan way to preserve Social Security for future generations.

Protects Social Security. The President recognizes that Social Security is indispensable to workers, the disabled, seniors, and survivors and is probably the most important and most successful program that our country has ever established. Social Security can pay full benefits until 2041. The President is committed to ensuring that Social Security is solvent and viable for the American people, now and in the future. He is strongly opposed to privatizing Social Security and looks forward to working in a bipartisan way to preserve it for future generations.

Provides a 10 Percent Funding Increase to Target Crucial Workloads and Process a Rising Number of Claims for Disability and Retirement Benefits. The Social Security Administration (SSA) is responsible for paying benefits to more than 55 million people each month. Each year, SSA processes more than 4.2 million retirement, survivor, and Medicare claims; 2.6 million disability claims; and over 300,000 Supplemental Security Income (SSI) claims. The Budget proposes $11.6 billion for SSA, an increase of $1.1 billion, or 10 percent, above the 2009 likely enacted level of $10.5 billion. This amount includes resources to ensure increased staffing in 2010 and will allow SSA to increase the level of work processed in key service delivery areas to the American public, such as processing initial retirement and disability claims, and disability appeals. In addition, this amount includes resources to enable SSA to more effectively and efficiently verify hundreds of millions of Social Security Numbers and issue about 18 million Social Security cards.

ensure that SSI recipients continue to meet the non-medical factors of eligibility.

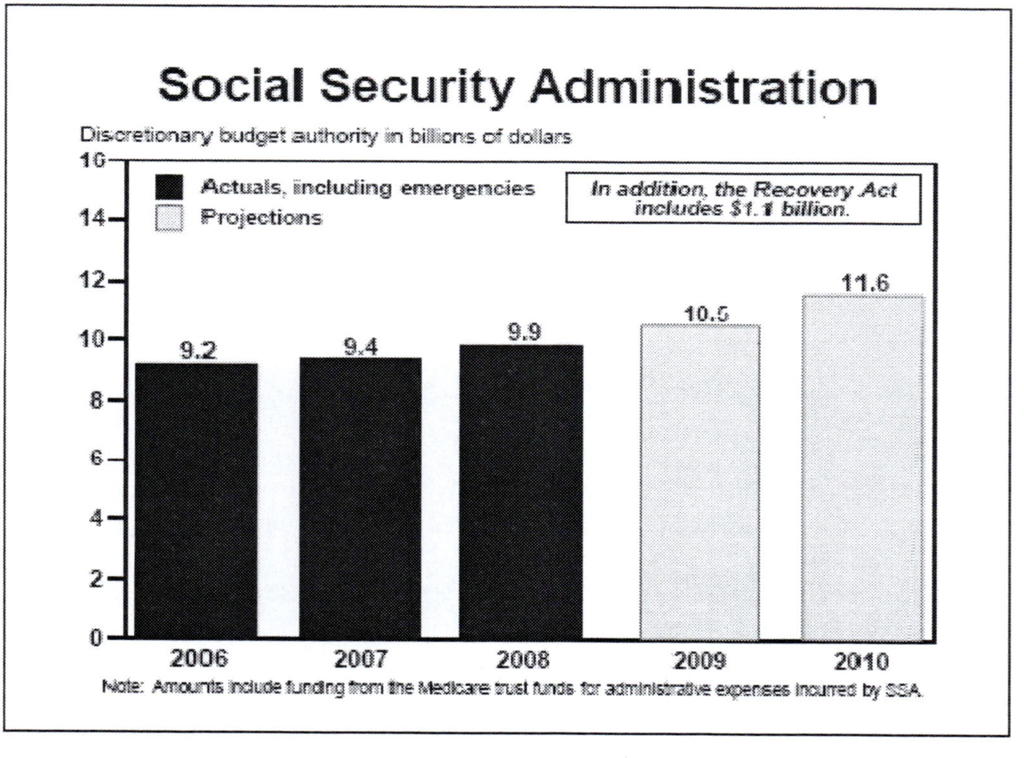

Significantly Increases Program Integrity Efforts. The President's 2010 Budget provides $759 million for SSA program integrity that will reverse a decline in these activities. SSA's program integrity efforts will be part of a strong framework for making sure Government is spending tax dollars efficiently and that benefits are paid only to those beneficiaries who are eligible and are paid in the correct amounts. Continuing Disability Reviews ensure that Disability Insurance and SSI recipients continue to meet the medical criteria. SSI redeterminations

Restructures the Federal Wage Reporting Process. The President's 2010 Budget proposes to restructure the Federal wage reporting process to increase the frequency with which wages are reported to SSA. Currently, wages are reported to the Federal Government once a year. Increasing the timeliness of wage reporting would enhance tax administration, improve program integrity for a range of programs, and facilitate implementation of automatic workplace pensions. The Administration will work with the States so that the overall reporting burden on employers is not increased.

Corporation for National and Community Service

Funding Highlights

- Makes a substantial investment in national service, setting the program on a path for expansion to 250,000 slots.
- Creates a new Social Innovation Fund to invest in and scale up innovative non-profits and solutions to address the Nation's most pressing social problems.
- Engages more retiring Americans in service, harnessing their skills and knowledge.
- Expands service-learning in the Nation's schools, helping students become contributing citizens and community members through service.

The Corporation for National and Community Service (CNCS) provides opportunities for Americans to serve their community and country while meeting the Nation's greatest national challenges. Through CNCS programs, Americans of all ages can help strengthen our country in different ways, from tutoring at-risk youth to responding to natural disasters to building the capacity of community organizations. The President's Budget proposes $1.13 billion for CNCS, an increase of $261 million from the 2009 likely enacted level, to give more Americans the opportunity to serve and to build the capacity of the nonprofit sector to find innovative solutions to social problems.

Expands National Service. The President's Budget makes a substantial investment in National Service, giving more individuals the opportunity to make an intensive commitment to giving back to their communities. The Budget would set AmeriCorps on a path to expand from its current 75,000 funded slots to 250,000, and would ensure the availability of service opportunities to achieve demonstrable results. The Budget would also increase the amount of the Eli Segal Education Award, which has not been adjusted since the program's inception in 1993.

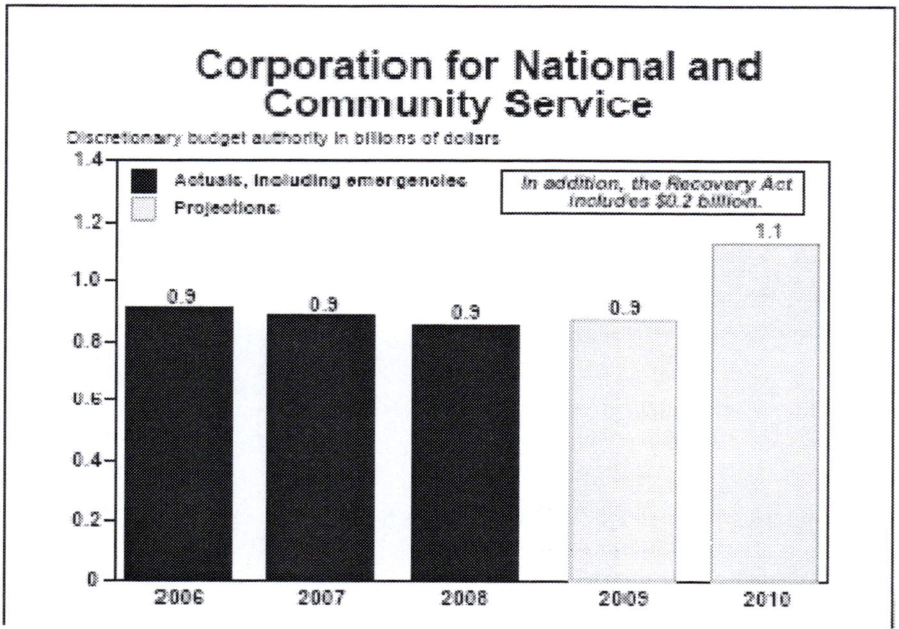

Creates a New Social innovation Fund. Innovators often come up with great ideas for addressing critical national challenges, but too often lack the capital to develop, evaluate, and scale up successful ideas. The Budget would create a new social innovation fund, charged with testing promising new approaches to major challenges, leveraging private and foundation capital to meet these needs, and scaling up research- proven programs.

Engages Retiring Americans in Service. Older Americans have a wide range of skills and knowledge to contribute to the Nation's communities. New efforts are needed to tap the idealism and experience of this "Baby Boomer" generation – the largest and healthiest generation to enter retirement in history. The President's Budget would expand and improve Senior Corps programs, which connect individuals over the age of 55 to local volunteer opportunities, allowing more retirees to help meet the needs and challenges in their communities.

Expands Service-Learning in the Nation's Schools. Service learning is an approach that connects classroom lessons with meaningful community service opportunities. The Budget includes additional resources for Learn and Serve America, which supports programs in schools, higher education institutions and community- based organizations that engage students, their teachers, and others in service-learning.

Strengthens the Management Capacity of the Corporation. The Budget provides needed resources to strengthen the capacity of CNCS to manage its programs, measure performance, and conduct rigorous evaluations of the impact of CNCS programs. Coupled with a strong Administration commitment to management reform, the Budget will ensure that CNCS can support both growth and excellence in service.

SUMMARY TABLES

Table S–1. Budget Totals (In billions of dollars and as a percent of GDP)

													Totals	
	2008	**2009**	**2010**	**2011**	**2012**	**2013**	**2014**	**2015**	**2016**	**2017**	**2018**	**2019**	**2010-2014**	**2010-2019**
Budget Totals in Billions of Dollars:														
Receipts	2,524	2,186	2,381	2,713	3,081	3,323	3,500	3,675	3,856	4,042	4,234	4,446	14,997	35,250
Outlays	2,983	3,938	3,552	3,625	3,662	3,856	4,069	4,258	4,493	4,678	4,868	5,158	18,764	42,219
Deficit .	459	1,752	1,171	912	581	533	570	583	637	636	634	712	3,767	6,969
Debt held by the public	5,803	8,364	9,509	10,436	10,985	11,505	12,070	12,659	13,297	13,932	14,557	15,370		
Debt net of financial assets	5,297	6,943	8,072	8,960	9,541	10,073	10,642	11,224	11,860	12,495	13,129	13,840		
Gross domestic product (GDP)	14,222	14,240	14,729	15,500	16,470	17,498	18,386	19,205	20,060	20,952	21,884	22,858		
Budget Totals as a Percent of GDP:														
Receipts	17.7%	15.4%	16.2%	17.5%	18.7%	19.0%	19.0%	19.1%	19.2%	19.3%	19.3%	19.5%	18.1%	18.7%
Outlays	21.0%	27.7%	24.1%	23.4%	22.2%	22.0%	22.1%	22.2%	22.4%	22.3%	22.2%	22.6%	22.8%	22.6%
Deficit	3.2%	12.3%	8.0%	5.9%	3.5%	3.0%	3.1%	3.0%	3.2%	3.0%	2.9%	3.1%	4.7%	3.9%
Debt held by the public .	40.8%	58.7%	64.6%	67.3%	66.7%	65.8%	65.6%	65.9%	66.3%	66.5%	66.5%	67.2%		
Debt net of financial assets	37.2%	48.8%	54.8%	57.8%	57.9%	57.6%	57.9%	58.4%	59.1%	59.6%	60.0%	60.5%		

Table S–2. Effect of Budget Proposals on Projected deficits (Deficit increases (+) or decreases (–) in billions of dollars)

	2009	2010	2011	2012	2013	2014	2015	2016	2017	2018	2019	Totals 2010–2014	Totals 2010–2019
Projected deficits in the baseline projection of current policy[1]	**1,509.1**	**1,178.0**	**1,033.1**	**757.5**	**734.0**	**791.0**	**811.0**	**877.6**	**892.6**	**906.3**	**1,002.1**	**4,493.6**	**8,983.2**
Percent of GDP	10.6%	8.0%	6.7%	4.6%	4.2%	4.3%	4.2%	4.4%	4.3%	4.1%	4.4%	5.6%	4.9%
Reserve funds:													
Health reform:													
Health savings[2]	......	*–1.8*	*–5.1*	*–18.0*	*–24.5*	*–34.3*	*–40.0*	*–47.1*	*–49.5*	*–44.8*	*–50.8*	*–83.7*	*–316.0*
Limit the rate at which itemized reductions reduce tax liability to 28 percent[2]	......	......	*–11.1*	*–30.8*	*–33.5*	*–35.5*	*–37.3*	*–39.3*	*–41.4*	*–43.4*	*–45.6*	*–110.8*	*–317.8*
Net total with additional savings and cost of health care benefits	......	......	......	......	......	......	......	......	......	......	......	......	......
Climate revenues:[3]													
Dedicated to climate policy (clean energy technologies)	......	......	......	–15.0	–15.0	–15.0	–15.0	–15.0	–15.0	–15.0	–15.0	–45.0	–120.0
Dedicated to Making Work Pay	......	......	......	–63.7	–64.1	–64.7	–65.3	–66.0	–66.7	–67.3	–68.0	–192.5	–525.7
Placeholder for potential additional financial stabilization efforts	250.0	......	......	......	......	......	......	......	......	......	......	......	......
Tax cuts for families and businesses[4]	28.5	49.0	19.3	90.3	96.3	102.3	106.3	113.2	116.9	120.4	124.2	357.3	940.2
Other revenue changes and loophole closers	–0.0	–1.0	–16.6	–28.0	–37.1	–42.9	–43.7	–44.5	–45.3	–46.3	–48.0	–125.7	–353.5
Proposed changes in mandatory programs and user fees	0.2	–5.0	5.1	0.7	–2.1	–2.5	1.4	4.7	7.1	9.9	11.3	–3.6	30.7
Proposed changes in appropriated ("discretionary") programs:													
Cost of overseas contingency operations	–31.2	–60.3	–118.6	–138.9	–149.7	–156.9	–163.1	–168.1	–173.1	–178.3	–183.5	–624.3	–1,490.4
Department of Defense (051) excluding overseas contingency operations	......	5.7	6.1	3.7	1.7	1.5	1.8	0.8	0.7	0.7	0.6	18.8	23.4
Other appropriated programs	3.8	19.8	16.2	29.2	39.5	45.7	52.4	54.8	55.8	56.7	58.7	150.4	426.7
Subtotal, appropriated programs	–27.4	–34.8	–96.2	–106.0	–108.5	–109.6	–108.9	–112.5	–116.6	–120.9	–124.2	–455.2	–1,038.3
Subtotal, policy proposals	**251.2**	**8.2**	**–88.4**	**–121.6**	**–130.5**	**–132.4**	**–123.2**	**–120.1**	**–119.7**	**–119.3**	**–119.6**	**–464.7**	**–1,066.5**
Upper-income tax provisions dedicated to deficit reduction	**0.2**	**–1.1**	**–28.5**	**–49.0**	**–58.2**	**–67.3**	**–74.6**	**–80.6**	**–86.6**	**–92.3**	**–98.6**	**–204.0**	**–636.7**
Debt service	–8.4	–13.7	–4.4	–5.5	–12.8	–21.6	–30.6	–40.0	–49.9	–60.7	–71.9	–57.9	–311.0
Total reduction in projected deficits	**243.0**	**–6.5**	**–121.3**	**–176.2**	**–201.4**	**–221.2**	**–228.3**	**–240.7**	**–256.2**	**–272.3**	**–290.1**	**–726.6**	**–2,014.3**
Resulting deficits in 2010 Budget	**1,752.1**	**1,171.4**	**911.9**	**581.3**	**532.6**	**569.7**	**582.6**	**636.9**	**636.4**	**634.0**	**712.0**	**3,767.0**	**6,968.9**
Percent of GDP	12.3%	8.0%	5.9%	3.5%	3.0%	3.1%	3.0%	3.2%	3.0%	2.9%	3.1%	4.7%	3.9%

Table S–2. (Continued)

	2009	2010	2011	2012	2013	2014	2015	2016	2017	2018	2019	Totals 2010–2014	Totals 2010–2019
Memorandum, proposed changes in appropriated ("discretionary") budget authority:													
Funding for overseas contingency operations	–50.3	–64.6	–148.3	–152.6	–157.2	–161.9	–166.7	–171.6	–176.6	–181.8	–187.1	–684.6	–1,568.4
Department of Defense (051) excluding overseas contingency operations	......	10.3	6.9	3.1	......	......	......	......	......	......	......	20.3	20.3
Other appropriated programs	7.1	31.3	29.5	47.5	49.7	53.9	53.3	54.2	53.6	53.6	55.6	212.0	482.2
Total, appropriated funding (budget authority)	–43.2	–23.0	–111.9	–102.0	–107.4	–107.9	–113.3	–117.4	–123.0	–128.2	–131.6	–452.3	–1,065.9

[1] See Tables S–3 and S–5 for information on the baseline projection of current policy.

[2] Non–additive.

[3] Shown here are those proceeds from auctioning emission allowances that are reserved for clean energy technology initiatives and to compensate families through the Making Work Pay tax cut. These proceeds are included in the grand totals as receipts, though they could alternatively be considered offsets to outlays. All additional net proceeds will be used to further compensate the public.

[4] Includes refundable tax credits.

Table S–3. Baseline Projection of Current Policy by Category[1] (In billions of dollars)

													Totals	
	2008	2009	2010	2011	2012	2013	2014	2015	2016	2017	2018	2019	2010-2014	2010-2019
Outlays:														
Appropriated ("discretionary") programs:														
Department of Defense (051) including cost of overseas contingency operations	593	697	728	727	739	757	773	792	811	831	851	872	3,723	7,881
Other appropriated programs	528	609	675	656	624	621	622	630	642	656	671	686	3,199	6,483
Subtotal, appropriated programs	1,120	1,307	1,403	1,383	1,363	1,378	1,395	1,422	1,453	1,487	1,522	1,558	6,922	14,364
Mandatory programs:														
Social Security	612	662	695	721	749	790	839	891	948	1,008	1,072	1,141	3,794	8,854
Medicare	386	425	453	498	501	556	605	651	724	756	781	872	2,613	6,397
Medicaid	201	259	290	274	280	299	322	347	375	404	435	468	1,466	3,495
Troubled Asset Relief Program (TARP)	......	247	......	......	......	......	......	......	......	......	......	......	......	......
Other mandatory programs	411	673	575	540	437	446	479	479	495	499	508	537	2,477	4,994
Subtotal, mandatory programs	1,610	2,266	2,014	2,033	1,967	2,091	2,244	2,369	2,541	2,668	2,796	3,018	10,349	23,741
Net interest	253	148	178	287	383	447	495	539	579	614	651	694	1,790	4,866
Disaster costs[2]	......	4	11	16	18	20	23	25	26	27	29	30	88	226
Total outlays	2,983	3,724	3,606	3,718	3,732	3,936	4,157	4,354	4,599	4,795	4,998	5,300	19,149	43,196
Receipts:														
Individual income taxes .	1,146	972	1,081	1,218	1,378	1,493	1,595	1,690	1,786	1,888	1,995	2,109	6,763	16,232
Corporation income taxes	304	180	249	292	348	387	391	423	442	461	486	511	1,667	3,990
Social insurance and retirement receipts:														
Social Security payroll taxes	658	654	682	719	756	803	842	879	925	962	1,004	1,048	3,801	8,620
Medicare payroll taxes	194	191	196	210	222	235	247	258	272	283	295	308	1,110	2,525

Table S–3. (Continued)

Unemployment insurance	40	44	52	58	65	67	66	61	57	62	58	62	307	607
Other retirement	9	9	9	8	9	9	9	9	9	9	9	9	43	86
Excise taxes	67	71	78	83	87	88	90	91	92	93	94	95	427	893
Estate and gift taxes	29	26	20	23	25	27	27	29	31	33	36	38	121	288
Customs duties	28	24	24	29	33	37	40	43	46	47	49	50	164	399
Deposits of earnings, Federal reserve System	34	28	22	29	36	39	42	43	45	47	48	50	168	402
Other miscellaneous receipts	17	16	16	16	17	17	17	17	18	18	18	18	84	172
Total receipts	2,524	2,215	2,428	2,685	2,975	3,202	3,366	3,543	3,722	3,903	4,091	4,298	14,656	34,213
deficit	459	1,509	1,178	1,033	757	734	791	811	878	893	906	1,002	4,494	8,983
On-budget deficit	642	1,647	1,313	1,187	931	928	991	1,009	1,080	1,087	1,094	1,180	5,350	10,801
Off-budget surplus (-)	–183	–138	–135	–154	–174	–194	–200	–198	–203	–194	–188	–178	–857	–1,818
Memorandum, funding (budget authority) for appropriated programs:														
Department of Defense (051) including funding for overseas contingency operations	666	712	718	733	750	768	786	805	825	845	865	887	3,756	7,983
Other appropriated programs	554	826	568	579	592	606	620	634	649	664	680	696	2,965	6,288
Total, appropriated funding	1,219	1,538	1,286	1,312	1,342	1,374	1,406	1,440	1,474	1,509	1,545	1,583	6,721	14,271

[1] See Table S-5 for information on adjustments to the Budget Enforcement Act (BEA) baseline.

[2] These amounts represent the statistical probability of a major disaster requiring federal assistance for relief and reconstruction. Such assistance might be provided in the form of discretionary or mandatory outlays or tax relief. These amounts are included as outlays for convenience.

Table S–4. Proposed Budget by Category (In billions of dollars)

													Totals	
	2008	**2009**	**2010**	**2011**	**2012**	**2013**	**2014**	**2015**	**2016**	**2017**	**2018**	**2019**	**2010-2014**	**2010-2019**
Outlays:														
Appropriated ("discretionary") programs:														
Department of Defense (051) including cost of overseas contingency operations	593	666	673	614	604	609	618	631	644	659	674	689	3,118	6,414
Other appropriated programs	528	613	695	672	653	661	668	682	697	711	727	745	3,349	6,911
Subtotal, appropriated programs	1,120	1,279	1,368	1,286	1,257	1,269	1,286	1,313	1,341	1,370	1,401	1,434	6,467	13,325
Mandatory programs:														
Social Security	612	662	695	719	747	787	835	887	944	1,006	1,070	1,139	3,784	8,831
Medicare	386	425	453	498	500	555	603	650	723	756	781	872	2,608	6,391
Medicaid	201	259	290	274	280	299	322	347	374	403	435	468	1,464	3,492
Troubled Asset Relief Program (TARP)	......	247	......	......	......	......	......	......	......	......	......	......	......	......
Placeholder for potential additional financial stabilization efforts	......	250	......	......	......	......	......	......	......	......	......	......	......	......
Other mandatory programs	411	673	571	549	482	491	527	527	545	552	562	594	2,620	5,400
Subtotal, mandatory programs	1,610	2,516	2,009	2,040	2,009	2,132	2,287	2,412	2,587	2,717	2,848	3,073	10,477	24,113
Net interest	253	139	164	283	378	434	474	509	539	564	590	622	1,732	4,555
Disaster costs [1]	......	4	11	16	18	20	23	25	26	27	29	30	88	226
Total outlays	2,983	3,938	3,552	3,623	3,662	3,856	4,069	4,258	4,493	4,678	4,868	5,158	18,764	42,219
Receipts:														
Individual income taxes	1,146	958	1,061	1,243	1,393	1,516	1,625	1,719	1,817	1,923	2,033	2,152	6,837	16,480
Corporation income taxes	304	165	222	302	369	414	423	455	474	494	518	544	1,730	4,215
Social insurance and retirement receipts:														
Social Security payroll taxes	658	654	682	719	756	804	843	879	926	963	1,005	1,049	3,804	8,627
Medicare payroll taxes	194	191	196	210	222	235	247	258	272	283	295	308	1,111	2,527
Unemployment insurance	40	44	53	58	65	67	66	60	57	62	57	62	309	606
Other retirement	9	9	9	8	9	9	9	9	9	9	9	9	43	86
Excise taxes	67	71	77	75	78	79	80	81	82	83	83	84	390	804
Estate and gift taxes	29	26	20	23	25	27	27	29	31	33	36	38	121	288
Customs duties	28	24	23	28	33	37	40	43	46	47	49	50	163	397

Table S–4. (Continued)

													Totals	
	2008	2009	2010	2011	2012	2013	2014	2015	2016	2017	2018	2019	2010-2014	2010-2019
Deposits of earnings, Federal reserve System	34	28	22	29	36	39	42	43	45	47	48	50	168	402
Other miscellaneous receipts	17	16	16	16	17	17	18	17	17	17	17	18	85	172
Total receipts	2,524	2,186	2,381	2,713	3,081	3,323	3,500	3,675	3,856	4,042	4,234	4,446	14,997	35,250
deficit	459	1,752	1,171	912	581	533	570	583	637	638	634	712	3,767	6,969
On-budget deficit	642	1,647	1,313	1,187	931	928	991	1,009	1,080	1,087	1,094	1,180	5,350	10,801
Off-budget surplus (-)	–183	–138	–135	–154	–174	–194	–200	–198	–203	–194	–188	–178	-857	–1,818
Memorandum, funding (budget authority) for appropriated programs:														
Department of Defense (051) including funding for overseas contingency operations	666	712	718	733	750	768	786	805	825	845	865	887	3,756	7,983
Other appropriated programs	554	826	568	579	592	606	620	634	649	664	680	696	2,965	6,288
Total, appropriated funding	1,219	1,538	1,286	1,312	1,342	1,374	1;406	1,440	1,474	1,509	1,545	1,583	6,721	14,271

[1] See Table S-5 for information on adjustments to the Budget Enforcement Act (BEA) baseline.

[2] These amounts represent the statistical probability of a major disaster requiring federal assistance for relief and reconstruction. Such assistance might be provided in the form of discretionary or mandatory outlays or tax relief. These amounts are included as outlays for convenience.

Table S –5. Bridge from Budget Enforcement Act Baseline to Baseline Projection of Current Policy (In billions of dollars)

	2008	2009	2010	2011	2012	2013	2014	2015	2016	2017	2018	2019	Totals 2010–2014	Totals 2010–2019
BEA baseline deficit/surplus (–)	**458.6**	**1,211.7**	**650.7**	**459.2**	**194.3**	**101.1**	**83.7**	**53.1**	**71.3**	**30.1**	**–23.4**	**–5.7**	**1,488.9**	**1,814.4**
Adjustments to reflect current policies:														
Index to inflation the 2009 parameters of the AMT as enacted in the American Recovery and Reinvestment Act	......	......	14.7	71.6	34.0	39.2	46.1	54.3	63.1	72.6	83.9	96.3	205.6	575.9
Continue the 2001 and 2003 tax cuts[1]	......	0.2	6.2	154.0	234.1	264.3	294.4	315.2	330.0	344.7	360.5	377.8	953.1	2,681.3
Account for additional expected Medicare physician payments	......	......	13.6	24.4	29.4	37.2	42.3	43.3	41.1	34.5	30.6	32.9	147.1	329.6
Continue Transitional Medical Assistance and Qualified Individuals programs	......	*	0.9	1.3	1.5	1.5	1.6	1.7	1.9	2.0	2.2	2.3	6.9	16.9
Correct baseline growth rates for pay and social insurance administrative expenses	......	......	–2.1	–2.4	–2.4	–2.5	–2.6	–2.9	–3.2	–3.5	–3.9	–4.3	–12.0	–29.8
Subtotal	......	0.2	33.6	248.9	296.5	339.8	381.8	411.6	432.8	450.3	473.5	505.0	1,300.7	3,573.9
Adjustments to reflect legislation this session:														
American Recovery and Reinvestment Act	......	202.3	353.3	139.8	98.7	30.0	27.7	11.4	–0.5	–1.7	–1.1	–1.1	583.5	590.5
2009 full-year appropriations	......	13.3	10.4	24.6	23.9	24.6	25.3	25.9	26.5	27.1	27.7	28.4	108.7	244.2
Subtotal	......	215.5	363.7	158.4	62.5	54.6	52.9	37.3	26.0	25.4	26.6	27.3	692.2	834.7
Adjustments to reflect costs of overseas contingency operations and disasters:														
Remove part-year overseas contingency operations funding (as enacted for 2009)	......	–40.6	–60.8	–64.7	–66.8	–68.6	–70.0	–71.2	–72.5	–73.8	–75.1	–76.5	–330.8	–700.0
Insert full-year overseas contingency operations funding (as enacted for 2008)	......	118.1	177.4	189.6	196.8	202.6	207.8	212.6	217.5	222.6	227.7	232.9	974.3	2,087.6
Remove part-year international funding (as enacted for 2009)	......	–2.2	–3.1	–3.8	–4.0	–4.1	–4.3	–4.4	–4.5	–4.6	–4.7	–4.8	–19.4	–42.4
Insert international emergency funding (as enacted for 2008)	......	4.7	7.1	8.2	8.7	9.0	9.4	9.6	9.6	10.0	10.2	10.4	42.4	92.5
Remove non-recurring emergency funding	......	–2.5	–7.7	–12.7	–16.3	–17.4	–17.8	–18.2	–18.6	–19.0	–19.4	–19.9	–71.8	–167.0
Insert statistical probability of future major disaster costs[2]	......	3.6	10.9	15.9	18.3	20.5	22.6	24.8	26.2	27.5	28.8	30.1	88.2	225.5
Subtotal	......	81.0	123.7	132.6	126.7	142.2	147.7	153.2	158.0	162.6	167.4	172.3	682.8	1,496.3
Adjustment to Pell Status, for comparability:[3]														
Remove Pell Grants from appropriated category	–14.7	–16.8	–23.5	–19.5	–17.6	–18.1	–18.4	–18.7	–19.1	–19.4	–19.8	–20.1	–97.4	–194.5
Add Pell Grants to mandatory category	14.7	16.8	23.5	19.5	17.6	18.1	18.4	18.7	19.1	19.4	19.8	20.1	97.4	194.5
Subtotal	......	......	......	......	......	......	......	......	......	......	......	......	......	......
Total program adjustments	......	296.7	521.0	539.9	495.8	536.6	582.5	602.1	616.8	638.3	667.5	704.6	2,675.7	5,905.0
Debt service on adjustments	......	0.6	6.3	34.1	67.5	96.4	124.8	155.8	189.5	224.3	262.2	303.2	329.0	1,463.9
Total adjustments	......	297.3	527.2	574.0	563.2	633.0	707.3	757.8	806.3	862.5	929.7	1,007.8	3,004.7	7,368.8
Baseline projection of current policy deficit	**458.6**	**1,509.1**	**1,178.0**	**1,033.1**	**757.5**	**734.0**	**791.0**	**811.0**	**877.6**	**892.6**	**906.3**	**1,002.1**	**4,493.6**	**8,983.2**

* $50 million or less.

[1]In continuing the 2001 and 2003 tax cuts, the estate tax is maintained at its 2009 parameters.

[2]These amounts represent the statistical probability of a major disaster requiring federal assistance for relief and reconstruction.

[3]The amount of the reclassification equals the existing and projected amounts of Pell as increased on a one-time basis by the recovery Act.

Table S–6. Mandatory and Receipt Proposals (Deficit increases (+) or decreases (–) in millions of dollars)

	2009	2010	2011	2012	2013	2014	2015	2016	2017	2018	2019	Totals 2010–2014	Totals 2010–2019
ax Provisions:[1]													
Tax cuts for families and individuals:													
Provide Making Work Pay Tax Credit[2]	......	......	11,017	63,682	64,119	64,661	65,291	66,001	66,671	67,307	67,979	203,479	536,728
Expand Earned Income Tax Credit[2]	......	......	19	4,013	3,961	3,961	4,006	4,090	4,176	4,268	4,364	11,954	32,858
Expand refundability of the Child Tax Credit[2]	......	......	......	8,714	8,616	8,609	8,703	8,786	8,902	9,020	9,119	25,939	70,469
Expand saver's credit and automatic enrollment in IRAs and 401(k)s[2]	......	......	257	3,018	4,707	5,926	6,909	7,722	8,371	8,916	9,406	13,908	55,232
Provide American Opportunity Tax Credit[2]	......	......	932	6,770	7,487	8,144	9,237	10,086	10,312	10,646	11,295	23,333	74,859
Total, tax cuts for families and individuals	......	......	12,225	86,197	88,890	91,301	94,146	96,635	98,432	100,157	102,163	278,613	770,146
Tax cuts for businesses:													
Eliminate capital gains taxation on small businesses	......	......	......	......	......	297	734	1,026	1,345	1,695	2,076	297	7,173
Make research and experimentation tax credit permanent	......	3,111	5,486	6,142	6,785	7,384	7,960	8,530	9,103	9,680	10,281	28,908	74,462
Expand net operating loss carryback	27,800	35,700	–10,700	–10,200	–7,900	–5,600	–3,900	–2,700	–1,800	–1,300	–900	1,300	–9,300
Modify Federal Aviation Administration financing[3]	......	......	7,225	7,599	7,980	8,260	8,559	8,869	9,190	9,527	9,873	31,064	77,082
Total, tax cuts for businesses	27,800	38,811	2,011	3,541	6,865	10,341	13,353	15,725	17,838	19,602	21,330	61,569	149,417
Continue remaining expiring provisions through calendar year 2010[2]	668	10,183	5,088	607	578	623	798	883	612	604	688	17,079	20,664
Other revenue changes and loophole closers:													
Reinstate Superfund Taxes	......	......	–1,213	–1,667	–1,803	–1,896	–1,970	–2,040	–2,113	–2,203	–2,300	–6,579	–17,205
Tax carried interest as ordinary income	......	......	–2,742	–4,347	–4,168	–3,494	–2,803	–2,204	–1,725	–1,351	–1,060	–14,751	–23,894
Codify "Economic Substance Doctrine"	–23	–70	–140	–240	–346	–438	–552	–656	–743	–834	–930	–1,234	–4,949
Repeal LIFO	......	......	......	–2,992	–6,748	–8,080	–8,431	–8,590	–8,545	–8,630	–9,036	–17,820	–61,052
Implement international enforcement, reform deferral, and other tax reform policies	......	......	–10,000	–15,000	–20,000	–25,000	–26,000	–27,000	–28,000	–29,000	–30,000	–70,000	–210,000
Require information reporting for rental payments	......	–319	–339	–357	–374	–390	–408	–426	–445	–465	–486	–1,779	–4,009
Eliminate oil and gas company preferences:													
Levy excise tax on Gulf of Mexico oil and gas (limits excess royalty relief)	......	......	–582	–623	–542	–526	–537	–510	–632	–649	–682	–2,273	–5,283
Repeal enhanced oil recovery credit[4]	......	......	......	......	......	......	......	......	......	......	......	......	......
Repeal marginal well tax credit[4]	......	......	......	......	......	......	......	......	......	......	......	......	......
Repeal expensing of intangible drilling costs	......	......	–347	–595	–526	–395	–269	–226	–237	–266	–488	–1,863	–3,349
Repeal deduction for tertiary injectants	......	......	–5	–9	–9	–8	–7	–6	–6	–6	–6	–31	–62

Table S–6. (Continued)

	2009	2010	2011	2012	2013	2014	2015	2016	2017	2018	2019	Totals 2010–2014	Totals 2010–2019
Repeal passive loss exception for working interests in oil and natural gas properties	......	......	–2	–5	–6	–6	–6	–6	–6	–6	–6	–19	–49
Repeal manufacturing tax deduction for oil and natural gas companies	......	......	–757	–1,311	–1,392	–1,464	–1,531	–1,600	–1,670	–1,745	–1,823	–4,924	–13,293
Increase geological and geophysical amortization period for independent producers to seven years	......	......	–41	–154	–240	–233	–187	–140	–91	–56	–47	–668	–1,189
Repeal percentage depletion for oil and natural gas	......	......	–316	–752	–925	–960	–996	–1,033	–1,065	–1,091	–1,113	–2,953	–8,251
Subtotal, eliminate oil and gas company preferences	......	......	–2,050	–3,449	–3,640	–3,592	–3,533	–3,521	–3,707	–3,819	–4,165	–12,731	–31,476
Eliminate Advanced Earned Income Tax Credit [2]	......	–588	–163	8	–10	–15	–20	–23	–24	–23	–23	–769	–882
Total, other revenue changes and loophole closers	–23	–977	–16,647	–28,044	–37,089	–42,906	–43,717	–44,460	–45,302	–46,325	–48,000	–125,663	–353,467
Upper-income tax provisions dedicated to deficit reduction:													
Reinstate the 36 percent and 39.6 percent rates for those taxpayers earning over $250,000 (married) and $200,000 (single)	......	......	–15,818	–29,604	–32,755	–35,653	–38,429	–41,588	–45,020	–48,217	–51,676	–113,830	–338,760
Reinstate the personal exemption phaseout and limitation on itemized deductions for those taxpayers earning over $250,000 (married) and $200,000 (single)	......	......	–7,227	–15,752	–17,848	–19,383	–20,844	–22,364	–23,955	–25,491	–26,984	–60,210	–179,848
Impose 20 percent rate on capital gains and dividends for those taxpayers earning over $250,000 (married) and $200,000 (single)	182	–1,102	–5,416	–3,656	–7,550	–12,235	–15,322	–16,607	–17,663	–18,625	–19,940	–29,959	–118,116
Total, upper-income tax provisions dedicated to deficit reduction	182	–1,102	–28,461	–49,012	–58,153	–67,271	–74,595	–80,559	–86,638	–92,333	–98,600	–203,999	–636,724
Total, tax provisions	**28,627**	**46,915**	**–25,784**	**13,289**	**1,091**	**–7,912**	**–10,015**	**–11,776**	**–15,058**	**–18,295**	**–22,419**	**27,599**	**–49,964**
Climate Revenues:													
Dedicated to climate policy (clean energy technologies)	......	......	......	–15,000	–15,000	–15,000	–15,000	–15,000	–15,000	–15,000	–15,000	–45,000	–120,000
Dedicated to Making Work Pay	......	......	......	–63,682	–64,119	–64,661	–65,291	–66,001	–66,671	–67,307	–67,979	–192,462	–525,711
Total, climate revenues [5]	......	......	......	**–78,682**	**–79,119**	**–79,661**	**–80,291**	**–81,001**	**–81,671**	**–82,307**	**–82,979**	**–237,462**	**–645,711**

Table S–6. (Continued)

	2009	2010	2011	2012	2013	2014	2015	2016	2017	2018	2019	Totals 2010–2014	Totals 2010–2019
Mandatory Initiatives and Savings:[6]													
Agriculture:													
Reduce direct payments to farms with sales above $500,000	......	–85	–480	–625	–1,225	–1,225	–1,225	–1,225	–1,225	–1,225	–1,225	–3,640	–9,765
Reduce Crop Insurance premiums/underwriting gains and increase fees	......	......	–429	–427	–595	–599	–610	–620	–627	–634	–642	–2,050	–5,184
Reform payments to high-income farmers	......	–58	–24	–10	–9	–7	–5	–4	–3	–3	–3	–106	–126
Eliminate Cotton Storage payments	......	–52	–58	–56	–56	–57	–57	–58	–58	–59	–59	–279	–570
Reauthorize Child Nutrition	......	850	1,000	1,000	1,000	1,000	1,000	1,000	1,000	1,000	1,000	4,850	9,850
Reform Market Access Program	......	–4	–34	–40	–40	–40	–40	–40	–40	–40	–40	–158	–358
Total, Agriculture	......	651	–25	–158	–925	–928	–937	–947	–953	–961	–969	–1,385	–6,152
Defense:													
Implement concurrent receipt policy:													
Effect on military retirement	......	194	318	419	521	574	607	640	673	710	749	2,026	5,405
Accrual payments to the Military Retirement Fund (non-PAYGO)	......	361	376	389	402	415	429	444	459	475	491	1,943	4,241
Military Retirement Fund offsetting receipts (non-PAYGO)	......	–361	–376	–389	–402	–415	–429	–444	–459	–475	–491	–1,943	–4,241
Total, Defense	......	194	318	419	521	574	607	640	673	710	749	2,026	5,405
Education:													
Make Pell Grant funding mandatory and increase and index maximum awards	......	7	6,625	9,728	11,298	14,150	12,445	13,649	14,881	16,197	17,804	41,808	116,784
Eliminate entitlements for financial intermediaries under the Family Federal Education Loan Program	......	–4,123	–6,577	–5,655	–4,186	–3,717	–4,033	–4,392	–4,640	–4,958	–5,262	–24,258	–47,543
Modernize Perkins loans	......	–868	–570	–467	–564	–692	–686	–677	–674	–659	–633	–3,161	–6,490
Create a new College Access and Completion Fund	......	100	500	500	500	500	400	......	......	......	......	2,100	2,500
Total, Education		–4,884	–22	4,106	7,048	10,241	8,126	8,580	9,567	10,580	11,909	16,489	65,251
Energy:													
Repeal ultra-deepwater oil and gas research and development program	......	–20	–40	–50	–50	–50	–30	–10	......	......	......	–210	–250
Health and Human Services (HHS):													
Create nurse home visitation program	......	87	213	362	528	710	904	1,112	1,332	1,564	1,753	1,900	8,565
Extend TANF supplemental grants	......	......	319	319	319	319	319	319	319	319	319	1,276	2,871
Create a LIHEAP trigger	......	329	414	437	450	450	450	450	450	450	450	2,080	4,330
Total, HHS	......	416	946	1,118	1,297	1,479	1,673	1,881	2,101	2,333	2,522	5,256	15,766

Table S–6. (Continued)

[illegible]

	2009	2010	2011	2012	2013	2014	2015	2016	2017	2018	2019	Totals 2010–2014	Totals 2010–2019
Housing and Urban Development:													
Provide funding for the Affordable Housing Trust Fund	......	20	140	250	250	240	100	......	......	......	......	900	1,000
Expand HOPE for Homeowners program	225	1,375	900	......	......	......	......	......	......	......	......	2,275	2,275
Total, Housing and Urban Development	225	1,395	1,040	250	250	240	100	......	......	......	......	3,175	3,275
Interior:													
Increase return from minerals on Federal lands:													
Fee on nonproducing leases ("use or lose")	......	–122	–121	–115	–107	–109	–112	–114	–116	–119	–121	–574	–1,156
Abandoned Mine Lands (AML) Payments to Certified States	......	–142	–164	–208	–210	–206	–90	–90	–94	–158	–161	–928	–1,520
Repeal Energy Policy Act fee prohibition and mandatory permit funds	......	–43	–32	–32	–32	–32	–32	–9	–9	–9	–9	–171	–239
Reserve funds for insular affairs assistance	......	7	6	6	5	5	4	4	4	4	4	28	45
Recover Pick-Sloan project cost	......	–23	–23	–23	–23	–23	–23	–23	–23	–23	–23	–115	–230
Total, Interior	......	–323	–333	–372	–366	–366	–253	–232	–238	–305	–311	–1,761	–3,100
Labor:													
Reform Trade Adjustment Assistance	......	......	116	360	472	550	584	604	629	649	678	1,498	4,642
Change Extended Unemployment Insurance benefits trigger	......	......	8,700	2,500	600	600	1,300	1,700	1,700	1,800	2,100	12,400	21,000
Implement Unemployment Insurance integrity legislation[7]	......	......	–519	–573	–384	–394	–233	–238	–241	594	–30	–1,869	–2,017
Total, Labor	......	......	8,297	2,287	688	756	1,651	2,066	2,088	3,043	2,748	12,029	23,625
Treasury:													
Create placeholder for potential additional financial stabilization effort	250,000	......	......	......	......	......	......	......	......	......	......	......	......
Levy payments to federal contractors with delinquent tax debt (receipt effect)[7]	......	–49	–73	–77	–80	–84	–88	–92	–96	–100	–105	–363	–844
Revise Terrorism Risk Insurance program[7]	......	110	134	408	–168	–920	–309	–193	–99	–18	1	–436	–1,054
Make technical correction to JOBS Act (receipt effect)[7]	......	–19	–28	–29	–30	–31	–32	–33	–34	–35	–36	–137	–307
Total, Treasury	250,000	42	33	302	–278	–1,035	–429	–318	–229	–153	–140	–936	–2,205
Veterans Affairs:													
Implement concurrent receipt policy:													
Effect on Veterans disability payments	......	47	49	51	53	54	54	54	53	53	52	254	520
Use discretionary funds for contract examinations for disability compensation eligibility (not subject to PAYGO)	......	–141	–148	–155	–163	–171	–180	–189	–198	–208	–219	–778	–1,772

Table S–6. (Continued)

	2009	2010	2011	2012	2013	2014	2015	2016	2017	2018	2019	Totals 2010–2014	Totals 2010–2019
Total, Veterans Affairs	......	–94	–99	–104	–110	–117	–126	–135	–145	–155	–167	–524	–1,252
Federal Communications Commission (FCC):													
Provide permanent auction authority	......	......	......	......	–200	–200	–200	–200	–200	–200	–200	–400	–1,400
Auction domestic satellite spectrum	......	–100	–75	–25	......	......	......	......	......	......	......	–200	–200
Total, FCC	......	–100	–75	–25	–200	–200	–200	–200	–200	–200	–200	–600	–1,600
Postal Service:													
Realign USPS employee/employer benefit contributions	......	–752	–814	–830	–870	–913	–959	–1,007	–1,056	–1,110	–1,167	–4,179	–9,478
Social Security Administration:													
Program integrity: require States and localities to provide pension information (not subject to PAYGO)	......	......	......	......	–166	–362	–480	–512	–472	–449	–418	–528	–2,859
Multi-Agency:													
Implement program integrity allocation adjustments[7]	......	–1,072	–3,536	–5,587	–8,054	–10,981	–6,553	–4,373	–3,282	–2,620	–2,440	–29,230	–48,498
Total, mandatory initiatives and savings	**250,225**	**–4,547**	**5,690**	**1,356**	**–1,215**	**–1,661**	**2,190**	**5,433**	**7,854**	**10,712**	**12,116**	**–378**	**37,928**
Enact User Fees:[8]													
Agriculture:													
Grain Inspection, Packers, and Stockyards Administration (GIPSA) fees	......	–27	–30	–30	–31	–31	–31	–32	–32	–32	–33	–149	–308
Animal Plant and Health Inspection Service (APHIS) fees	......	–20	–27	–27	–26	–29	–30	–31	–32	–33	–34	–131	–291
Food Safety and Inspection Service (FSIS) performance fee	......	–4	–4	–4	–4	–4	–4	–5	–5	–5	–5	–20	–44
Corps of Engineers:													
Replace the inland waterways fuel tax with a lock usage fee (receipt effect)	......	–128	–128	–107	–195	–129	–116	–115	–115	–114	–112	–687	–1,259
Environmental Protection Agency:													
Pesticide and pre-manufacture notification (PMN) fees	......	–52	–56	–55	–45	–47	–47	–49	–49	–51	–51	–255	–502
FCC:													
Spectrum license user fee	–50	–200	–300	–425	–550	–550	–550	–550	–550	–550	–550	–2,025	–4,775
HHS (Centers for Medicare and Medicaid Services):													
Survey and certification revisit user fee[9]	......	......	......	......	......	......	......	......	......	......	......	......	......
Survey and certification recertification user fee[9]	......	......	......	......	......	......	......	......	......	......	......	......	......
Total, user fees	**–50**	**–431**	**–545**	**–648**	**–853**	**–790**	**–778**	**–782**	**–783**	**–785**	**–785**	**–3,267**	**–7,180**
Total, mandatory and receipt proposals and climate policies	**278,802**	**41,938**	**–20,639**	**–64,686**	**–80,096**	**–90,025**	**–88,894**	**–88,126**	**–89,658**	**–90,675**	**–94,067**	**–213,508**	**–664,927**

Table S–6. (Continued)

Health Reform Reserve Fund

	2009	2010	2011	2012	2013	2014	2015	2016	2017	2018	2019	Totals 2010–2014	Totals 2010–2019
Aligning incentives toward quality:													
Encourage hospitals serving Medicare beneficiaries to reduce readmission rates	......	......	......	–680	–840	–930	–1,020	–1,110	–1,200	–1,280	–1,370	–2,450	–8,430
Create hospital quality incentive payments	......	......	–400	–570	–840	–1,160	–1,540	–1,700	–1,830	–1,960	–2,090	–2,970	–12,090
Encourage primary care physicians to administer the flu vaccine to Medicare beneficiaries	......	*	*	*	*	*	*	*	*	*	*	*	*
Enable physicians to form voluntary groups that coordinate care for Medicare beneficiaries and to receive performance-based payments for the coordinated care	......	*	*	*	*	*	*	*	*	*	*	*	*
Total, aligning incentives toward quality	......	......	–400	–1,250	–1,680	–2,090	–2,560	–2,810	–3,030	–3,240	–3,460	–5,420	–20,520
Promoting efficiency and accountability:													
Establish competitive bidding for Medicare Advantage	......	......	......	–11,240	–16,610	–18,980	–21,550	–25,940	–26,140	–25,870	–30,270	–46,830	–176,600
Promote efficient provision of acute care through bundled Medicare payments covering hospital and post-acute settings	......	......	......	......	–180	–770	–1,910	–2,790	–3,750	–4,080	–4,360	–950	–17,840
Address financial conflicts of interest in physician-owned specialty hospitals	......	*	*	*	*	*	*	*	*	*	*	*	*
Ensure that Medicare makes appropriate payments for imaging services through the use of radiology benefit managers	......	......	–10	–20	–20	–20	–30	–30	–40	–40	–50	–70	–260
Provide private sector enhancements to ensure Medicare pays accurately	......	–60	–110	–160	–190	–200	–230	–240	–260	–280	–310	–720	–2,040
Promote cost-effective purchase and delivery of Medicaid prescription drugs by (1) increasing the Medicaid rebate amounts, (2) extending to and collecting rebates on behalf of managed care plans, and (3) applying rebates to new formulations of existing drugs	......	–1,185	–1,630	–1,690	–1,770	–1,890	–2,040	–2,130	–2,260	–2,420	–2,540	–8,165	–19,555
Promote increased generic medication utilization by establishing a pathway for FDA approval of generic biologics	......	......	......	......	20	–10	–680	–1,550	–1,920	–2,330	–2,770	10	–9,240
Expand availability of family planning services under Medicaid	......	5	5	......	–5	–15	–20	–25	–35	–45	–55	–10	–190
Ensure appropriate Medicaid payments through use of the National Correct Coding Initiative (NCCI) edits	......	–10	–25	–40	–45	–55	–75	–85	–90	–95	–100	–175	–620
Improve Medicare home health payments to align with costs	......	–550	–2,540	–3,010	–3,850	–3,710	–4,080	–4,450	–4,780	–5,120	–5,480	–13,160	–37,070
Reallocate Medicare and Medicaid Improvement Funds	......	......	......	......	......	–5,810	–5,940	–6,070	–6,090	–30	......	–5,810	–23,940

Table S–6. (Continued)

	2009	2010	2011	2012	2013	2014	2015	2016	2017	2018	2019	Totals 2010–2014	Totals 2010–2019
Total, promoting efficiency and accountability	......	–1,800	–4,310	–16,160	–22,150	–31,460	–36,555	–43,310	–45,365	–40,310	–45,935	–75,880	–287,355
Encouraging Shared Responsibility:													
Require certain higher-income beneficiaries enrolled in the Medicare drug benefit to pay higher premiums, as is currently required for physician and outpatient services	......	......	–400	–590	–680	–770	–870	–990	–1,120	–1,270	–1,440	–2,440	–8,130
Total, Medicare/Medicaid savings (–)[a]	......	**–1,800**	**–5,110**	**–18,000**	**–24,510**	**–34,320**	**–39,985**	**–47,110**	**–49,515**	**–44,820**	**–50,835**	**–83,740**	**–316,005**
Limit the tax rate at which itemized deductions reduce tax liability	......	......	–11,081	–30,808	–33,464	–35,478	–37,322	–39,269	–41,366	–43,402	–45,564	–110,831	–317,754
Total, specified savings (–)	......	**–1,800**	**–16,191**	**–48,808**	**–57,974**	**–69,798**	**–77,307**	**–86,379**	**–90,881**	**–88,222**	**–96,399**	**–194,571**	**–633,759**
Additional savings not yet determined	**TBD**	**TBD**	**TBD**	**TBD**	**TBD**	**TBD**	**TBD**	**TBD**	**TBD**	**TBD**	**TBD**	**TBD**	**TBD**
Benefits not yet determined	**TBD**	**TBD**	**TBD**	**TBD**	**TBD**	**TBD**	**TBD**	**TBD**	**TBD**	**TBD**	**TBD**	**TBD**	**TBD**
Net total of health reform	......	......	......	......	......	......	......	......	......	......	......	......	......

[a] Estimates exclude effects of Medicare and Medicaid provisions included in the American Recovery and Reinvestment Act of 2009.

* Savings negligible or undetermined at this time.

Table S–6. (Continued)

Note: For receipt effects, positive figures indicate lower receipts. For outlay effects, positive figures indicate higher outlays. For net costs, positive figures indicate higher deficits.

[1] Receipt effects unless otherwise noted.

[2] The estimates for this proposal include effects on outlays. The outlay effects included in the totals above are listed below:

	2009	2010	2011	2012	2013	2014	2015	2016	2017	2018	2019	2010–2014	2010–2019
Provide Making Work Pay tax credit	......	......	761	22,528	22,429	22,400	22,561	22,834	22,974	23,172	23,430	68,118	183,089
Expand Earned Income Tax Credit	......	......	......	3,935	3,882	3,881	3,929	4,014	4,097	4,188	4,263	11,698	32,209
Expand refundability of the Child Tax Credit	......	......	......	8,714	8,616	8,609	8,703	8,786	8,902	9,020	9,119	25,939	70,469
Expand saver's credit and automatic enrollment in IRAs and 401(k)s	......	......	87	743	848	866	900	940	976	1,008	1,048	2,544	7,416
Provide American Opportunity Tax Credit	......	......	......	2,928	3,256	3,629	4,144	4,645	4,890	5,018	5,310	9,813	33,820
Continue remaining expiring provisions through calendar year 2010	......	62	21	......	......	......	......	......	......	......	......	83	83
Eliminate Advanced Earned Income Tax Credit	......	–588	–163	8	–10	–16	–20	–23	–24	–23	–23	–769	–882
Total outlay effects of receipt proposals	......	–526	706	38,856	39,021	39,369	40,217	41,196	41,815	42,383	43,167	117,426	326,204

[3] The Budget proposes repealing some aviation excise taxes and replacing these taxes with direct user charges. The cost of repealing the excise taxes is reflected here. The user charges are considered discretionary and offset discretionary budget authority and outlays.

[4] This provision is estimated to have zero receipt effect under the Administration's current projections for energy prices.

[5] Shown here are those proceeds from auctioning emission allowances that are reserved for clean energy technology initiatives and to compensate families through the Making Work Pay tax cut. These proceeds are included in the grand totals as receipts, though they could alternatively be considered offsets to outlays. All additional net proceeds will be used to further compensate the public.

[6] Outlay effects unless otherwise noted.

[7] The estimates for this proposal include effects on receipts. The receipt effects included in the totals above are listed below:

	2009	2010	2011	2012	2013	2014	2015	2016	2017	2018	2019	2010–2014	2010–2019
Implement Unemployment Insurance integrity legislation:													
Subject to PAYGO	......	......	–32	–34	–22	–22	–21	–19	–18	–18	–19	–110	–206
Not subject to PAYGO	......	......	–2	6	42	25	187	187	192	1,041	432	71	2,110
Revise Terrorism Risk Insurance program	......	110	175	514	99	–440	253	325	314	266	174	458	1,790
Levy payments to federal contractors with delinquent tax debt	......	–49	–73	–77	–80	–84	–88	–92	–96	–100	–105	–363	–844
Make technical correction to JOBS Act	......	–19	–28	–29	–30	–31	–32	–33	–34	–35	–36	–137	–307
Implement program integrity allocation adjustments – IRS	......	–290	–1,119	–2,348	–3,864	–5,729	–1,460	–617	–462	–371	–380	–13,350	–16,640
Total receipt effects of mandatory proposals	......	–248	–1,079	–1,969	–3,855	–6,281	–1,161	–249	–104	782	66	–13,431	–14,097

[8] Spending of proposed mandatory user fee equals projected collections, for a net zero impact.

Table S–7. funding Levels for Appropriated ("discretionary") Programs by Agency (Budget authority in billions of dollars)

	2009 Estimate	2009-2010 Recovery Act	2010 Request	Outyears				Totals	
				2011	2012	2013	2014	2010-2014	2010-2019
Base discretionary Policy by Agency:									
Departments:									
Agriculture	23.9	6.9	26.0	27.2	27.9	28.4	29.1	138.6	299.0
Commerce	9.3	7.9	13.8	8.1	7.9	8.5	8.7	46.9	94.3
Defense (DOD -- excluding Overseas Contingency Operations)	513.3	7.4	533.7	541.8	550.7	561.1	574.5	2,761.8	5,854.9
Education[1]	41.4	81.1	46.7	53.6	58.5	61.6	64.5	284.9	626.4
Energy	26.4	38.7	26.3	26.3	27.2	27.7	28.3	135.8	285.9
Health and Human Services [2]	80.1	22.4	78.7	83.7	85.5	87.5	90.7	426.1	908.5
Homeland Security	42.2	2.8	42.7	42.4	41.9	41.4	40.9	209.3	426.3
Housing and Urban Development	40.1	13.6	47.5	47.6	47.5	47.6	48.2	238.3	498.8
Interior	11.3	3.0	12.0	12.3	12.5	12.7	13.0	62.4	131.8
Justice	25.5	4.0	23.9	27.7	27.9	28.0	28.2	135.7	284.6
Labor	12.7	4.8	13.3	13.4	13.5	13.6	13.7	67.5	139.8
State and Other International Programs[3]	36.7	0.6	51.7	56.0	60.3	64.8	69.3	302.1	687.7
Transportation [4, 5]	70.5	48.1	72.5	64.2	64.1	65.2	66.3	332.2	681.8
Treasury	12.7	0.3	13.3	13.7	14.1	14.7	15.3	71.1	157.8
Veterans Affairs [6]	47.6	1.4	52.5	53.7	55.1	56.6	58.2	276.2	588.8
Major Agencies:									
Corps of Engineers	5.3	4.6	5.1	5.2	5.2	5.3	5.5	26.3	56.6
Environmental Protection Agency	7.8	7.2	10.5	10.6	10.7	10.8	10.9	53.4	110.8
General Services Administration	0.7	5.9	0.6	0.7	0.6	0.6	0.6	3.2	6.4
National Aeronautics and Space Administration	17.8	1.0	18.7	18.6	18.6	18.6	18.9	93.4	191.6
National Science Foundation	6.9	3.0	7.0	7.2	8.5	9.1	9.7	41.6	97.9

Table S–7. (Continued)

	2009 Estimate	2009-2010 Recovery Act	2010 Request	Outyears				Totals	
				2011	2012	2013	2014	2010-2014	2010-2019
Small Business Administration	0.7	0.7	0.7	0.8	0.8	0.8	1.0	4.1	9.6
Social Security Administration [2]	8.8	1.1	9.7	10.5	11.0	11.6	12.2	54.9	122.3
Corporation for National and Community Service	0.9	0.2	1.1	1.3	1.7	2.0	2.4	8.6	25.9
National Infrastructure Bank	......	......	5.0	5.0	5.0	5.0	5.0	25.0	25.2
Climate Policy (Clean Energy Technologies)	......	......	......	......	15.0	15.0	15.0	45.0	120.0
Other Agencies	19.1	0.2	19.8	18.8	18.6	18.4	18.4	93.8	192.3
Total, Base discretionary	**1,061.6**	**267.0**	**1,132.8**	**1,150.3**	**1,190.3**	**1,216.7**	**1,248.2**	**5,938.3**	**12,625.2**
Other discretionary Costs:									
Funding for Overseas Contingency Operations (DOD) - Enacted	65.9	......	......	......	......	......	......	......	......
Funding for Overseas Contingency Operations (DOD) - Proposed [7]	75.5	......	130.0	50.0	50.0	50.0	50.0	330.0	580.0
International Supplemental Funding—Enacted [8]	4.1	......	......	......	......	......	......	......	......
International Supplemental Funding—Proposed [8]	7.1	......	......	......	......	......	......	......	......
One-time Costs:									
Energy.	7.5	......	......	......	......	......	......	......	......
Corps of Engineers	5.8	......	......	......	......	......	......	......	......
Veterans Affairs and Other	0.2	......	......	......	......	......	......	......	......
Total, Overseas Operations, international, and One-time									
Costs	**166.2**	**......**	**130.0**	**50.0**	**50.0**	**50.0**	**50.0**	**330.0**	**580.0**
Grand Total, discretionary funding	**1,227.7**	**267.0**	**1,262.8**	**1,200.3**	**1,240.3**	**1,266.7**	**1,298.2**	**6,268.3**	**13,205.2**

[1] Adjusted for advance appropriations, 2009 funding is $46.2 billion. All numbers exclude funding for Pell Grants.

[2] Funding from the Hospital Insurance and Supplementary Medical Insurance trust funds for administrative expenses incurred by the Social Security Administration that support the Medicare program are included in the Health and Human Services total and not in the Social Security Administration total.

[3] The Administration requests that Congress enact an increase in the Government's quota subscription to the International Monetary Fund valued at approximately $8 billion. Because this is an exchange of financial assets, the Administration does not propose to score this transaction as discretionary budget authority or outlays.

[4] The Administration proposes that all discretionary budgetary resources for transportation be scored as discretionary budget authority, as is the case for other programs.

[5] Starting in 2011, the Budget proposes to replace some aviation excise taxes with direct user charges. The direct user charges are considered to be discretionary and offset discretionary budget authority and outlays, while the aviation excise taxes are considered to be a receipt. Because of this budgetary treatment, this reform results in lower discretionary budget authority starting in 2011, which is reflected here. It also reduces aviation excise taxes. This is shown in Table S-6.

[6] The Veterans Affairs total is net of medical care collections.

[7] The Budget includes placeholder estimates of $50 billion per year for Overseas Contingency Operations in 2011 and beyond. These estimates do not reflect any specific policy decisions.

[8] Enacted and proposed supplementals include emergency food aid funded by the Department of Agriculture.

Table S–8. Comparison of Economic Assumptions (Calendar years)

	2008	2009	2010	2011	2012	2013	2014	2015	2016	2017	2018	2019
Nominal GDP:												
2010 Budget	14,281	14,291	14,902	15,728	16,731	17,739	18,588	19,415	20,279	21,181	22,124	23,108
Congressional Budget Office (January 2009)[1]	14,304	14,241	14,591	15,347	16,293	17,280	18,211	19,077	19,909	20,749	21,617	22,500
February Blue Chip Consensus	14,282	14,176	14,676	15,395	16,184	17,009	17,859	18,734	19,643	20,597	21,598	22,646
Real GDP:[2]												
2010 Budget	1.3	−1.2	3.2	4.0	4.6	4.2	2.9	2.6	2.6	2.6	2.6	2.6
Congressional Budget Office (January 2009)[1]	1.2	−2.2	1.5	4.2	4.4	4.1	3.5	2.8	2.5	2.3	2.2	2.2
February Blue Chip Consensus	1.3	−1.9	2.1	2.9	2.9	2.8	2.7	2.7	2.7	2.7	2.7	2.7
GDP Price Index:[2]												
2010 Budget	2.2	1.2	1.1	1.5	1.7	1.8	1.8	1.8	1.8	1.8	1.8	1.8
Congressional Budget Office (January 2009)[1]	2.4	1.8	0.9	1.0	1.7	1.8	1.8	1.9	1.8	1.9	1.9	1.9
February Blue Chip Consensus	2.2	1.0	1.3	1.9	2.2	2.2	2.2	2.1	2.1	2.1	2.1	2.1
Consumer Price Index (CPI-U):[2]												
2010 Budget	3.8	−0.6	1.6	1.8	2.0	2.1	2.1	2.1	2.1	2.1	2.1	2.1
Congressional Budget Office (January 2009)[1]	4.1	0.1	1.7	1.8	2.0	2.2	2.2	2.2	2.2	2.2	2.2	2.2
February Blue Chip Consensus	3.8	−0.8	1.8	2.4	2.5	2.4	2.5	2.4	2.3	2.3	2.3	2.3
Unemployment Rate:[3]												
2010 Budget	5.8	8.1	7.9	7.1	6.0	5.2	5.0	5.0	5.0	5.0	5.0	5.0
Congressional Budget Office (January 2009)[1]	5.7	8.3	9.0	8.0	6.8	5.8	5.1	4.9	4.8	4.8	4.8	4.8
February Blue Chip Consensus	5.8	8.3	8.7	5.8	5.5	5.3	5.2	5.1	5.1	5.1	5.1	5.1
Interest Rates:[3]												
91-Day Treasury Bills (discount basis):												
2010 Budget	1.4	0.2	1.6	3.4	3.9	4.0	4.0	4.0	4.0	4.0	4.0	4.0
Congressional Budget Office (January 2009)[1]	1.4	0.2	0.6	2.1	4.0	4.7	4.7	4.7	4.7	4.7	4.7	4.7
February Blue Chip Consensus	1.4	0.3	1.1	4.2	4.3	4.4	4.4	4.4	4.4	4.4	4.4	4.4
10-Year Treasury Notes:												
2010 Budget	3.7	2.8	4.0	4.8	5.1	5.2	5.2	5.2	5.2	5.2	5.2	5.2
Congressional Budget Office (January 2009)[1]	3.7	3.0	3.2	3.6	4.7	5.4	5.4	5.4	5.4	5.4	5.4	5.4
February Blue Chip Consensus	3.7	2.8	3.6	5.1	5.2	5.3	5.2	5.2	5.2	5.2	5.2	5.2

Sources: Administration; CBO, The *Budget and Economic Outlook: January 2009; February 2009 Blue Chip Economic Indicators*, Aspen Publishers, Inc. (2011-2019 from October 2008 Blue Chip long run extension).

[1] CBO economic projections do not include the effects of the American recovery and reinvestment Act of 2009.

[2] year-over-year percent change.

[3] Annual averages, percent.

Table S–9. Federal Government Financing and Debt (In billions of dollars)

	Actual	Estimate										
	2008	2009	2010	2011	2012	2013	2014	2015	2016	2017	2018	2019
financing:												
Unified budget deficit	459	1,752	1,171	912	581	533	570	583	637	636	634	712
Other transactions affecting borrowing from the public:												
Changes in financial assets and liabilities:[1]												
Change in Treasury operating cash balance	296	–302	......	......	......	......	......	......	......	......	......	......
Net disbursements of credit financing accounts:												
Direct loan accounts	27	482	57	88	80	83	78	77	71	68	67	95
Guaranteed loan accounts	6	2	–8	–3	4	6	7	5	3	1	–4	–6
Troubled Asset relief Program (TARP) equity purchase accounts	......	202	–16	–8	–53	–38	–25	–9	–5	–2	–2	4
Financing accounts for potential additional financial stabilization efforts	......	432	–59	–60	–61	–62	–63	–65	–66	–67	–68	9
Net purchases of non-Federal securities by the National railroad retirement Investment Trust (NRRIT)	–7	–6	–1	–1	–1	–1	–1	–1	–1	–1	–1	–1
Net change in other financing assets and liabilities[2]	–12	......	......	......	......	......	......	......	......	......	......	......
Subtotal, changes in financial assets and liabilities	310	810	–27	16	–31	–12	–4	7	2	–1	–9	102
Seigniorage on coins	–1	–1	–1	–1	–1	–1	–1	–1	–1	–1	–1	–1
Total, other transactions affecting borrowing from the public	309	810	–27	15	–32	–12	–5	7	2	–2	–9	101
Total, requirement to borrow from the public (equals change in debt held by the public)	768	2,562	1,144	927	549	520	565	589	638	634	625	813

Table S–9. (Continued)

	Actual	Estimate										
	2008	2009	2010	2011	2012	2013	2014	2015	2016	2017	2018	2019
Changes in debt Subject to Statutory Limitation:												
Change in debt held by the public	768	2,562	1,144	927	549	520	565	589	638	634	625	813
Change in debt held by Government accounts	267	157	229	267	371	402	384	372	354	358	364	328
Change in other factors	3	2	1	1	2	2	1	2	2	2	2	1
Total, change in debt subject to statutory limitation .	1,039	2,720	1,374	1,196	923	925	950	963	994	995	991	1,142
Debt Subject to Statutory Limitation, End of year:												
Debt issued by Treasury	9,961	12,679	14,053	15,248	16,169	17,093	18,042	19,003	19,996	20,990	21,981	23,122
Adjustment for discount, premium, and coverage [3]	–1	1	1	2	3	5	6	7	8	9	9	10
Total, debt subject to statutory limitation [4]	9,960	12,680	14,054	15,250	16,173	17,097	18,048	19,010	20,004	20,999	21,990	23,132
Debt Outstanding, End of year:												
Gross Federal debt:5												
Debt issued by Treasury	9,961	12,679	14,053	15,248	16,169	17,093	18,042	19,003	19,996	20,990	21,981	23,122
Debt issued by other agencies	25	25	25	24	24	23	23	22	22	20	18	18
Total, gross Federal debt	9,986	12,704	14,078	15,272	16,193	17,116	18,065	19,026	20,018	21,011	21,999	23,140
Held by:												
Debt held by Government accounts	4,183	4,340	4,569	4,837	5,208	5,610	5,995	6,367	6,720	7,079	7,443	7,770
Debt held by the public[6]	5,803	8,364	9,509	10,436	10,985	11,505	12,070	12,659	13,297	13,932	14,557	15,370
Debt held by the Public Net of financial Assets:												
Debt held by the public	5,803	8,364	9,509	10,436	10,985	11,505	12,070	12,659	13,297	13,932	14,557	15,370
Less financial assets net of liabilities:												
Treasury operating cash balance	372	70	70	70	70	70	70	70	70	70	70	70

Table S–9. (Continued)

		Estimate										
	Actual 2008	2009	2010	2011	2012	2013	2014	2015	2016	2017	2018	2019
Credit financing account balances:												
Direct loan accounts	196	678	734	822	902	985	1,063	1,140	1,211	1,279	1,346	1,441
Guaranteed loan accounts	–42	–40	–48	–51	–48	–42	–34	–29	–26	–26	–30	–35
TARP equity purchase accounts	......	202	186	178	125	87	62	53	48	46	44	49
Financing accounts for potential additional financial stabilization efforts	......	432	374	314	253	191	127	63	–3	–70	–138	–129
Government Sponsored Enterprise preferred stock..	2	108	149	173	173	173	173	173	173	173	173	173
Non-Federal securities held by NRRIT	25	19	18	16	16	15	14	13	11	10	9	7
Other assets net of liabilities	–46	–46	–46	–46	–46	–46	–46	–46	–46	–46	–46	–46
Total, financial assets net of liabilities .	505	1,422	1,436	1,476	1,444	1,433	1,428	1,435	1,438	1,436	1,428	1,530
Debt held by the public net of financial assets	5,297	6,943	8,072	8,960	9,541	10,073	10,642	11,224	11,860	12,495	13,129	13,840

[1] A decrease in assets, such as the Treasury operating cash balance, is a means of financing a deficit and therefore has a negative sign. An increase in liabilities, such as checks outstanding, is also a means of financing a deficit and therefore also has a negative sign.

[2] Besides checks outstanding, includes accrued interest payable on Treasury debt, uninvested deposit fund balances, allocations of special drawing rights, and other liability accounts; and, as an offset, cash and monetary assets (other than the Treasury operating cash balance), other asset accounts, and profit on sale of gold.

[3] Consists mainly of debt issued by the Federal Financing Bank (which is not subject to limit), debt held by the Federal Financing Bank, the unamortized discount (less premium) on public issues of Treasury notes and bonds (other than zero–coupon bonds), and the unrealized discount on Government account series securities.

[4] The statutory debt limit is $12,104 billion, enacted on February 17, 2009.

[5] Treasury securities held by the public and zero–coupon bonds held by Government accounts are almost all measured at sales price plus amortized discount or less amortized premium. Agency debt securities are almost all measured at face value. Treasury securities in the Government account series are otherwise measured at face value less unrealized discount (if any).

[6] At the end of 2008, the Federal reserve Banks held $491.1 billion of Federal securities and the rest of the public held $5,311.6 billion. Debt held by the Federal reserve Banks is not estimated for future years.

U.S. GOVERNMENT PRINTING OFFICE
KEEPING AMERICA INFORMED

Order Processing Code: 3538

Easy Secure Internet: bookstore.gpo.gov

Toll Free: 866 512–1800
DC Area: 202 512–1800
Fax: 202 512–2104

Mail: US Government Printing Office
P.O. Box 979050
St. Louis, MO 63197–9000

Qty	Stock Number	Publication Title	Unit Price	Total Price
	041-001-00660-5	A New Era of Responsibility: Renewing America's Promise	$26.00	
			Total Order	

Personal name (Please type or print)

Company name

Street address

City, State, Zip code

Daytime phone including area code

☐ Check payable to *Superintendent of Documents*

☐ SOD Deposit Account ☐☐☐☐☐☐☐ — ☐

☐ VISA ☐ MasterCard ☐ Discover/NOVUS ☐ American Express

☐☐☐☐☐☐☐☐☐☐☐☐☐☐☐☐☐☐☐☐

☐☐☐☐ (expiration date)

Thank you for your order!

AUTHORIZING SIGNATURE 02/09

End Notes

[1] This page corrects an amount erroneously included in the printed version of *A New Era of Responsibility*.

In: Call for A New Era in the U.S. Budget
Editor: Benjamin J. Walters
ISBN: 978-1-60741-883-2

Chapter 2

A PRELIMINARY ANALYSIS OF THE PRESIDENT'S BUDGET AND AN UPDATE OF CBO'S BUDGET AND ECONOMIC OUTLOOK

Congress of the United States, Congressional Budget Office

This report presents the Congressional Budget Office's (CBO's) latest projections for the budget and economic outlook, updating the projections published in early January 2009. In addition, CBO has reviewed the President's budgetary proposals contained in the February publication *A New Era of Responsibility: Renewing America's Promise,* and this report summarizes CBO's preliminary analysis of that budget plan. (CBO will review the complete plan after the Administration submits it to the Congress later this spring.)

CBO's updated budget projections indicate that:

- Largely as a result of the enactment of recent legislation and the continuing turmoil in financial markets, CBO's baseline projections of the deficit have risen by more than $400 billion in both 2009 and 2010 and by smaller amounts thereafter. Those projections assume that current laws and policies remain in place. Under that assumption, CBO now estimates that the deficit would total almost $1.7 trillion (11.9 percent of gross domestic product, or GDP) this year and $1.1 trillion (7.9 percent of GDP) next year—the largest deficits as a share of GDP since 1945. Deficits would shrink to about 2 percent of GDP by 2012 and remain in that vicinity through 2019.
- Under current laws and policies, outlays are projected to decline from 27.4 percent of GDP in 2009 to about 22 percent in 2012 and subsequent years, as spending related to the current recession phases out, problems in the financial markets fade, and discretionary spending—under the assumptions used for the baseline— declines as a share of GDP.
- At the same time, under current laws and policies, revenues are estimated to rise from 15.5 percent of GDP in 2009 to about 20 percent in 2012 and subsequent years. Much of that projected increase in revenues results from the growing impact of the alternative minimum tax (AMT) and, even more significant, the scheduled expiration

in December 2010 of provisions enacted in the recent economic stimulus legislation and in the Economic Growth and Tax Relief Reconciliation Act of 2001 (EGTRRA) and the Jobs and Growth Tax Relief Reconciliation Act of 2003 (JGTRRA).

CBO's analysis of the President's budget proposals indicates that:

- As estimated by CBO and the Joint Committee on Taxation, the President's proposals would add $4.8 trillion to the baseline deficits over the 2010– 2019 period. CBO projects that if those proposals were enacted, the deficit would total $1.8 trillion (13.1 percent of GDP) in 2009 and $1.4 trillion (9.6 percent of GDP) in 2010. It would decline to about 4 percent of GDP by 2012 and remain between 4 percent and 6 percent of GDP through 2019.
- The cumulative deficit from 2010 to 2019 under the President's proposals would total $9.3 trillion, compared with a cumulative deficit of $4.4 trillion projected under the current-law assumptions embodied in CBO's baseline. Debt held by the public would rise, from 41 percent of GDP in 2008 to 57 percent in 2009 and then to 82 percent of GDP by 2019 (compared with 56 percent of GDP in that year under baseline assumptions).
- Proposed changes in tax policy would reduce revenues by an estimated $2.1 trillion (or 6.1 percent) over the next 10 years. The proposals with the greatest effect on the budget include modifications to and the permanent extension of provisions of the 2001 and 2003 tax legislation (EGTRRA and JGTRRA); extension of the Making Work Pay tax credit; indexing of the exemption amounts for the AMT; implementation of a cap-and-trade program to reduce greenhouse-gas emissions; and limits on itemized deductions.
- Proposed changes in spending programs would add $1.7 trillion (excluding debt service) to outlays over the next 10 years, an increase of 4.4 percent above baseline levels. Outlays for refundable tax credits, higher spending for payments to physicians under Medicare, and increased discretionary spending for a variety of annually appropriated programs account for the bulk of those changes. Interest costs associated with greater borrowing would add another $1.0 trillion to deficits over the 2010–2019 period.
- CBO's estimates of deficits under the President's budget exceed those anticipated by the Administration by $2.3 trillion over the 2010–2019 period. The differences arise largely because of differing projections of baseline revenues and outlays. CBO's projection of baseline deficits exceeds the Administration's estimate (prepared on a comparable basis) by about $1.6 trillion.

CBO's current assessment of economic developments indicates that:

- Although the economy is likely to continue to deteriorate for some time, the enactment of the American Recovery and Reinvestment Act and very aggressive actions by the Federal Reserve and the Treasury are projected to help end the recession in the fall of 2009. In CBO's forecast, on a fourth-quarter-to-fourthquarter basis, real (inflation-adjusted) GDP falls by 1.5 percent in 2009 before growing by 4.1 percent in both 2010 and 2011.

- For the next two years, CBO anticipates that economic output will average about 7 percent below its potential—the output that would be produced if the economy's resources were fully employed. That shortfall is comparable with the one that occurred during the recession of 1981 and 1982 and will persist for significantly longer—making the current recession the most severe since World War II. In CBO's forecast, the unemployment rate peaks at 9.4 percent in late 2009 and early 2010 and remains above 7.0 percent through the end of 2011. With a large and sustained output gap, inflation is expected to be very low during the next several years.

1. CBO's Baesline and Estimate of the President's Budget

Since the Congressional Budget Office (CBO) last issued its baseline projections, in January 2009, the outlook for the budget deficit has deteriorated further.[1] Enactment of stimulus legislation and omnibus appropriations, a worsening of the economic outlook, and other factors have increased CBO's projections of the deficit by more than $400 billion in both 2009 and 2010 and by smaller amounts thereafter. As a result, if current policies remain the same, CBO now anticipates that the deficit will total almost $1.7 trillion (11.9 percent of gross domestic product, or GDP) this year and $1.1 trillion (7.9 percent of GDP) next year, the largest deficits as a share of GDP since 1945 (see Table 1-1).

CBO has also analyzed the policy proposals outlined in the President's preliminary budget request.[2] Under those policies, the deficit would total $1.8 trillion (13.1 percent of GDP) in 2009 and $1.4 trillion (9.6 percent of GDP) in 2010. The cumulative deficit over the 2010–2019 projection period would equal $9.3 trillion and would average 5.3 percent of GDP. Debt held by the public would rise from 57 percent of GDP in 2009 to 82 percent of GDP in 2019.

CBO's Baseline Budget Projections

CBO's baseline projections are estimates of federal revenues and spending for the next 10 years under the assumption that current laws and policies remain in place. The projected deficit for fiscal year 2009 under that assumption—$1.7 trillion—is up significantly from the $1.2 trillion projected in January. (Additional fund-ing likely to be requested for military operations in Iraq and Afghanistan would add to that total.) The increase in the projected deficit results primarily from legislation enacted since January and from an updated assessment of the costs of actions taken in response to the turmoil affecting the financial markets. In particular, enactment of the economic stimulus legislation—the American Recovery and Reinvestment Act of 2009 (ARRA, Public Law 111-5)—will boost outlays in 2009 by $120 billion and reduce revenues by $65 billion, CBO and the Joint Committee on Taxation (JCT) estimate. In addition, CBO has increased its estimate of outlays in 2009 associ-ated with the Troubled Asset Relief Program (TARP) by over $150 billion.[3] Most of the remaining change in CBO's baseline estimate for 2009 reflects lower tax receipts as well as higher costs for federal operation of Fannie Mae and Freddie Mac, the two government-sponsored enterprises that guarantee mortgages and mortgage-backed securities and that have now been taken over by the government.

Under current laws and policies, the budget deficit in 2010 would total $1.1 trillion, CBO estimates—$436billion higher than projected in January. The cumulative deficit for the 2010–2019 period has also increased significantly since January. Under the assump-tion that current laws remain in place over the next 10years, CBO projects baseline deficits totaling $4.4 tril-lion (2.5 percent of GDP) from 2010 to 2019, roughly $1.3trillion higher than its previous projection of $3.1trillion. Most of the change in the 10-year deficit projection is attributable to recent legislative actions, with changes in other factors having largely offsetting effects on projected deficits.

As a percentage of GDP, the baseline budget deficit peaks in 2009 and then falls in each year through 2013, when it reaches 1.8 percent of GDP (see Table 1-2). The baseline deficit is projected to roughly stabilize as a share of output thereafter, ranging between 1.6 percent and 2.0 percent of GDP through 2019.

Revenues in CBO's baseline grow from a low of 15.5 percent of GDP this year to 19.9 percent in 2013 and remain at roughly 20 percent of GDP thereafter. Much of that increase results from the growing impact of the alternative minimum tax (AMT) and, even more significant, the scheduled expiration in December 2010 of provisions originally enacted in the Economic Growth and Tax Relief Reconciliation Act of 2001 (EGTRRA) and the Jobs and Growth Tax Relief Reconciliation Act of 2003 (JGTRRA), as well as tax provisions enacted in ARRA.

As a percentage of GDP, outlays in the baseline peak in 2009 at 27.4 percent of GDP and then fall to 21.7 percent in 2012. They remain roughly constant thereafter, at about 22 percent of GDP from 2013 to 2019.

CBO generally constructs its baseline in accordance with the provisions set forth in the Balanced Budget and Emergency Deficit Control Act of 1985 and the Congressional Budget and Impoundment Control Act of 1974. (Although the provisions of the Deficit Control Act that pertain to the baseline expired at the end of September 2006, CBO has continued to use that law's specifications as guidance in preparing its baseline.) The resulting baseline projections are not intended to be a prediction of future budget outcomes. Rather, they serve as a benchmark that lawmakers can use to measure the effects of spending or revenue proposals, such as those in the President's budget.

To project revenues and mandatory spending, CBO assumes that current laws continue unchanged in the future, with only a few exceptions.[4] That approach includes the assumption that various changes in tax law enacted since 2001 expire as scheduled, by the end of December 2010, causing revenues to rise thereafter.

Table 1.1. Comparison of Projected Revenues, Outlays, and Deficits in CBO's March 2009 Baseline and CBO's Estimate of the President's Budget

(Billions of dollars)

	Actual 2008	2009	2010	2011	2012	2013	2014	2015	2016	2017	2018	2019	Total, 2010-2014	Total, 2010-2019
							CBO's Baseline							
Revenues	2,524	2,186	2,334	2,783	3,086	3,281	3,436	3,610	3,761	3,927	4,083	4,247	14,921	34,550
Outlays	2,983	3,853	3,473	3,476	3,417	3,581	3,746	3,892	4,088	4,239	4,408	4,671	17,693	38,991
Total Deficit	**-459**	**-1,667**	**-1,139**	**-693**	**-331**	**-300**	**-310**	**-282**	**-327**	**-312**	**-325**	**-423**	**-2,772**	**-4,441**
							CBO's Estimate of the President's Budget							
Revenues	2,524	2,159	2,289	2,586	2,917	3,095	3,231	3,387	3,522	3,669	3,807	3,950	14,118	32,452
Outlays	2,983	4,004	3,669	3,556	3,575	3,767	3,979	4,172	4,417	4,619	4,830	5,139	18,546	41,723
Total Deficit	**-459**	**-1,845**	**-1,379**	**-970**	**-658**	**-672**	**-749**	**-785**	**-895**	**-949**	**-1,023**	**-1,189**	**-4,429**	**-9,270**
							Difference Between the President's Budget and CBO's Baseline							
Revenues	n.a.	-26	-45	-198	-169	-187	-205	-223	-240	-257	-276	-297	-804	-2,097
Outlays	n.a.	151	196	80	158	186	233	280	329	380	422	468	853	2,732
Total Deficit[a]	**n.a.**	**-177**	**-241**	**-278**	**-327**	**-373**	**-438**	**-503**	**-568**	**-637**	**-698**	**-765**	**-1,657**	**-4,829**
Memorandum:														
Total Deficit as a Percentage of GDP														
CBO's baseline	-3.2	-11.9	-7.9	-4.6	-2.1	-1.8	-1.8	-1.6	-1.8	-1.6	-1.6	-2.0	-3.5	-2.5
CBO's estimate of the President's budget	-3.2	-13.1	-9.6	-6.4	-4.2	-4.1	-4.3	-4.4	-4.8	-4.9	-5.1	-5.7	-5.6	-5.3

Table 1.1. (Continued)

	Actual 2008	2009	2010	2011	2012	2013	2014	2015	2016	2017	2018	2019	Total, 2010-2014	Total, 2010-2019
Debt Held by the Public as a Percentage of GDP														
CBO's baseline	40.8	54.8	60.1	62.0	61.6	60.7	60.2	59.5	59.0	58.5	56.1	56.1	n.a.	n.a.
CBO's estimate of the President's budget	40.8	56.8	64.7	68.3	70.1	71.4	73.2	75.2	77.5	79.9	79.3	82.4	n.a.	n.a.

Source Congressional Budget Office.

Note: GDP = gross domestic product;n.a. = not applicable.

a. Negative numbers indicate an increase relative to the baseline deficit.

Table 1.2. CBO's Baseline Budget Projections

	Actual 2008	2009	2010	2011	2012	2013	2014	2015	2016	2017	2018	2019	Total, 2010-2014	Total, 2010-2019
						In Billions of Dollars								
Revenues														
Individual income taxes	1,146	968	1,043	1,359	1,525	1,658	1,767	1,878	1,986	2,101	2,205	2,317	7,352	17,838
Corporate income taxes	304	174	206	281	339	339	328	338 .	335	334	336	332	1,493	3,167
Social insurance taxes	900	891	926	972	1,022	1,074	1,117	1,154	1,190	1,231	1,275	1,322	5,111	11,284
Other	174	153	160	171	200	211	223	239	250	261	268	277	965	2,261
Total Revenues	**2,524**	**2,186**	**2,334**	**2,783**	**3,086**	**3,281**	**3,436**	**3,610**	**3,761**	**3,927**	**4,083**	**4,247**	**14,921**	**34,550**
On-budget	1,866	1,533	1,666	2,089	2,360	2,515	2,634	2,776	2,897	3,029	3,151	3,279	11,264	26,396
Off-budget	658	653	668	695	726	766	802	834	864	898	932	968	3,657	8,154

Table 1.2. (Continued)

	Actual 2008	2009	2010	2011	2012	2013	2014	2015	2016	2017	2018	2019	Total, 2010-2014	Total, 2010-2019
Outlays														
Mandatory spending	1,595	2,463	2,004	1,988	1,921	2,023	2,118	2,205	2,345	2,450	2,558	2,753	10,053	22,365
Discretionary spending	1,135	1,221	1,302	1,285	1,240	1,239	1,244	1,256	1,279	1,300	1,320	1,352	6,310	12,816
Net interest	253	170	167	203	256	320	385	431	464	489	530	566	1,330	3,810
Total Outlays	**2,983**	**3,853**	**3,473**	**3,476**	**3,417**	**3,581**	**3,746**	**3,892**	**4,088**	**4,239**	**4,408**	**4,671**	**17,693**	**38,991**
On-budget	2,508	3,330	2,920	2,904	2,825	2,964	3,101	3,216	3,376	3,485	3,609	3,823	14,713	32,223
Off-budget	475	523	553	572	592	618	645	676	712	754	799	848	2,980	6,768
Deficit (-) or Surplus	**-459**	**-1,667**	**-1,139**	**-693**	**-331**	**-300**	**-310**	**-282**	**-327**	**-312**	**-325**	**-423**	**-2,772**	**-4,441**
On-budget	-642	-1,798	-1,254	-815	-464	-448	-468	-440	-479	-456	-458	-544	-3,449	-5,827
Off-budget	183	130	115	123	134	148	157	158	152	144	133	121	677	1,385
Debt Held by the Public	5,803	7,703	8,658	9,340	9,712	10,016	10,372	10,684	11,034	11,365	11,334	11,753	n.a.	n.a.
Memorandum:														
Gross Domestic Product	14,222	14,057	14,405	15,061	15,774	16,496	17,241	17,957	18,688	19,436	20,191	20,966	78,977	176,215
As a Percentage of Gross Domestic Product														
Revenues														
Individual income taxes	8.1	6.9	7.2	9.0	9.7	10.0	10.2	10.5	10.6	10.8	10.9	11.0	9.3	10.1
Corporate income taxes	2.1	1.2	1.4	1.9	2.1	2.1	1.9	1.9	1.8	1.7	1.7	1.6	1.9	1.8
Social insurance taxes	6.3	6.3	6.4	6.5	6.5	6.5	6.5	6.4	6.4	6.3	6.3	6.3	6.5	6.4
Other	1.2	1.1	1.1	1.1	1.3	1.3	1.3	1.3	1.3	1.3	1.3	1.3	1.2	1.3
Total Revenues	**17.7**	**15.5**	**16.2**	**18.5**	**19.6**	**19.9**	**19.9**	**20.1**	**20.1**	**20.2**	**20.2**	**20.3**	**18.9**	**19.6**
On-budget	13.1	10.9	11.6	13.9	15.0	15.2	15.3	15.5	15.5	15.6	15.6	15.6	14.3	15.0
Off-budget	4.6	4.6	4.6	4.6	4.6	4.6	4.7	4.6	4.6	4.6	4.6	4.6	4.6	4.6
Outlays														
Mandatory spending	11.2	17.5	13.9	13.2	12.2	12.3	12.3	12.3	12.5	12.6	12.7	13.1	12.7	12.7
Discretionary spending	8.0	8.7	9.0	8.5	7.9	7.5	7.2	7.0	6.8	6.7	6.5	6.4	8.0	7.3
Net interest	1.8	1.2	1.2	1.3	1.6	1.9	2.2	2.4	2.5	2.5	2.6	2.7	1.7	2.2
Total Outlays	**21.0**	**27.4**	**24.1**	**23.1**	**21.7**	**21.7**	**21.7**	**21.7**	**21.9**	**21.8**	**21.8**	**22.3**	**22.4**	**22.1**

Table 1.2. (Continued)

	Actual 2008	2009	2010	2011	2012	2013	2014	2015	2016	2017	2018	2019	Total, 2010-2014	Total, 2010-2019
On-budget	17.6	23.7	20.3	19.3	17.9	18.0	18.0	17.9	18.1	17.9	17.9	18.2	18.6	18.3
Off-budget	3.3	3.7	3.8	3.8	3.8	3.7	3.7	3.8	3.8	3.9	4.0	4.0	3.8	3.8
Deficit (-) or Surplus	**-3.2**	**-11.9**	**-7.9**	**-4.6**	**-2.1**	**-1.8**	**-1.8**	**-1.6**	**-1.8**	**-1.6**	**-1.6**	**-2.0**	**-3.5**	**-2.5**
On-budget	-4.5	-12.8	-8.7	-5.4	-2.9	-2.7	-2.7	-2.5	-2.6	-2.3	-2.3	-2.6	-4.4	-3.3
Off-budget	1.3	0.9	0.8	0.8	0.8	0.9	0.9	0.9	0.8	0.7	0.7	0.6	0.9	0.8
Debt Held by the Public	40.8	54.8	60.1	62.0	61.6	60.7	60.2	59.5	59.0	58.5	56.1	56.1	n.a.	n.a.

Source Congressional Budget Office.

Note: n.a. = not applicable.

The Deficit Control Act also provides guidelines for CBO's projections of discretionary spending, so CBO normally assumes that appropriations each year are equal to the current year's budget authority adjusted for inflation and for certain other factors. However, CBO, with the agreement of the budget committees, deviated from that procedure for its current baseline. Because of the unusual size and nature of the funding provided in ARRA, the $283 billion in discretionary budget authority provided in that act has not been extrapolated in CBO's baseline (that is, funding projected for subsequent years is based on enacted appropriations excluding those in ARRA).

Changes in CBO's Baseline since January 2009

Revision to CBO's baseline incorporate enacted legislation as well as economic data and technical information that have become available since CBO completed its pre-vious baseline projections in January.

Since January, CBO has increased its current-law estimate of the 2009 deficit by $481 billion, to $1.7 trillion (see Table1-3). Much of that change stems from lower esti-mated revenues and the increased costs attributable to the TARP. Over the 2010–2019 period, CBO has increased its estimate of the cumulative deficit by $1.3 trillion—mostly because of recently enacted legislation. Nearly half of that projected increase occurs in 2010 and 2011, largely as a result of the 2009 stimulus legislation (ARRA). Revisions stemming from CBO's updated eco-nomic forecast are substantial but are mostly offsetting between the revenue and outlay sides of the budget; changes in economic assumptions reduce projections of revenues and outlays by $1.3 trillion to $1.4 trillion over the 10-year period. Changes resulting from technical adjustments are roughly $177 billion for 2009, primarily because of revised estimates of the cost of the TARP and the conservatorship of Fannie Mae and Freddie Mac, as well as reductions in estimated revenue. Technical adjust-ments have much smaller effects in subsequent years.

Legislative Changes

CBO estimates that enacted legislation will increase the deficit by $195 billion in 2009 and by $1.3 trillion over the 2010–2019 period. Nearly all of that increase is attributable to the economic stimulus legislation.[5]

Changes in Outlays. Legislation enacted since January will increase outlays by $134 billion in 2009 and by $1.2 trillion over the 2010–2019 period, according to CBO's estimates. Much of that change results from the enactment of ARRA, but some is attributable to passage of the Omnibus Appropriations Act of 2009 (P.L. 111-8) and the reauthorization of the Children's Health Insur-ance Program (CHIP).

Economic Stimulus. Provisions in ARRA will increase outlays in 2009 by $120 billion in CBO's estimates; $90 billion of that total is classified as mandatory outlays, and the remaining $30 billion affects discretionary programs. Over the 10-year period, additional outlays resulting from the stimulus package are estimated to total $456 billion, nearly evenly split between mandatory and discretionary programs[6]

Children's Health Insurance. The Children's Health Insurance Program Reauthorization Act of 2009 (P.L. 111-3) reauthorized and expanded CHIP through 2013 and increased federal funding for the program, relative to January baseline figures. CBO estimates that the act will increase mandatory outlays by $2 billion in 2009 and by $38 billion between 2010 and 2019.

Omnibus Appropriations. The Omnibus Appropriations Act of 2009, enacted in March, provided funding for the rest of fiscal year 2009 for all agencies except the Departments of Defense, Homeland Security, and Veterans Affairs, which received their appropriations last fall. The funding in that bill (on an annualized basis) is about $20 billion greater than the amount in the continuing resolution, which provided funding for the first part of the fiscal year and was the basis for CBO's January baseline projections. CBO therefore estimates that the omnibus legislation will increase discretionary outlays by $9 billion for 2009; assuming similar appropriations (adjusted for inflation) over the 2010–2019 period adds $260 billion to the baseline totals.

Net Interest. Recently enacted legislation directly increased the deficit for 2009 by an estimated $195 billion and the cumulative baseline deficit by $863 billion. Interest costs on the additional debt required to fund those deficits are estimated to boost net interest costs by $404 billion over the 10-year period. Therefore, projected outlays between 2010 and 2019 have risen by $1.3 trillion as the result of enacted legislation.

Changes in Revenues. As a result of recemtly enacted legislation, CBO has reduced its estimate of revenues by $61 billion for 2009 and by $76 billion for the 2010–2019 period. The largest change occurs in 2010, for which CBO has reduced its projection by $173 billion; over the following nine years, however, legislation accounts for an upward revision to revenues of $97 billion.

Economic Stimulus. The largest legislative changes stem from enactment of ARRA. Several provisions of that law account for most of the impact on revenues: the new Making Work Pay tax credit, which is in effect through 2010; one year of relief to individuals from the AMT; and business tax provisions related to depreciation and income from cancellation of indebtedness. JCT and CBO estimate that ARRA will lower revenues by $245 billion over the 2009–2010 period and produce small gains beginning in 2012, yielding a net reduction of revenues totaling $212 billion over the 2009–2019 period.[7]

Children's Health Insurance. CBO also adjusted its base-line projections of revenues to incorporate the effects of an increase in the tobacco tax enacted in the Children's Health Insurance Program Reauthorization Act of 2009; those increases will raise revenues by $4 billion in 2009 and $71 billion over the 2010–2019 period, CBO estimates.

Table 1.3. Changes in CBO's Baseline Projections of the Deficit Since January 2009

(Billions of dollars)	2009	2010	2011	2012	2013	2014	2015	2016	2017	2018	2019	Total, 2010-2014	Total, 2010-2019
Total Deficit as Projected in January 2009	**-1,186**	**-703**	**-498**	**-264**	**-257**	**-250**	**-234**	**-272**	**-234**	**-188**	**-235**	**-1,972**	**-3,135**
Legislative Changes													
Revenues	-61	-173	-1	17	10	13	14	13	12	12	7	-133	-76
Outlays													
Mandatory outlays													
Stimulus	90	116	56	12	10	16	6	-4	-3	-1	-1	209	205
CHIP	2	5	7	8	9	3	1	1	1	1	1	33	38
Other	2	*	*	1	1	4	5	5	6	6	7	5	34
Subtotal, mandatory	95	120	63	20	20	23	12	3	4	6	6	247	277
Discretionary outlays													
Stimulus	30	103	71	35	20	12	6	2	1	1	*	241	251
Other Defense	1	1	1	1	1	1	1	1	1	1	1	6	13
Other Nondefense	8	19	23	24	24	25	25	26	26	27	27	115	246
Subtotal, discretionary	39	124	95	60	46	38	33	29	28	29	29	362	510
Net interest	1	5	13	22	31	41	48	54	59	63	69	112	404
Subtotal, outlays	134	250	171	102	97	101	92	86	91	98	104	720	1,191
Total, Legislative Changes[a]	**-195**	**-422**	**-172**	**-84**	**-86**	**-89**	**-78**	**-73**	**-79**	**-86**	**-97**	**-853**	**-1,267**
Economic Changes													
Revenues	-45	-14	-24	-45	-71	-109	-145	-175	-201	-232	-259	-263	-1,276
Outlays													
Mandatory outlays													
Social Security	0	0	-6	-17	-28	-39	-48	-54	-58	-62	-67	-90	-378
Other COLA programs	0	*	-2	-6	-9	-12	-15	-21	-18	-19	-20	-29	-122
Medicare	-1	*	-2	-6	-12	-17	-22	-26	-31	-36	-42	-37	-194
Medicaid	1	*	-3	-6	-9	-14	-17	-19	-22	-24	-27	-31	-140

Table 1.3. (Continued)

(Billions of dollars)	2009	2010	2011	2012	2013	2014	2015	2016	2017	2018	2019	Total, 2010-2014	Total, 2010-2019
Unemployment	5	2	1	*	-1	-2	-2	-3	-3	-3	-3	-1	-15
Other	-1	-2	-2	-1	-2	-1	-2	*	-4	-4	-4	-8	-22
Subtotal, mandatory	4	*	-14	-36	-61	-84	-105	-123	-136	-148	-164	-195	-871
Discretionary outlays	*	1	-4	-13	-27	-41	-51	-58	-64	-70	-76	-84	-404
Net interest													
Debt service	*	1	1	2	1	-1	-3	-4	-4	-4	-4	3	-17
Rate effect and inflation	-5	5	3	-19	-38	-24	-13	-5	-2	3	5	-73	-85
Subtotal, net interest	-5	5	5	-18	-37	-25	-16	-9	-6	-2	2	-71	-101
Subtotal, outlays	-1	6	-13	-67	-126	-150	-172	-190	-206	-220	-238	-350	-1,377
Total, Economic Changes[a]	**-43**	**-20**	**-11**	**23**	**55**	**41**	**27**	**15**	**5**	**-12**	**-21**	**87**	**101**
Technical Changes													
Revenues	-66	-12	-17	-11	-11	-11	-6	-5	-6	-6	-5	-62	-89
Outlays													
Mandatory outlays													
TARP	152	15	0	0	0	0	0	0	0	0	0	15	15
Fannie Mae and Freddie Mac	52	5	7	8	8	2	1	*	-1	-1	-1	30	28
Medicare	-2	-2	4	11	13	19	13	11	15	21	17	45	123
Deposit Insurance	-5	6	10	11	7	*	-6	-6	-7	-6	*	34	9
Other	3	2	4	2	2	2	3	2	3	3	5	12	27
Subtotal, mandatory	200	26	25	31	31	23	11	7	10	17	20	137	201
Discretionary outlays	-2	-10	5	*	1	1	*	*	*	*	*	-4	-4
Net interest													
Debt service	1	3	4	8	16	27	33	38	44	50	56	57	278
Other	-21	-37	-39	-44	-48	-49	-52	-53	-55	-33	-12	-218	-424
Subtotal, net interest	-21	-35	-35	-37	-32	-22	-19	-15	-12	16	44	-161	-146

Table 1.3. (Continued)

(Billions of dollars)	2009	2010	2011	2012	2013	2014	2015	2016	2017	2018	2019	Total, 2010-2014	Total, 2010-2019
Subtotal, outlays	177	-19	-5	-5	*	1	-9	-8	-1	33	64	-28	51
Total, Technical Changes[a]	**-243**	**7**	**-11**	**-5**	**-11**	**-12**	**3**	**3**	**-4**	**-38**	**-69**	**-34**	**-140**
Total Impact on the Deficit[a]	**-481**	**-436**	**-194**	**-67**	**-43**	**-61**	**-48**	**-55**	**-78**	**-136**	**-188**	**-801**	**-1,307**
Total Deficit as Projected in March 2009	**-1,667**	**-1,139**	**-693**	**-331**	**-300**	**-310**	**-282**	**-327**	**-312**	**-325**	**-423**	**-2,772**	**-4,441**
Memorandum:													
Total Revenue Changes	-172	-199	-41	-38	-72	-108	-137	-168	-195	-226	-258	-458	-1,441
Total Outlay Changes	310	237	153	29	-29	-47	-88	-113	-117	-90	-70	342	-135

Source: Congressional Budget Office.

Note: * = between -$500 million and $500 million; CHIP = Children's Health Insurance Program; COLA = cost-of-living adjustment; TARP = Troubled Asset Relief Program.

a. Negative numbers indicate an increase in the deficit.

Economic Changes

In its updated economic forecast, CBO modified projections of real GDP, inflation, interest rates, the unemployment rate, and other economic variables (for details, see Chapter 2). The weaker outlook for the economy generates an upward revision of $43 billion to the estimated 2009 deficit. Over the following 10 years, economic changes significantly affect estimates of revenues and outlays; those changes largely offset each other, however, because lower projections of inflation have reduced CB O's estimates of both revenues and outlays. CBO has lowered its projection of revenues by nearly $1.3 trillion but its estimate of outlays by $1.4 trillion. Overall, CBO's updated economic forecast leads to a $101 billion reduction in the cumulative budget deficit over the next 10 years.

Changes in Revenues. As a result of changes to its economic outlook since January, revenues under current law would be lower by $45 billion in 2009, by $14 billion in 2010, and by $1.3 trillion, or 3.5 percent, over the 20 10– 2019 period, CBO estimates. Baseline revenues are now lower because the projection for nominal GDP has decreased by more than $7 trillion, or 3.9 percent, over the 10-year period. Compared with the previous forecast, the outlook for lower nominal GDP stems from a reduction in the level of real economic activity in 2009 as well as lower inflation in 2009 and beyond. Lower projected GDP, in turn, leads to a drop in estimated wages and salaries, corporate profits, and other taxable income.

Changes in Outlays. Changes in CBO's economic forecast have little effect on projected outlays in 2009. However, economic changes—particularly a reduction in various measures of inflation—have significantly decreased projected spending over the following 10 years; CBO has lowered its estimate of outlays by $1.4 trillion, or 3.5 percent, for that period. Over 60 percent of that total change ($871 billion) results from adjustments to spending for mandatory programs, particularly Social Security, retirement benefits for federal employees, Medicare, and Medicaid. About 30 percent ($404 billion) results from reduced estimates of discretionary outlays because the inflation rates used to project future funding are now lower. The remaining change ($101 billion) stems from a decrease in estimated interest on the federal debt.

Social Security and Other Indexed Programs. Over the 10-year baseline period, CBO has reduced estimated outlays by $500 billion for federal retirement and benefit programs, including Social Security, because projected cost-of-living adjustments (COLAs) have fallen since January. No COLAs are currently projected for such programs from 2010 through 2012; the COLA would amount to less than 2 percent in all future years (an average of 0.8 percentage points below CBO's previous projections for years after 2011). As a result, estimated outlays for 2010 to 2019 are $378 billion lower for Social Security benefits and $122 billion lower for other federal programs that incorporate a COLA in their benefit calculations (such as civil service retirement, veterans' compensation and pensions, and other federal retirement programs).

Medicare. Payment rates for most Medicare services are adjusted each year on the basis of the estimated rate of inflation. Because inflation is estimated to be lower, payment rates for most Medicare services are now projected to drop over the 2010–2019 period. By 2019, payment rates will be about 6 percent lower than previously estimated. CBO has therefore reduced projected Medicare spending over that period by $194 billion.

Medicaid. The lower inflation forecast has trimmed projections of Medicaid payment rates over the 2010–2019 period, thus reducing estimated Medicaid outlays by approximately $140 billion.

Discretionary Programs Reductions in the factors used to extrapolate discretionary spending (the GDP price index and the employment cost index for wages and salaries) diminish projected discretionary outlays by $404 billion over the 10-year period.

Net Interest. From 2010 to 2019, CBO's projection of net interest has been reduced by $101 billion. About one- third of that change stems from lower anticipated inflation adjustments on Treasury Inflation-Protected Securities (TIPS); the rest results from lower projections of other interest rates (mostly for the 2012–2014 period) and from debt-service costs related to other economic changes.

Technical Changes

In updates to CBO's baselines, changes not attributable to economic or legislative activity are classified as technical. For 2009, such revisions increase the deficit by $243 billion; they result from adjustments to expected outlays ($177 billion) and expected revenues ($66 billion). Over the following 10 years, technical changes account for small increases in deficit projections, averaging about $14 billion a year.

Changes in Revenue. Adjustments to CBO's technical assumptions reduce projected revenues by $66 billion in 2009 and by $89 billion from 2010 to 2019. The most significant change stems from smaller-than-expected collections from employers' withholding of income and payroll (social insurance) taxes from employees' paychecks. Starting in December, those collections dropped significantly compared with a year ago, presumably reflecting, at least in part, substantial decreases in year-end bonuses and increasing job losses. However, the year-over-year declines in withholding have continued past the traditional bonus season and are greater than implied by macroeconomic data on labor market activity. CBO assumes that this downward effect on revenues will diminish over the next few years, as most forms of taxable income return to their historical relationship to GDP.

Changes in Outlays. in 2009, technical adjustments increase estimated outlays by $177 billion. Increased subsidy costs estimated for the TARP, Fannie Mae, and Freddie Mac total roughly $200 billion. That increase is partially offset by a reduction in net interest of $21 billion.

Over the 2010–2019 period, technical changes boost estimated outlays by $51 billion (0.1 percent)—the result of a $201 billion increase in mandatory outlays (dominated by a $123 billion increase in Medicare outlays) that is partially offset by a $146 billion decrease in net interest outlays.

Troubled Asset Relief Program. Since January, CBO has raised its estimate of the net cost (on a present-value basis) of the transactions covered by the TARP by $152 billion for 2009 and by $15 billion for 2010. Those revisions stem from three factors—changes in financial market conditions, new transactions, and a small shift in the anticipated timing of disbursements.

Since CBO's previous estimate was completed, market yields on securities issued by the firms that have received TARP funds have increased, thereby boosting the estimated subsidy cost of the Treasury's purchases of preferred stock, asset guarantees, and loans to automakers. Also, the Treasury announced additional deals with Bank of America and American International Group (AIG) as well as participation of up to $50 billion in the Administration's foreclosure mitigation plan, all of which involve subsidy rates that are higher than the averages in the previous baseline.[8]

Finally, CBO assumed that more transactions would occur after October 1, which pushes the recognition of more of the subsidy cost into fiscal year 2010.

Fannie Mae and Freddie Mac. As a result of the degree of management and financial control that the federal government currently exercises over Fannie Mae and Freddie Mac, CBO has determined that the two corporations should now be included in the federal budget. In January, CBO estimated the subsidy cost for their existing business when the takeover occurred ($200 billion recorded in 2009) and the estimated subsidy costs for future activities (nearly $40 billion for 2009 and smaller amounts thereafter). Since January, however, the condition of the two entities has turned out to be worse than expected; as a result, CBO has increased its estimate of the present value of future losses for Fannie Mae and Freddie Mac by $52 billion for 2009—most of which stems from loans and guarantees inherited at the time of the conservatorship—and by $28 billion for their activities between 2010 and 2019.[9]

Medicare. CBO has raised its projection of Medicare outlays over the 2010–2019 period by $123 billion because of technical factors (although that increase is largely offset by the decrease in estimated Medicare outlays resulting from CB O's updated economic forecast). The technical changes in the Medicare baseline are the net effect of a $167 billion increase in projected spending for Parts A and B and a $46 billion reduction in projected spending for Part D. (Parts A and B cover medical and surgical benefits; Part D covers prescription drugs.) The major component of the higher projected spending for Parts A and B is a 2 percent increase in projected enrollment because of greater participation in Social Security's Disability Insurance (DI) program. (Beginning two years after they become eligible for DI, participants in that program are automatically eligible for benefits through Medicare.) The lower projected spending for the Part D program reflects the expectation that growth in spending for prescription drugs—which has been lower in recent years than CBO had expected—will continue to be lower than CBO had previously projected.

Deposit Insurance. Estimated outlays for 2009 are $5 billion lower than in CBO's January baseline, primarily because of the Federal Deposit Insurance Corporation's (FDIC's) recent actions to increase insurance premiums (which are recorded as offsets to spending). CBO expects that net outlays for deposit insurance will be about $29 billion higher through 2014 than projected in January; by 2019, most of that increase would be offset by income from higher premiums and proceeds from selling the assets of failed institutions. On balance, net outlays over the 2010–2019 period are projected to be about $9 billion higher than was estimated in January.

Table 1-4. CBO's Estimate of the President's Budget

	Actual 2008	2009	2010	2011	2012	2013	2014	2015	2016	2017	2018	2019	Total, 2010-2014	Total, 2010-2019
							In Billions of Dollars							
Revenues														
On-budget	1,866	1,506	1,621	1,891	2,192	2,329	2,429	2,554	2,658	2,772	2,875	2,982	10,461	24,302
Off-budget	658	653	668	695	726	766	802	833	864	897	932	968	3,656	8,151
Total	2,524	2,159	2,289	2,586	2,917	3,095	3,231	3,387	3,522	3,669	3,807	3,950	14,118	32,452
Outlays														
Mandatory spending	1,595	2,588	2,135	2,025	2,020	2,121	2,225	2,318	2,466	2,581	2,694	2,895	10,526	23,480
Discretionary spending	1,135	1,246	1,362	1,315	1,273	1,279	1,294	1,319	1,351	1,377	1,402	1,438	6,523	13,409
Net interest	253	170	172	216	282	367	460	536	601	661	734	806	1,497	4,834
Total	2,983	4,004	3,669	3,556	3,575	3,767	3,979	4,172	4,417	4,619	4,830	5,139	18,546	41,723
On-budget	2,508	3,481	3,115	2,983	2,982	3,148	3,333	3,496	3,704	3,864	4,030	4,290	15,562	34,946
Off-budget	475	523	553	573	594	619	646	676	713	755	800	849	2,984	6,777
Deficit (-) or Surplus	-459	-1,845	-1,379	-970	-658	-672	-749	-785	-895	-949	-1,023	-1,189	-4,429	-9,270
On-budget	-642	-1,975	-1,494	-1,092	-790	-819	-905	-942	-1,046	-1,092	-1,155	-1,308	-5,101	-10,644
Off-budget	183	130	115	122	132	147	156	157	151	143	132	119	672	1,374
Debt Held by the Public	5,803	7,987	9,319	10,292	11,055	11,770	12,628	13,508	14,491	15,523	16,013	17,277	n.a.	n.a.
Memorandum:														
Gross Domestic Product	14,222	14,057	14,405	15,061	15,774	16,496	17,241	17,957	18,688	19,436	20,191	20,966	78,977	176,215
							As a Percentage of Gross Domestic Product							
Revenues														
On-budget	13.1	10.7	11.3	12.6	13.9	14.1	14.1	14.2	14.2	14.3	14.2	14.2	13.2	13.8
Off-budget	4.6	4.6	4.6	4.6	4.6	4.6	4.7	4.6	4.6	4.6	4.6	4.6	4.6	4.6
Total	17.7	15.4	15.9	17.2	18.5	18.8	18.7	18.9	18.8	18.9	18.9	18.8	17.9	18.4
Outlays														
Mandatory spending	11.2	18.4	14.8	13.4	12.8	12.9	12.9	12.9	13.2	13.3	13.3	13.8	13.3	13.3
Discretionary spending	8.0	8.9	9.5	8.7	8.1	7.8	7.5	7.3	7.2	7.1	6.9	6.9	8.3	7.6
Net interest	1.8	1.2	1.2	1.4	1.8	2.2	2.7	3.0	3.2	3.4	3.6	3.8	1.9	2.7
Total	21.0	28.5	25.5	23.6	22.7	22.8	23.1	23.2	23.6	23.8	23.9	24.5	23.5	23.7
On-budget	17.6	24.8	21.6	19.8	18.9	19.1	19.3	19.5	19.8	19.9	20.0	20.5	19.7	19.8
Off-budget	3.3	3.7	3.8	3.8	3.8	3.8	3.7	3.8	3.8	3.9	4.0	4.0	3.8	3.8
Deficit (-) or Surplus	-3.2	-13.1	-9.6	-6.4	-4.2	-4.1	-4.3	-4.4	-4.8	-4.9	-5.1	-5.7	-5.6	-5.3
On-budget	-4.5	-14.1	-10.4	-7.3	-5.0	-5.0	-5.2	-5.2	-5.6	-5.6	-5.7	-6.2	-6.5	-6.0
Off-budget	1.3	0.9	0.8	0.8	0.8	0.9	0.9	0.9	0.8	0.7	0.7	0.6	0.9	0.8
Debt Held by the Public	40.8	56.8	64.7	68.3	70.1	71.4	73.2	75.2	77.5	79.9	79.3	82.4	n.a.	n.a.

Source: Congressional Budget Office.
Note: n.a. = not applicable.

The annual budgetary impact of deposit insurance activity depends on several factors, including the expenses stemming from failed institutions, the methods used to resolve those failures, and the timing of industry payments to recoup any losses. CBO estimates that losses from FDIC-insured institutions could total about $100 billion through 2014, roughly double the amount projected in January. CBO's projections assume that the FDIC will continue to raise premiums as needed to maintain sufficient balances in the insurance funds and will manage costs in ways that reduce the volatility of annual outlays—for example, by resolving failures of large institutions through cost-sharing arrangements, which tend to spread costs over a longer period.

Net Interest. Technical changes to net interest mostly stem from an adjustment to the treatment of interest transactions with credit financing accounts (nonbudgetary accounts that record cash flows for federal credit programs), the borrowing activities of the Federal Financing Bank, and a shift in the maturity structure of federal borrowing. Such changes reduce interest costs by $424 billion between 2010 and 2019; added debt-service costs stemming from other technical changes increase interest payments by $278 billion over the 10-year period.

CBO's Estimate of the President's Budget

The President's budget provides a broad outline of his policy proposals that will be followed by a more detailed budget presentation in April. Nevertheless, most of the proposals were specific enough that CBO and JCT could estimate the budgetary impact using their own technical assumptions and CBO's economic forecast. For discretionary funding, the budget outline provided only aggregate amounts of budget authority, which CBO used as a basis for estimating such spending.

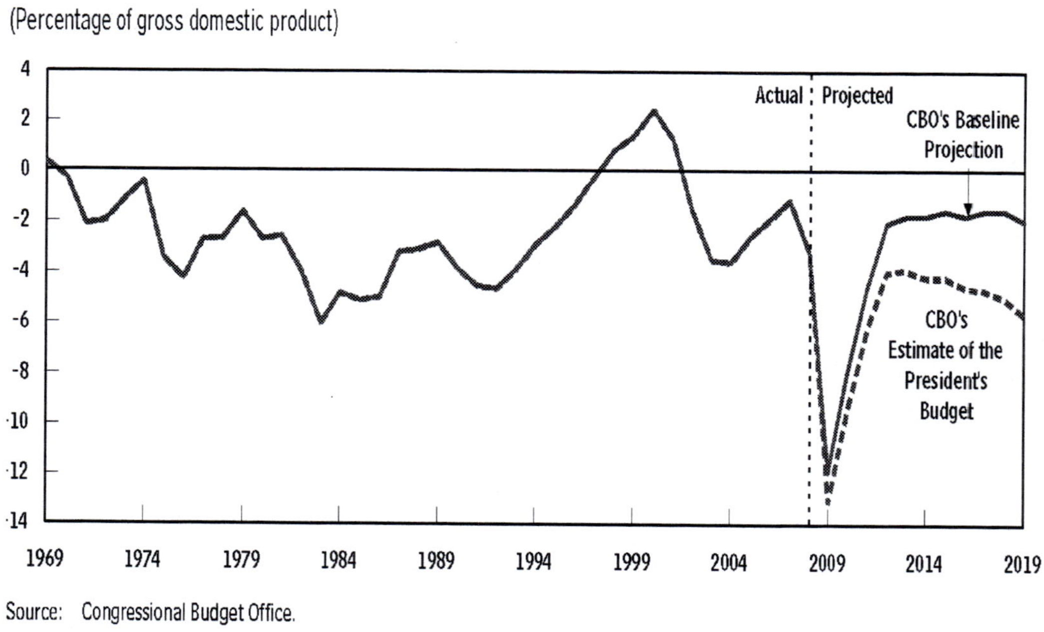

Figure 1.1. Total Deficits or Surpluses, 1969 to 2019.

Overview of the President's Budget

If the President's proposals were enacted, the government would record a deficit of $1.8 trillion in 2009, CBO estimates (see Table 1-4). The deficit for 2009 would equal 13.1 percent of GDP, with revenues totaling 15.4 percent and outlays equal to 28.5 percent of GDP.[10] Relative to CBO's baseline budget projections for 2009, the proposals in the President's budget request would reduce revenues by $26 billion and boost outlays by $151 billion (mostly for additional efforts aimed at stabilizing the financial system). As a result, the deficit for this year would be $177 billion larger than the deficit that CBO anticipates under current law.

In 2010, the deficit under the President's budget would fall to 9.6 percent of GDP, or nearly $1.4 trillion, CBO estimates—$241 billion more than the deficit of $1.1 trillion that CBO projects under current laws and policies (see Figure 1-1). That difference is largely attributable to additional spending for the government's actions to stabilize financial markets ($125 billion); defense spending, primarily for ongoing military operations in Iraq and Afghanistan and other activities related to the war on terrorism ($50 billion); and various revenue reductions ($45 billion). In total, outlays next year would measure 25.5 percent of GDP under the President's policies, and revenues would amount to 15.9 percent.

From 2010 to 2019, the cumulative deficit under the President's proposals would total $9.3 trillion, more than double the cumulative deficit projected under the current-law assumptions embodied in CBO's baseline (see Table 1-5). Over the 10-year period, proposed tax policies—such as extending some of the expiring provisions enacted in EGTRRA and JGTRRA—would reduce revenues relative to the baseline by an estimated $ 2.1 trillon, an average of 1.2 percent of GDP. In addition, under the President's proposals, spending other than interest outlays would be $1.7 trillion higher (about 1.0 percent of GDP). Discretionary spending would be $0.6 trillion above CBO's baseline projection; nondefense programs would receive more than 70 percent of that increase. Mandatory spending would be $1.1 trillion above the baseline total. The resulting higher deficits would require additional federal borrowing; net interest paid on that borrowing would add $1.0 trillion over the 10-year period relative to the baseline. Debt held by the public would rise, from 41 percent of GDP in 2008 to 57 percent in 2009 and to 82 percent of GDP by 2019.

Under the President's proposals, revenues would climb from 17.2 percent of GDP in 2011 to 18.8 percent in 2013 and remain near 19.0 percent thereafter (see Figure 1-2 and Table 1-4). That level is slightly above the average of 18.3 percent over the past 40 years and below the baseline projection of 20.3 percent for 2019. The same factors that push up the share of receipts in the baseline—including the anticipated recovery from the recession, which results in taxable income rising as a share of GDP, and the expiration of certain provisions of ARRA, EGTRRA, and JGTRRA—also cause revenues to rise as a share of GDP in the President's budget.

Outlays under the President's policies would increase from 23.6 percent of GDP in 2011 to 24.5 percent in 2019. Both of those figures are above the average of 20.7 percent over the past 40 years; higher mandatory spending as a percentage of GDP (especially for Medicare and refundable tax credits) would be only partly offset by lower discretionary spending. Spending for mandatory programs would fall in 2010 and 2011 (largely because of reduced spending to stabilize the financial markets and gradually declining spending from ARRA and for unemployment insurance) and then rise by an average of 4.7 percent annually (about three-fourths of a percentage point above the growth rate of nominal GDP) through 2019

Table 1.5. CBO's Estimate of the Effect of the President's Budget on Baseline Deficits

	2009	2010	2011	2012	2013	2014	2015	2016	2017	2018	2019	Total, 2010-2014	Total, 2010-2019
Total Deficit as Projected in CBO's March 2009 Baseline	-1,667	-1,139	-693	-331	-300	-310	-282	-327	-312	-325	-423	-2,772	-4,441
Effect of the President's Proposals													
Revenues													
Provisions related to EGTRRA and JGTRRA													
Modify individual income tax rates[a]	0	0	-68	-99	-104	-109	-114	-119	-124	-129	-134	-379	-999
Modify capital gains and dividend tax rates[b]	0	*	-5	-20	-25	-27	-28	-29	-30	-31	-32	-77	-226
Modify estate and gift tax rates	0	*	-2	-20	-23	-27	-31	-34	-37	-40	-43	-72	-256
Other provisions	0	0	-28	-46	-47	-48	-49	-50	-51	-52	-54	-170	-427
Subtotal, proposed extensions	0	*	-103	-185	-199	-211	-222	-231	-242	-252	-263	-698	-1,907
Permanently extend Making Work Pay credit	0	0	-29	-42	-43	-43	-44	-44	-44	-45	-45	-156	-378
Index the AMT starting from 2009 levels	0	-7	-69	-31	-34	-37	-41	-46	-52	-60	-70	-177	-447
Revenues from climate policy	0	0	0	77	77	78	78	79	79	80	80	232	629
Other proposals	-26	-39	3	12	12	8	5	3	2	1	*	-5	7
Total Effect on Revenues	**-26**	**-45**	**-198**	**-169**	**-187**	**-205**	**-223**	**-240**	**-257**	**-276**	**-297**	**-804**	**-2,097**
Outlays													
Mandatory													
Expand earned income and child tax credits	0	*	*	36	36	36	36	36	37	37	37	108	292
Provide Making Work Pay and other tax credits	0	0	*	23	24	24	24	24	24	24	24	72	193
Freeze Medicare physician payment rates	0	7	17	22	18	23	28	35	42	45	47	87	285
Support financial stabilization	125	125	0	0	0	0	0	0	0	0	0	125	125
Modify the Family Federal Education Loan Program	0	-5	-10	-12	-11	-10	-9	-9	-9	-9	-10	-47	-94
Modify Pell grants[c]	0	5	20	28	30	33	32	33	35	37	39	116	293
Other proposals	*	-1	9	2	1	*	1	1	2	3	3	11	22
Subtotal, mandatory	125	131	37	99	98	107	112	121	131	136	142	472	1,115
Discretionary													
Defense	25	50	24	14	7	6	7	9	10	12	13	100	151
Nondefense	*	9	6	19	33	45	56	62	67	70	74	113	442
Subtotal, discretionary	25	59	30	33	40	51	63	71	77	82	87	213	593
Net interest	1	6	13	26	48	75	105	137	172	204	239	167	1,023
Total Effect on Outlays	**151**	**196**	**80**	**158**	**186**	**233**	**280**	**329**	**380**	**422**	**468**	**853**	**2,732**
Total Effect on the Deficit[d]	**-177**	**-241**	**-278**	**-327**	**-373**	**-438**	**-503**	**-568**	**-637**	**-698**	**-765**	**-1,657**	**-4,829**
Total Deficit Under the President's Proposals as Estimated by CBO	-1,845	-1,379	-970	-658	-672	-749	-785	-895	-949	-1,023	-1,189	-4,429	-9,270
Memorandum:													
Health Reform Reserve Fund[e]													
Increased revenues from limiting the rate at which itemized deductions reduce tax liability	0	0	11	30	32	34	37	39	41	43	45	107	311
Reduced spending from specified health proposals	0	2	5	14	20	39	36	36	42	48	55	79	295
New, unspecified benefits from health reforms[e]	0	-2	-16	-44	-51	-73	-72	-75	-83	-91	-100	-185	-606
Net effect on the deficit of the health reform proposal	0	0	0	0	0	0	0	0	0	0	0	0	0
Total Deficit Under the President's Proposals as Estimated by OMB	-1,752	-1,171	-912	-581	-533	-570	-583	-637	-636	-634	-712	-3,767	-6,969

Source: Congressional Budget Office; Joint Committee on Taxation.

Note: * = between -$500 million and $500 million; EGTRRA = Economic Growth and Tax Relief Reconciliation Act of 2001; JGTRRA = Jobs and Growth Tax Relief Reconciliation Act of 2003; AMT = alternative minimum tax; OMB = Office of Management and Budget.

a. The estimates include the effects of maintaining, for taxpayers with income above certain levels, the income tax rates of 36 percent and 39.6 percent scheduled to go into effect in 2011 under current law. For the remaining taxpayers, tax rates would be at the 2010 levels specified in EGTRRA.

b. The estimates include the effects of imposing a 20 percent tax rate on capital gains and dividends for taxpayers with income above certain levels, starting in 2011. Tax rates for the remaining taxpayers would be at the 2010 levels specified in JGTRRA.

c. The current Pell grant program has discretionary and mandatory components. CBO's estimate of the costs of modifying Pell grants includes the costs of setting the maximum award at $5,550 in 2010, indexing that award level for future years, and reclassifying the entire program as mandatory spending. That reclassification would result in eliminating spending for Pell grants in CBO's discretionary baseline, which currently includes $195 billion in outlays for new grants over the 2010–2019 period.

d. Negative numbers indicate an increase in the deficit.

e. Health reform benefits may be a combination of revenue reductions and spending increases and are assumed to exactly offset the savings dedicated to the proposed fund on both the revenue and outlay sides of the budget.

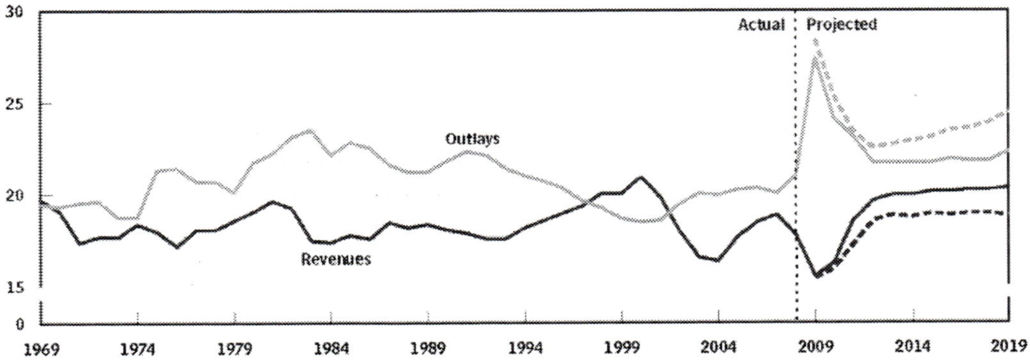

Source: Congressional Budget Office.

Note: Dashed lines represent CBO's estimate of revenues and outlays as a share of gross domestic product in the President's budget.

Figure 1.2. Total Revenues and Outlays as a Percentage of Gross Domestic Product in CBO's Baseline and the President's Budget.

Discretionary outlays would decline by $88 billion from 2010 to 2012—largely because of lower outlays related to ARRA and reduced war-related spending—and then grow slightly thereafter. Measured as a percentage of GDP, they would fall from 9.5 percent in 2010 to 6.9 percent in 2018 and 2019. CBO's estimates for discretionary spending reflect the President's proposal for $75.5 billion in additional funding for military operations in Iraq and Afghanistan in 2009 (bringing the total for that year to $141.4 billion), $130 billion for such purposes in 2010, and $50 billion a year thereafter.[11]

CBO's estimate of the deficits under the President's budget are higher each year than those estimated by the Administration—by $93 billion for 2009 and by about $2.3 trillion for the 2010–2019 period. Most of those differences stem from underlying baseline differences rather than from varying assessments of the effect of the President's policy proposals. Economic and technical factors affecting revenue projections account for the largest part of those baseline differences.

In its presentation of the budget, the Administration has compared its policy proposals with a "current-policy" baseline that assumes the continuation of certain policies that are currently in place but that would require further legislation in order to continue in future years. Those policies include extensions of most of the provisions of EGTRRA and JGTRRA and certain payments to physicians participating in the Medicare program. Because CBO's baseline for mandatory spending and revenues is predicated on current law, this estimate of the President's budget treats such continuations as policy proposals. The extended policies generally involve increased spending and reduced revenues; as a result, CBO's analysis generally shows larger spending increases and larger tax reductions—and thus larger increases in the deficit—than are shown in the Administration's presentation of its proposals (regardless of differences in economic and technical assumptions).[12]

Policy Proposals Affecting Revenues

The President's budget proposes a number of changes to tax law that would reduce revenues over the next decade relative to CBO's baseline. Compared with projected receipts under current law, total revenues would be $2.1 trillion lower over the 2010–2019 period, according to JCT and CBO.[13] The proposal to modify and extend provisions of EGTRRA and JGTRRA would have the largest effect, reducing revenues by $1.9 trillion, according to JCT. On net, the other proposals would lower revenues by about $190 billion, some reducing revenues by roughly $1.1 trillion and others raising revenues by roughly $900 billion. Those estimates do not reflect the effect on revenues of several of the President's proposals for which sufficient detail was not available. Those proposals include implementing international tax reform, for which the Administration estimates a revenue increase of $210 billion over 10 years. Until additional details are available, JCT and CBO treat those proposals as having no effect on revenues.

Provisions Related to EGTRRA and JGTRRA. Proposals related to modifying and permanently extending provisions of EGTRRA and JGTRRA that are set to expire in 2010 would reduce revenues by $1.9 trillion (or 1.1 percent of GDP) over the next 10 years relative to current law.[14] The provisions scheduled to expire include reductions in some individual income tax rates; reductions in tax rates on capital gains and dividends; changes to estate and gift taxation; limits on phaseouts for personal exemptions and itemized deductions for certain taxpayers; an increase in the child tax credit; relief from the so-called marriage penalty; and changes in the tax treatment of certain investments in equipment by small businesses.

The President proposes to permanently extend, at 2010 levels, tax rates on income, capital gains, and dividends for married taxpayers earning under $250,000 and single taxpayers earning under $200,000. For taxpayers with income above those levels, the President proposes to maintain the income tax rates, the phaseout of the personal exemption, and the limits on itemized deductions scheduled to go into effect in 2011 under current law; those higher-income taxpayers would also be subject to a tax rate of 20 percent on capital gains and dividends. In addition, the President proposes to modify estate, gift, and generation-skipping transfer taxes by extending 2009 law and indexing the estate tax exemption for inflation while maintaining the $1 million lifetime exclusion for gifts.

"Making Work Pay" Tax Credit. The President also proposes to permanently extend the Making Work Pay credit, which expires at the end of 2010 under current law. The credit equals 6.2 percent of earned income, up to a maximum credit amount of $800 for married taxpayers ($400 for single filers) and phasing out for married taxpayers with income above

$150,000 ($75,000 for single filers). Extending the credit would reduce revenues by $378 billion over the 2010–2019 period, according to JCT. (This proposal would also affect outlays because the credit is refundable. See *Tax Credits,* below.)

Alternative Minimum Tax. The President proposes to provide relief from the AMT by permanently setting the AMT exemption amount at 2009 levels, indexed for inflation, and permanently extending the unrestricted use of certain personal tax credits under the AMT.[15] The proposal would reduce revenues by $447 billion between 2010 and 2019, JCT estimates. That estimate does not include the interaction between the AMT provisions and the proposal to extend and modify the tax provisions related to EGTRRA and JGTRRA. That interaction is included in the estimate for the latter proposal.

Revenues from Climate Policy. The President's proposals include a plan to reduce greenhouse-gas emissions through the sales of emissions allowances in a cup-and-trade programme. The proceeds would raise enough revenue to cover the post-2011 cost of extending the Making Work Pay credit plus $120 billion intended for investment in clean energy technologies. CBO and JCT estimate that those proposed uses of the funds could cost $629 billion: $349 billion for the post-2011 reduction in revenues for the Making Work Pay credit, $159 billion in outlays for the refundable portion of that credit, and $120 billion for spending on clean energy technologies. CBO assumes that the proposed cap-and-trade program would generate $629 billion between 2012 and 2019 to cover the costs of extending that credit and to fund the clean energy investments. In fact, the revenues raised from a cap-and-trade program could be significantly higher or lower depending on how the program is structured.

Other Proposals Affecting Revenues. Other tax proposals in the President's budget include making the research and experimentation tax credit permanent; repealing the last-in/first-out inventory accounting method; taxing carried interest as income; and expanding the saver's credit and automatic enrollment in individual retirement accounts and 401(k) retirement plans.[16] The President's proposal to extend the period to which firms can carry back net operating losses to more than the current two years would reduce revenues in 2009 and 2010 and increase them thereafter.[17] Altogether, the President's other tax proposals for which CBO and JCT were able to provide estimates would increase revenues by an estimated $7 billion between 2010 and 2019.

Policy Proposals Affecting Mandatory Spending. If the proposals in the President's budger were enacted, they would, on balance, increase mandatory spending relative to the amounts in the baseline by $1.1 trillion (or 0.6 percent of GDP) over the next 10 years, CBO estimates. Costs and savings from those proposals are shown in Table 1-5 on page 12, and the most significant proposals are highlighted below.

Tax Credits. About $484 billion in increased outlays over the 10-year period would stem from tax proposals that would expand various refundable tax credits.[18] According to JCT's estimates, the permanent extension and modification of certain expiring tax provisions originally enacted in 2001 and 2003 would increase outlays by $197 billion over the 2010–2019 period, mostly for the refundable portions of the earned income and child tax credits. The proposal to extend the Making Work Pay tax credit would increase outlays by an estimated $159 billion between 2010 and 2019. The proposal to expand the refundability of the child tax credit would increase outlays by $74 billion over the 2010–2019 period, JCT estimates. Other tax proposals would increase outlays by $54 billion over the 2010–2019 period, JCT and CBO estimate.

Physicians' Payment Rates. A proposed change in the calculation of the rates paid to physicians under Medicare would result in additional outlays totaling an estimated $285 billion over the next 10 years.[19] Under current law, Medicare's payment rates for physicians' services will be reduced by about 21 percent in 2010 and by about 6 percent a year for most of the rest of the decade. The President's policy would freeze those payment rates at the 2009 level through at least 2019.

Reserve for Financial Stabilization Efforts. The Administration has included a placeholder of $250 billion in fiscal year 2009 to cover future efforts to stabilize the financial system. As with the current budgetary treatment of the TARP, those outlays reflect the estimated subsidy provided by the unspecified policies; the Administration calculates that the $250 billion would represent the net cost of purchases of $750 billion in assets. For the purposes of projecting federal debt, CBO assumes that the total proposed by the Administration would support asset purchases, loan guarantees, or other transactions totaling $500 billion, reflecting a subsidy cost similar to what CBO now estimates for the $700 billion already authorized for the TARP. CBO also assumes that such additional support, if enacted, would be disbursed over the next two years—$125 billion in estimated outlays in 2009 and the same amount in 2010.

Student Loans. The President's proposal would essentially eliminate the federal guaranteed student loan program, replacing such loans with direct loans made by the Department of Education. Under the Federal Credit Reform Act, the budgetary cost of direct loans and guaranteed loans reflects the total cash flows over the life of each loan. Under current law, the direct loan program is estimated to have a lower cost for each dollar loaned than does the guaranteed loan program. Thus, assuming that loan volume does not change, replacing the guaranteed loan program with additional direct loans would yield

2. The Economic Outlook

The current recession, which began in December 2007, took a sudden and severe turn for the worse late last year. Of the 4.4 million jobs lost since the recession began, more than half have been lost in just the past four months. According to the Congressional Budget Office's economic projections, the economy will continue to deteriorate for some time, although the adoption of the American Recovery and Reinvestment Act and very aggressive actions by the Federal Reserve and the Treasury will help end the recession this fall.

In CBO's forecast, on a fourth-quarter-to-fourth-quarter basis, real (inflation-adjusted) gross domestic product falls by 1.5 percent in 2009 before growing by 4.1 percent in both 2010 and in 2011 (see Table 2-1). During the next two years, economic output averages about 7 percent below its potential—the output that would be produced if the economy's resources were fully employed (see Figure 2-1). The shortfall in the nation's output relative to its potential is comparable with what occurred during the recession of 1981 and 1982 and will persist for significantly longer—making the current recession the most severe since World War II. In the forecast, the unemployment rate rises further, peaking at 9.4 percent in late 2009 and early 2010, and remains above 7 percent through the end of 2011 (see Figure 2-2). The deterioration in 2009 and the protracted nature of the recovery reflect a number of factors: tight credit, a large number of vacant houses continuing to suppress housing construction, large losses in wealth restraining households' spending, and weak economic growth overseas.

Table 2.1. CBO's Economic Projections for Calendar Years 2009 to 2019

	Estimated 2008[a]	Forecast			Projected Annual Average	
		2009	2010	2011	2012-2015	2016-2019
Year to Year (Percentage change)						
Nominal GDP (Billions of dollars)	14,257	14,047	14,576	15,233	18,138[b]	21,164[c]
Nominal GDP	3.3	-1.5	3.8	4.5	4.5	3.9
Real GDP	1.1	-3.0	2.9	4.0	3.6	2.3
GDP Price Index	2.2	1.5	0.8	0.5	0.9	1.6
PCE Price Index[d]	3.3	-0.1	1.1	1.0	1.0	1.6
Core PCE Price Index[e]	2.0	1.0	0.8	0.7	0.9	1.6
Consumer Price Index[f]	3.8	-0.7	1.4	1.2	1.2	1.9
Core Consumer Price Index[g]	2.3	1.5	1.1	0.9	1.1	1.9
Calendar Year Average (Percent)						
Unemployment Rate	5.8	8.8	9.0	7.7	5.6	4.8
Three-Month Treasury Bill Rate	1.4	0.3	0.9	1.8	4.0	4.7
Ten-Year Treasury Note Rate	3.7	2.9	3.4	4.0	5.1	5.6
Tax Bases (Billions of dollars)						
Economic profits	1,496	1,269	1,386	1,547	1,822[b]	1,940[c]
Wages and salaries	6,543	6,496	6,743	6,953	8,315[b]	9,709[c]
Tax Bases (Percentage of GDP)						
Economic profits	10.5	9.0	9.5	10.2	10.4	9.5
Wages and salaries	45.9	46.2	46.3	45.6	45.9	45.9
Fourth Quarter to Fourth Quarter (Percentage change)						
Nominal GDP	1.0	-0.3	4.9	4.6	4.4	3.9
Real GDP	-0.9	-1.5	4.1	4.1	3.4	2.3
GDP Price Index	1.9	1.3	0.8	0.5	0.9	1.6
PCE Price Index[d]	1.7	0.5	1.0	0.9	1.1	1.6
Core PCE Price Index[e]	1.8	0.7	0.8	0.7	1.0	1.6
Consumer Price Index[f]	1.5	0.6	1.3	1.1	1.3	1.9
Core Consumer Price Index[g]	2.0	1.4	1.0	0.8	1.2	1.9

Sources: Congressional Budget Office; Department of Commerce, Bureau of Economic Analysis; Department of Labor, Bureau of Labor Statistics; Federal Reserve Board.

Notes: GDP = gross domestic product; PCE = personal consumption expenditure.

Economic projections for each year from 2009 to 2019 appear in Appendix A.

a. Figures for the consumer price index, the unemployment rate, and the interest rates are actual values; the other 2008 figures are estimates.

b. Level in 2015.

c. Level in 2019.

d. The PCE chained price index.
e. The PCE chained price index excluding prices for food and energy.
f. The consumer price index for all urban consumers.
g. The consumer price index for all urban consumers excluding prices for food and energy.

Inflation in consumer prices has been extremely low recently and, given the projection of persistently weak demand and excess productive capacity, it is expected to be low over the next few years as well. Overall price indexes have fallen since September 2008, primarily because of the sharp drop in energy and commodity prices, but also because "core" inflation (for items besides food and energy) slowed. CBO anticipates that core consumer price inflation, which averaged 2.3 percent during 2007 and 2008, will fall to 1.5 percent this year and 1.1 percent in 2010 and remain low through 2012.

Because of the likely persistence of the various factors holding down economic activity, CBO does not expect the output gap—the difference between actual and potential output of goods and services—to close fully until about 2014. In the latter part of the decade, CBO projects, GDP will grow at its potential (an average rate of 2.3 percent); the unemployment rate will average 4.8 percent; and core inflation for consumer prices, 1.9 percent.

CBO's current forecast, particularly for the near term, is subject to a greater than normal degree of uncertainty. Figure 2-3, based on CBO's past forecasting errors, illustrates the usual uncertainty regarding forecasts of real GDP. However, the figure probably understates uncertainty today. Both the magnitude of the contractionary forces operating in the economy and the magnitude of the government's actions to stabilize the financial system and stimulate economic growth are outside the range of recent experience. The forecast assumes that financial markets will begin to function more normally and that the housing market will stabilize by early next year. The possibility that financial markets might not stabilize represents a major source of downside risk to the forecast. Households' and businesses' confidence is also difficult to predict. For example, if consumers begin to anticipate a period of deflation, they may choose to further postpone major discretionary purchases, thereby delaying the recovery; but evidence that economic conditions are stabilizing could encourage households and businesses to resume spending more rapidly than is envisioned in the forecast. Finally, although CBO's forecast incorporates the middle of the range of the agency's estimates of ARRA's impact on GDP and employment, that range is quite large. For instance, CBO's analysis suggests that by the fourth quarter of 2010, the stimulus legislation will raise real GDP by between 1.1 percent and 3.4 percent and increase employment by between 1.2 million and 3.6 million jobs.[20]

Recent Economic Developments

Economic conditions have deteriorated in the months since CBO prepared its last forecast, which was published in early January.[21] Job losses have mounted, with the unemployment rate jumping to a 25-year high of 8.1 percent. Real GDP fell at a 6.2 percent annual rate in the fourth quarter and appears likely to have declined substantially further in the first quarter. Housing starts, industrial production, and orders and shipments of durable goods all declined sharply in late 2008 and early 2009, although consumer spending rebounded somewhat early this year from a very weak holiday season. Inflation is low, but the extremely low rates reported at the end of last year appear to have been largely transitory.

The Housing Market

Even though house prices and housing starts continue to fall substantially, the inventory of unsold homes is still very high. Consequently, the prices of houses and the number of new homes being constructed are likely to be low for some time.

The Federal Housing Finance Authority's national purchase-only house price index, which covers prices of houses purchased with conventional conforming mortgage loans (those eligible for purchase by Fannie Mae and Freddie Mac), declined by 3.4 percent in the fourth quarter, the largest one-quarter decline in that index's history—leaving it about 10 percent off its early 2007 peak level. Also in the fourth quarter, the Standard & Poor's (S&P) Case-Shiller national home price index, which covers all types of mortgage loans but is more geographically limited, was down by a larger amount, 18 percent from a year earlier and 27 percent from its early 2006 peak. Most analysts believe that the correction in house prices is far from complete; for example, according to the February *Blue Chip* consensus (which is the average of) about 50 forecasts by private-sector economists), the 20- city version of the S&P Case-Shiller index will fall a further 14 percent in 2009.

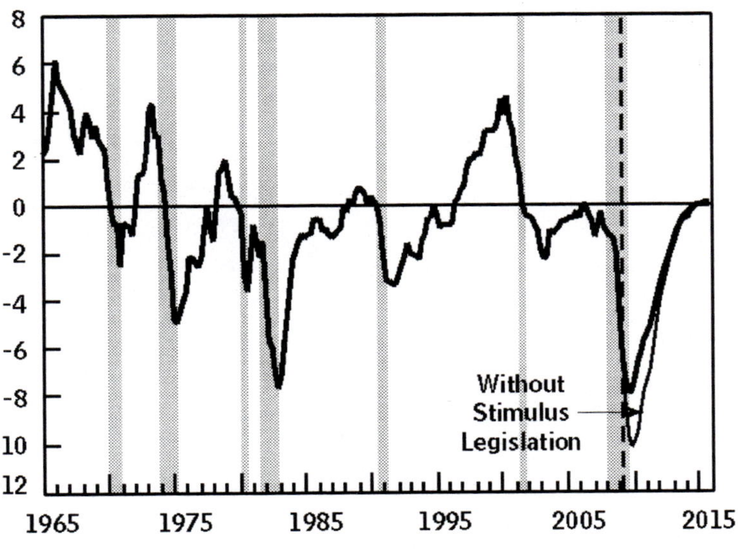

Source: Congressional Budget Office; Department of Commerce, Bureau of Economic Analysis.
Notes: The GDP gap is the difference between real (inflation-adjusted) gross domestic product and its estimated potential level (which corresponds to a high level of use of labor and capital resources). Data are quarterly and are plotted through 2015.

Figure 2.1. The GDP Gap, 1965 to 2015.

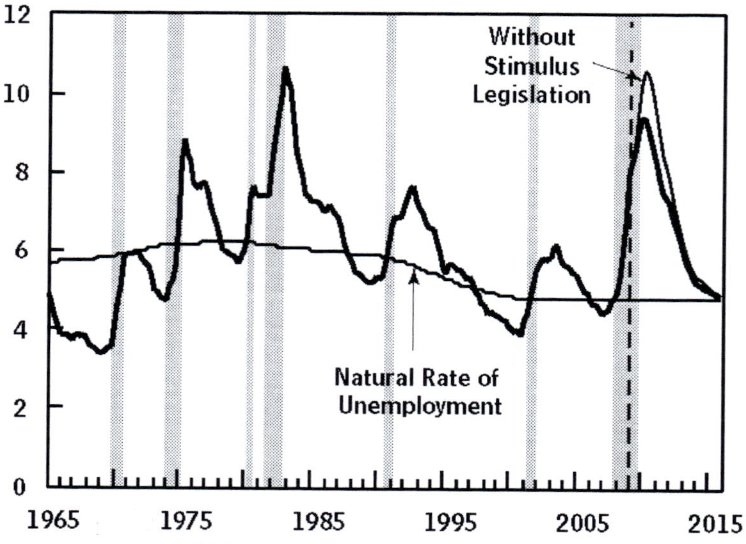

Sources: Congressional Budget Office; Department of Labor, Bureau of Labor Statistics.

Notes: CBO's estimate of the natural rate of unemployment is the rate of unemployment that is not due to the business cycle but to underlying characteristics of the labor market, such as normal rates of job turnover and the degree to which the job seekers' skills and locations match available openings.

Although the rate of unemployment is projected to peak at a lower level than in 1982, the peak unemployment gap (the difference between the unemployment rate and the estimate of the natural rate of unemployment) is projected to be about the same as in 1982.

Data are quarterly and are plotted through 2015.

Figure 2.2. The Unemployment Rate.

Housing starts in January plunged to 477,000 (at a seasonally adjusted annual rate), an all-time low since the U.S. Census Bureau started tabulating them in 1959. Although they rebounded somewhat, to 583,000 in February, that number contrasts with the more than2 million starts at the height of the boom in 2005. Even though the construction of new homes has been at an extremely low rate for more than a year, no progress has been made toward reducing the excess supply of vacant units. The number of vacant units per thousand households jumped from 143 at the end of 2005 to 170 at the end of 2008 (see Figure 2-4).

After rising for much of last year, mortgage rates—both for conforming loans and for larger, or jumbo, loans—fell late last year, and they have remained low thus far in 2009. Lower mortgage rates have spurred applications for refinancing; nevertheless, the number of applications for loans to finance purchases of homes has fallen this year.

Foreclosure rates continue to rise for all types of mortgages, especially for subprime adjustable-rate mortgages.

Those rates are likely to remain high as long as house prices continue to fall and the unemployment rate climbs. A rising number of homeowners—13.6 million in the fourth quarter, according to an estimate by Moody's Economy.com, compared with only 3.2 million at the end of 2006—have negative equity in their house (meaning that they currently owe more on their mortgage than the market value of their house).

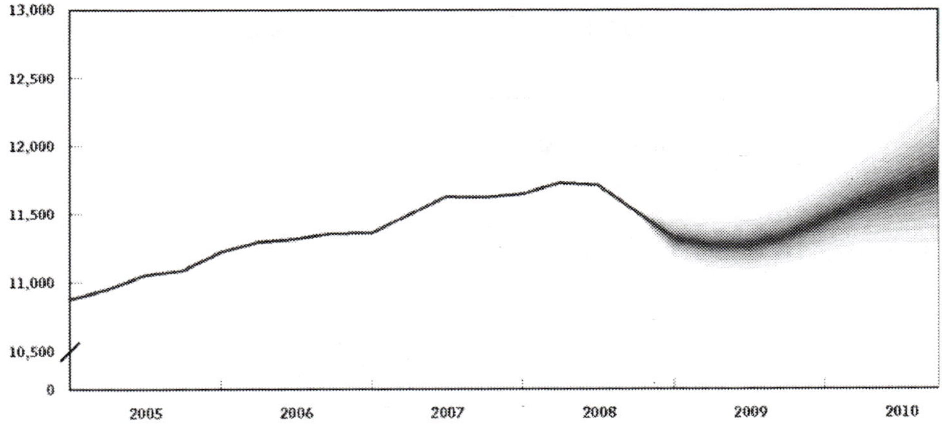

Sources: Congressional Budget Office; Department of Commerce, Bureau of Economic Analysis.

Note: This figure, based on CBO's past errors in forecasting real (inflation-adjusted) growth, shows a range of possible outcomes for real GDP. The projection described in this chapter falls in the middle of the darkest area of the figure. If the potential errors in the current forecast are similar to the errors in CBO's forecasts published between 1976 and 2006, the probability is 90 percent that real GDP will fall in the shaded area of the graph. In the current circumstances, larger errors are more likely to occur than usual.

Figure 2.3. Uncertainty in Projections of Real GDP (Billions of 2000 dollars).

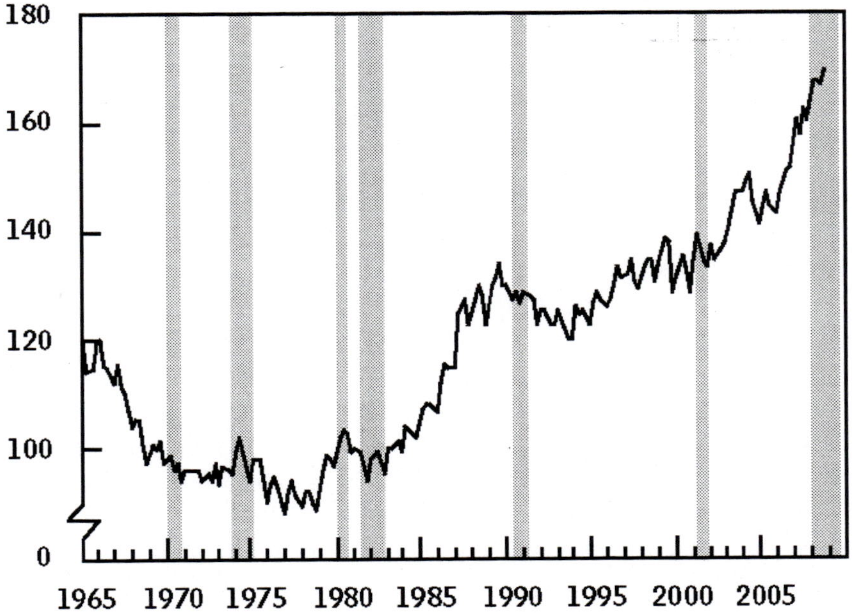

Sources: Congressional Budget Office; Department of Commerce, Bureau of the Census; Haver Analytics.

Notes: Total number of vacant housing units.

Data are quarterly and are plotted through 2008.

Figure 2.4. Vacant Homes, 1965 to 2008 (Vacant homes per thousand households).

Financial Markets

Although conditions in the financial markets have improved from the acute turmoil in September and October of last year, they remain strained. Large-scale efforts by the Federal Reserve and the Treasury following the collapse of the investment bank Lehman Brothers and the rescue of insurance conglomerate American Insurance Group (AIG) have brought down risk spreads (or differences in interest rates between risky and risk-free assets) from severely elevated levels. Those efforts also helped restore a considerable degree of activity to credit markets. However, many credit markets are not yet able to function normally without government assistance, and lending conditions remain tight, especially for financial firms.

Banks have tightened standards and terms for lending, although the pace of credit tightening may have eased a bit late last year. In the Federal Reserve's most recent survey of senior loan officers, in January 2009, 90 percent of the domestic banks reported that they had increased spreads on commercial and industrial loans in the fourth quarter, and about 70 percent reported tighter lending standards.[22] The percentage of banks reporting tighter standards on residential mortgages dropped sharply, perhaps reflecting efforts by the Federal Reserve and the Treasury to increase mortgage lending or less need to tighten standards further given previous tightening. For consumer loans, 60 percent of banks reported tighter lending standards, about the same as in the October survey.

In the fourth quarter of 2008, the commercial banking industry experienced its first aggregate loss since 1990, when many savings and loan institutions failed.[23] For 2008 as a whole, earnings fell to $16 billion, compared with $100 billion in 2007. The proportion of real estate loans that were 30 days or more past due, at 6.2 percent in the fourth quarter of last year, had risen steadily from a year earlier, when it was 3.2 percent. The performance of other types of consumer loans and commercial and industrial loans also deteriorated. Overall, of the $7.9 trillion in loans and leases outstanding at the end of 2008, 5 percent were 30 days or more past due—including 3 percent that were 90 days or more past due, about double the amount in the fourth quarter of 2007.

Risk spreads remain elevated. They reflect a higher risk of default amid both the continuing difficulties of the financial system and a recession that is already deeper and longer than the past several downturns. One important risk spread is the difference between the interest rates banks pay to borrow from each other (which can be measured by the three-month Libor, or London interbank offered rate) and market expectations of the federal funds rate (which can be measured from an overnight index swap contracts)[24] That indicator of the risk that banks will default on their loans was just over 1 percentage point in mid-March, well below its October 2008 peak of 3.6 percentage points but well above its normal level of 0.25 to 0.3 points and about where it was before the failure of Lehman Brothers in September 2008 (see Figure 2-5).

Conditions have improved in the market for commercial paper (that is, short-term borrowing by firms), as indicated by a narrower spread relative to Treasury bills. Like the three-month Libor spread, commercial paper spreads have narrowed substantially from October 2008, but that narrowing has stalled since early January. The amount of outstanding commercial paper issued by nonfinancial firms has increased since the start of 2008, but the amount issued by financial firms has fallen by 20 percent over that period, implying that problems with access to credit in the corporate sector are for the most part confined to the financial sector. Although the Federal Reserve continues to provide extensive support to the market for commercial paper, the funding required for the central bank's Commercial Paper Funding Facility has decreased steadily this year—a positive sign.[25]

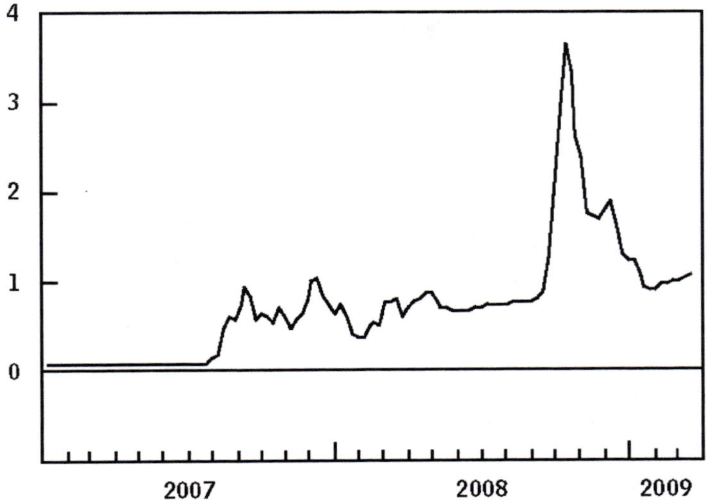

Sources: Congressional Budget Office; Bloomberg.

Notes: A spread is the difference between two interest rates. One, the three-month Libor (London interbank offered rate), is the interest rate major banks offer to other banks for loans of that duration. The other is the average federal funds rate expected over a three-month period as measured by the overnight index swap contract.

Data are weekly and are plotted through March 13, 2009.

Figure 2.5. Spread Between the Three-Month Libor and the Expected Federal Funds Rate, January 2007 to March 2009 (Percentage points).

The difference between interest rates on corporate bonds and Treasury securities remains wide, consistent with heightened concerns about credit markets and about the future course of the economy. Despite those concerns, the amount of corporate debt issued this year is well above that in the same period in 2008 for both investment- grade securities and high-yield debt.

An important credit channel, securitization, in which loans are pooled and converted into packages of securities, has yet to recover from its prolonged slump. The volume of new securities backed by auto loans, unpaid credit card balances, home equity loans, and student loans has plummeted from nearly $900 billion in 2007 to just $6 billion so far in 2009.

Diminished expectations of future profit growth because of the recession in the United States, the marked slowdown in economic activity in the rest of the world, and investors' reduced appetite for risk have hurt prices of corporate stocks. Through March 18, the Wilshire 5000 index, the broadest U.S. equity measure, has declined by about 12 percent since the beginning of 2009 and is down 46 percent since the beginning of 2008. Financial companies and automakers have been the worst performers, with share prices down about 70 percent since the beginning of 2008. The decline in stock prices makes it more expensive for companies to raise equity capital for the purpose of investing in new plant and equipment (that is, structures, equipment, and software). And the reduction in households' wealth attributable to falling equity and house prices has contributed to a decline in consumer spending.

Personal Consumption Spending

Personal Consumption Spending slumped sharply during the second half of last year; in the fourth quarter, spending was slightly more than 1-1/2 percent below its level of a year earlier (see Figure 2-6). However, the latest data suggest a slight uptick in early 2009. Some of last year's decline was in sales of light motor vehicles (automobiles and light trucks), which plunged from an average of about 17 million per year between 2000 and 2007 to an annual rate of just over 10 million in the fourth quarter of last year. But the decline in spending was broader, as spending on goods and services besides motor vehicles and parts fell by 1.4 percent in the second half of last year.

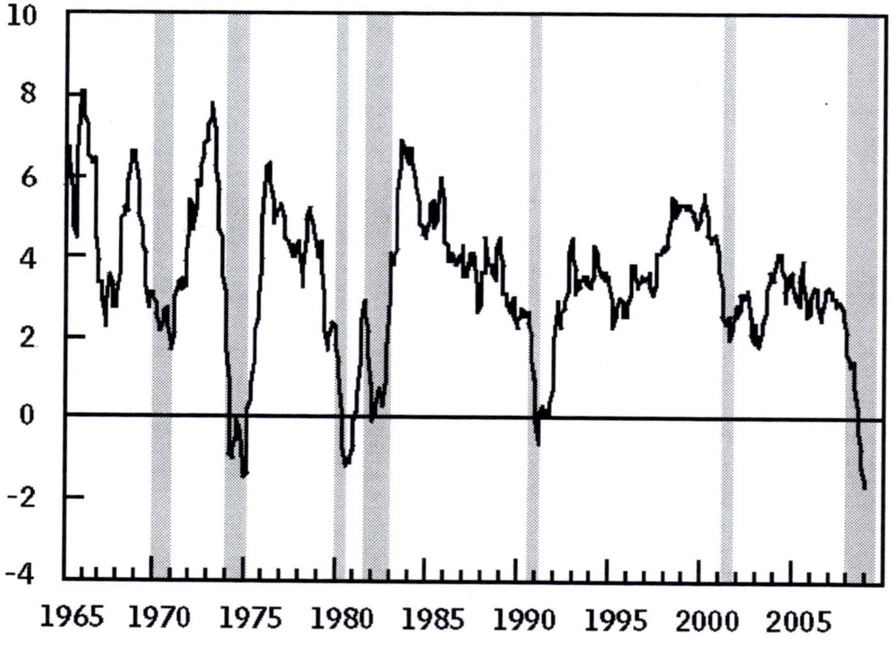

Sources: Congressional Budget Office; Department of Commerce, Bureau of Economic Analysis.
Note: Data are three-month moving averages of monthly data and are plotted through January 2009.

Figure 2-6. Real Personal Consumption Expenditures, January 1965 to January 2009 (Percentage change from previous year).

So far in 2009, sales of motor vehicles have fallen even further, to a 9.1 million annual rate in February. However, real personal consumption spending rose by 0.4 percent in January, and data on retail sales in February suggest another modest gain (and the likelihood that the January increase will be revised upward).

The weakness in consumer spending since mid-2008 (notwithstanding the slight rebound so far this year) reflects difficult conditions for consumers. Employment has fallen, households' wealth has dropped markedly, credit conditions are quite tight, the income tax rebate under last year's Emergency Economic Stabilization Act has run out, and consumer confidence has fallen to extremely low levels. But the sharp decline in the price of gasoline and other energy commodities since mid-2008 has boosted real disposable income, providing some support for consumer spending.

Over the past four months, the number of jobs has fallen by about 2.6 million (or nearly 2 percent), and aggregate income from wages and salaries fell 0.8 percent between October and January (or at an annual rate of 3.3 percent). The labor market shows no sign of stabilizing; in February and early March, initial claims for unemployment insurance averaged well over 600,000 per week— roughly twice their average from 2005 to 2007 (see Figure 2-7).

The ongoing decline in house prices and the drop in stock prices reduced the net worth of households by 20 percent between the middle of 2007 and the fourth quarter of 2008. By CBO's estimates, that decrease in wealth reduced the growth of spending by about 1 percentage point in 2008 and will have a similar effect in 2009. Weakness in the stock market and in house prices may further dampen consumer spending in 2009, with part of the effect extending into 2010.

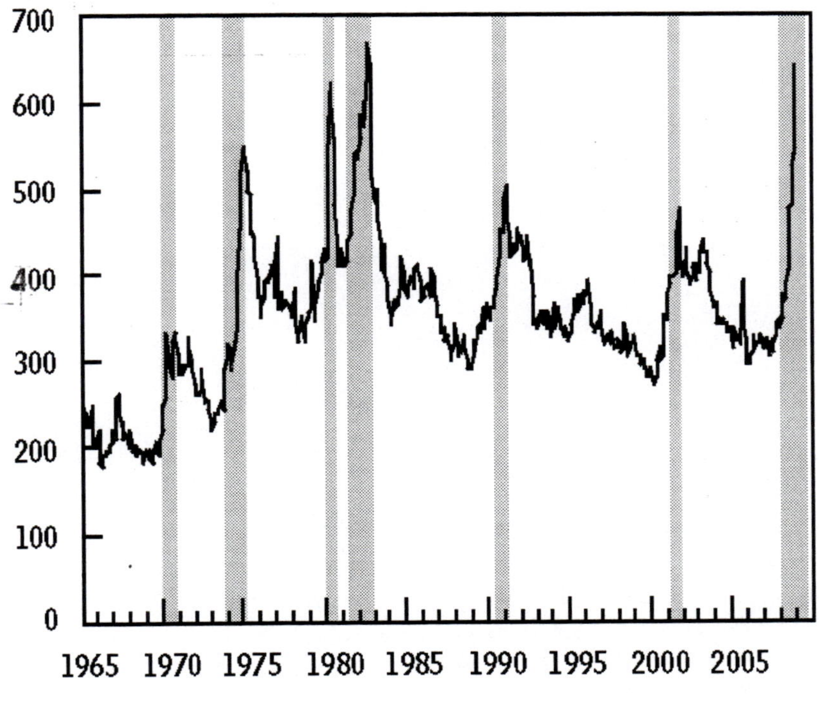

Sources: Congressional Buddet Office, Department of Labor, Employment and Training Administration, Unemployment Insurance Division.

Note: Data are monthly averages of weekly data and are plotted through February 2009.

Figure 2-7. Initial Claims for Unemployment Insurance, January 1965 to February 2009 (Thousands).

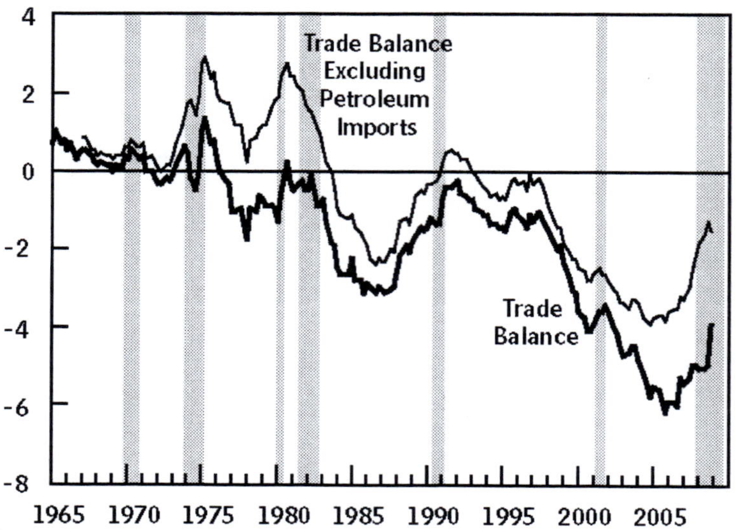

Source: Congressional Budget Office; Department of Commerce, Bureau of Economic Analysis.
Note: Data are quarterly and are plotted through 2008.

Figure 2.8. The Trade Balance, 1965 to 2008 (Percentage of gross domestic product).

The financial turmoil has also played a role in weakening households' spending by reducing the credit available to consumers, especially for those with limited opportunity to borrow or little collateral. According to the Federal Reserve's January 2009 survey of senior loan officers, banks had further tightened lending standards on credit cards and other consumer loans. A significant number of banks had also reduced the size of existing home equity lines of credit.

Investment and Net Exports

Business fixed investment (or spending by business on structures, equipment, and software), which had plateaued during the first three quarters of 2008, plunged at a 21 percent annual rate in the fourth quarter—a rate comparable to the worst declines observed in past post-war recessions. Shipments of nondefense capital goods and businesses' purchases of light vehicles both fell sharply in January, pointing to another large drop in investment in producers' durable equipment in the first quarter. Private nonresidential construction dropped significantly in January, and the American Institute of Architects' billings index, a leading indicator of such construction, suggests more of the same through midyear.

After hitting an all-time low in June 2008, the ratio of inventories to sales in the manufacturing and the wholesale and retail trade sectors had, by the end of the year, jumped to its highest level since the last recession. The ratio of inventories to sales in manufacturing and in wholesale trade continued to rise in January. The need to realign inventories with sales is currently dampening production.

A rise in net exports contributed positively to real growth of GDP from the end of 2005 through most of 2008 (see Figure 2-8). However, the global recession and the sharp rise in the value of the dollar since last summer are together undercutting that source of strength. In the fourth quarter of last year, exports fell even more (in real terms, 24 percent at an annual rate) than did imports (16 percent).

The outlook for growth in the rest of the world has continued to deteriorate, suggesting that trade is not likely to contribute to growth in the United States in the near term (see Table 2-2). Economies that have relied heavily on exports for economic growth—including many emerging Asian economies, as well as Germany's and Japan's—have been particularly hard hit as the global downturn and credit squeeze have crushed demand for their exports. The situation is especially dire in Japan, Taiwan, South Korea, and Singapore, evidenced by the double-digit rate (annualized) at which real GDP contracted in those countries in the last quarter of 2008.

Spending by State and Local Governments

State and local governments have reduced spending in response to shortfalls in their revenues, and CBO expects further cuts to slow economic activity over the next two years. Recent spending cuts have taken a variety of forms, including hiring and pay freezes, furloughs, layoffs, reductions in benefit programs, and decreases in purchases. States and localities have also tapped reserves and, in a few cases, increased taxes. Some states have increased borrowing, but in the aggregate, borrowing has been down, as unfavorable credit market conditions have made it more difficult to finance capital projects and to borrow for the sake of cash management in the short term.

Falling incomes, declining consumer spending, and continued decreases in house prices reduced all major sources of state and local revenue collections in 2008. In the fourth quarter, collections from personal income taxes fell by 0.4 percent (measured relative to those in the fourth quarter of 2007)—the first decline in more than five years. Corporate tax payments decreased by double digits over the year. Sales tax collections were also lower in the fourth quarter than a year earlier—the only such decline on record during the past half century. Although revenues from property taxes continued to grow, the rate of growth declined to 2.2 percent, contrasting with 5.4 percent a year earlier.

Table 2.2. Consensus Forecasts of Foreign Economies' Inflation-Adjusted Growth of GDP, 2009 (Percentage change from previous year)

Region/Country	Survey of		
	June 2008	Sept. 2008	Mar. 2009
Eurozone	1.4	0.9	-2.6
Germany	1.3	0.8	-3.2
United Kingdom	1.3	0.6	-3.0
Canada	2.1	1.8	-1.8
Asia Pacific	4.8	4.6	-0.2
Japan	1.5	0.9	-5.8
China	9.4	9.1	7.0
India	8.1	7.6	5.2
Latin America	3.9	3.7	-0.7
Brazil	4.1	3.8	-0.1
Mexico	3.0	2.6	-2.8

Source:Congressional Budget Office based on data from Consensus Economics, Inc.
Note: GDP = gross domestic product.

Inflation

Although recent movements in consumer prices have been dominated by the fall in commodity prices—for both energy and food—consumer price inflation slowed in a number of other spending categories as well. The precipitous drop in petroleum prices from an average of $133 per barrel in July 2008 to $39 per barrel in February 2009 had a particularly large effect on overall inflation, as motor fuel prices fell sharply. A decline in prices for agricultural commodities also reduced consumer prices. The food-at-home index of the consumer price index for all urban consumers (CPI-U) eased down slightly from its November 2008 peak.

Inflation rates for consumer goods and services other than energy and food (core inflation) also slowed during the past few months (see Figure 2-9). Although the core CPI-U grew at an average 2.4 percent rate through the first three quarters of 2008, it rose at just a 0.6 percent rate in the fourth quarter. Some of the reduction is likely to be temporary, because declines in energy prices affected prices in some categories (especially the index for public transportation) and because vehicle prices fell sharply—factors that are not likely to be repeated on such a scale in 2009. Some of the disinflation is likely to be persistent, however, as a general easing in core inflation is typical during recessions. In addition, the large number of vacant housing units dampened the growth of rents in recent months, and that condition is likely to persist for some time.

CBO's Short-Term Forecast

In CBO's forecast, the decline in output continues until the fall. But the rate of decline slows after the first quarter, in part because the effects of ARRA begin to take hold. Reduced tax-withholding rates and increased aid to low-income households in the form of expanded unemployment insurance and payments from the Supplemental Nutrition Assistance Program will support consumer spending in 2009, as will lower prices for energy. And the stimulus legislation will also contribute to growth via purchases of goods and services by the federal government and averted reductions in spending or increases in taxes that would have otherwise occurred at the state and local levels. However, CBO expects that high unemployment, tight credit conditions, and the declines in wealth will restrain the growth of consumption.

The forecast anticipates that business fixed investment will continue to decline in 2009, reflecting those tight lending conditions, much higher costs of funds (especially for equity), and weak demand for output that would be produced with new capital. Housing investment is also expected to continue declining this year. In addition, a continued drawdown of inventories and weakening foreign economies will restrain growth this year. By the end of 2009, the unemployment rate is projected to reach 9.4 percent, as employment declines by an additional 1-1/2 million jobs—for a total loss of nearly 6 million jobs since the recession started.

In the forecast, a recovery begins to take hold late in 2009 and quickens in 2010, as the drawdown of inventories ends, housing investment begins to recover, and business investment responds to the improvement in overall economic activity. And with labor markets no longer deteriorating, and the negative effects of the drop in wealth fading, consumer spending is expected to grow modestly. The unemployment rate declines to 8.5 percent by the end of 2010. In 2011, the projected output gap closes further, though GDP is still 4.3 percent below its potential by the end of that year, with the unemployment rate at 7.2 percent. (That recovery path assumes that policies aimed at stabilizing financial markets prove to be successful.)

With a large and sustained output gap, inflation is expected to be very low during the next several years. On a fourth-quarter-to-fourth quarter basis, the core consumer price index is forecast to increase just 1.4 percent in 2009, 1.0 percent in 2010, and 0.8 percent in 2011 (see Figure 2-9). Because energy prices are lower in 2009 than they were last year, the overall consumer price index is expected to rise just 0.6 percent in 2009. Even as energy prices are forecast to stabilize, growth in the consumer price index is expected to remain low, at 1.3 percent in 2010 and 1.1 percent in 2011. In fact, some private-sector analysts are now concerned about deflation—prices falling for a broad range of goods and services for a protracted period. Although CBO's forecast indicates a drop in the CPI-U between 2008 and 2009, that decline results from the fall in commodity prices— not in prices for a broad range of goods and services— and it is not persistent.

The rate for 3-month Treasury bills is expected to average only 0.3 percent in 2009; and for 10-year Treasury notes, 2.9 percent. Both of those rates are anticipated to rise in 2010 and 2011 but to remain well below their long-term averages. Although large federal budget deficits in CBO's baseline projections would tend to boost interest rates, the weakness in economic activity and the very low inflation rate should hold down nominal interest rates for the next few years.

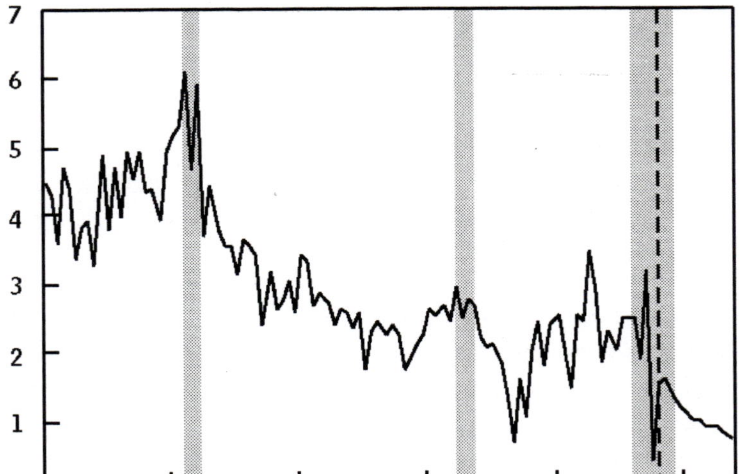

Source: Congressional Budget Office; Department of Labor, Bureau of Labor Statistics.
Notes: The core consumer price index excludes energy and food.
Data are quarterly and are plotted through 2011.

Figure 2.9. Core Consumer Price Index, 1985 to 2011 (Percentage change at annual rates).

The American Recovery and Reinvestment Act's Impact on the Near-Term Outlook

CBO's forecast incorporates the estimated impact of the spending increases and tax reductions provided by ARRA. The major provisions of that law provide for direct purchases of goods and services by the federal government, transfers to state and local governments (both for infrastructure and for other purposes), payments to individuals, and temporary tax reductions for individuals and businesses. CBO believes that, without such stimulus, the economy probably would have continued to contract sharply throughout 2009. The unemployment rate probably would have exceeded 10.0 percent by the end of the year and peaked at around 10.5 percent in the first half of next year.

In projecting the impact of ARRA, CBO assessed the likely magnitude and timing of federal outlays and revenue reductions, developing a range of estimates of the effects on real GDP. The agency grouped the various provisions into a number of general categories, each of which was assumed to have a range of effects on the economy that could be summarized by "multipliers," or the cumulative impact that a dollar in stimulus would have on output.[26] For example, CBO determined that, with a multiplier of 1.0 to 2.5, a one-time increase in federal purchases of goods and services of $1.00 in the second quarter of this year would raise GDP by $1.00 to $2.50 in total over several quarters. The range of estimates for each category of stimulus is quite wide, reflecting a diversity of views among economists as to their effectiveness. CBO's forecast is based on roughly the midpoint between the low and high estimated multipliers within each category.

Even after the fact, it will be quite difficult to assess the impact of ARRA on the economy. Uncertainty is great about both how the economy would perform in the absence of fiscal stimulus and the impact of stimulus. The best estimates of the impact of stimulus will come later, from studies carefully designed to isolate the effects of particular categories of stimulus from other influences on the economy.[27]

In CBO's forecast, the enactment of ARRA boosts real GDP relative to that in a forecast of what would have happened in the absence of stimulus by about 2-1/2 percent in the fourth quarter of 2009 and by about 2-1/4 percent in the fourth quarter of 2010 (see Table 2-3). The unemployment rate is lower than it would otherwise be by about 0.9 percentage points in the fourth quarter of 2009 and 1.3 points in the fourth quarter of 2010. The boost to total employment peaks at about 2-1/2 million jobs in the second half of 2010.

Steps to Stabilize Financial Markets

CBO's forecast assumes that the Federal Reserve and the Treasury, along with the Federal Deposit Insurance Corporation, will continue to act vigorously to address the problems in financial markets. Programs created by those entities have provided funds or issued guarantees in large amounts to financial institutions. Those programs have improved conditions in some financial markets and have reduced the risk of a collapse of the financial system. The forecast also assumes that the Federal Reserve will keep the federal funds rate close to zero and will continue to supply very large amounts of credit to financial markets until financial conditions and the availability of credit begin to return to normal. In addition, the forecast assumes that the central bank will act quickly to address any adverse developments that threaten liquidity or the stability of the financial system.

The Federal Reserve has announced that it will provide large amounts of additional funding to financial markets this year. After its March policy meeting, the Federal Reserve stated that it will purchase up to an additional $400 billion of securities for its portfolio—$300 billion in longer-term Treasury securities and $100 billion in debt issued by the government-owned corporations Fannie Mae and Freddie Mac. In addition to its more traditional way of purchasing government-related securities to expand its balance sheet, the Federal Reserve has created two new programs for that purpose. In the first program, designed in part to lower mortgage rates, the central bank will purchase up to $1.25 trillion of mortgage-backed securities (MBSs) issued by Fannie Mae, Freddie Mac, and Ginnie Mae. Through March 11, the Federal Reserve had purchased a net $217 billion of MBSs. The second program, called the Term Asset- Backed Security Loan Facility (TALF), is designed to increase the securitization of certain types of loans, including commercial mortgages, auto loans, and student loans. Under the TALF, the Federal Reserve will lend funds to private purchasers of top-rated securities backed by such loans for up to a three-year period using those securities as collateral; the total amount provided by the facility may be as much as $1 trillion.

The Treasury had bought about $107 billion of MBSs as of February 28, 2009, and it continues to purchase them. To support the TALF, the Treasury will allocate funds from the Troubled Asset Relief Program to offset the Federal Reserve's potential losses in the event of default. In addition to the funds allocated so far for the TALF, roughly $250 billion remained uncommitted under the TARP as of mid-March and could be used to inject additional capital into banks or to support new programs.

Table 2.3. Estimated Macroeconomic Impacts of the American Recovery and Reinvestment Act of 2009. Fourth Quarters of Calendar Years 2009 to 2019

	2009	2010	2011	2012	2013	2014	2015	2016	2017	2018	2019
Real GDP (Percentage change from baseline)											
Low estimate of effect	1.4	1.1	0.4	0.1	0	0	-0.1	-0.2	-0.2	-0.2	-0.2
High estimate of effect	3.8	3.4	1.2	0.5	0.3	0.2	0.1	0	0	0	0
GDP Gap[a] (Percent)											
Baseline	-7.4	-6.3	-4.1	-2.2	-0.7	-0.1	0	0	0	0	0
Low estimate of effect	-6.1	-5.3	-3.7	-2.0	-0.6	-0.1	0	0	0	0	0
High estimate of effect	-3.9	-3.2	-2.9	-1.7	-0.5	0	0.1	0	0	0	0
Unemployment Rate (Percent)											
Baseline	9.0	8.7	7.5	6.4	5.5	5.0	4.8	4.8	4.8	4.8	4.8
Low estimate of effect	8.5	8.1	7.2	6.3	5.4	5.0	4.8	4.8	4.8	4.8	4.8
High estimate of effect	7.8	6.8	6.6	6.0	5.3	4.9	4.8	4.8	4.8	4.8	4.8
Employment (Millions of jobs)											
Baseline	141.6	143.3	146.2	149.3	152.1	153.9	154.9	155.7	156.4	157.0	157.7
Low estimate of effect	142.4	144.5	146.8	149.6	152.2	153.9	155.0	155.7	156.4	157.0	157.7
High estimate of effect	143.9	146.9	148.0	150.0	152.4	154.1	155.0	155.7	156.4	157.0	157.7

Source:Congressional Budget Office.

a. Real GDP is gross domestic product, excluding the effects of inflation. The GDP gap is the percentage difference between gross domestic product and CBO's estimate of potential GDP. Potential GDP is the estimated level of output that corresponds to a high level of use of labor and capital resources. A negative gap indicates a high unemployment rate and low utilization rates for plant and equipment.

Table 2.4. Key Assumptions in CBO's Projection of Potential Output

(Percent)	Average Annual Growth						Projections		
	1950 - 1973	1974 - 1981	1982-1990	1991-2001	2002-2008	1950-2008	2009-2014	2015-2019	2009-2019
Overall Economy									
Potential Output	3.9	3.2	3.2	2.9	2.8	3.4	2.2	2.4	2.3
Potential Labor Force	1.6	2.5	1.7	1.1	1.1	1.6	0.8	0.4	0.6
Potential Labor Force Productivity[a]	2.3	0.7	1.5	1.7	1.7	1.8	1.4	1.9	1.6
Nonfarm Business Sector									
Potential Output	4.0	3.5	3.4	3.3	3.1	3.6	2.5	2.8	2.6
Potential Hours Worked	1.4	2.2	1.7	1.1	0.9	1.4	0.7	0.5	0.6
Capital Services	3.8	4.3	4.2	4.7	2.6	3.9	2.1	3.8	2.9
Potential TFP	1.9	0.7	0.9	1.1	1.6	1.4	1.3	1.3	1.3
Trend TFP	1.9	0.7	1.0	1.0	1.2	1.3	1.2	1.2	1.2
TFP adjustments	0	0	0	0.1	0.5	0.1	0.2	0.2	0.2
Price measurement[b]	0	0	0	0.1	0.2	0	0.2	0.2	0.2
Temporary adjustment[c]	0	0	0	0.1	0.3	0.1	0	0	0
Contributions to the Growth of Potential Output (Percentage points)									
Potential labor input	1.0	1.6	1.2	0.8	0.7	1.0	0.5	0.3	0.4
Capital services	1.1	1.3	1.3	1.4	0.8	1.2	0.6	1.1	0.9
Potential TFP	1.9	0.7	0.9	1.1	1.6	1.4	1.3	1.3	1.3
Total Contributions	**4.0**	**3.5**	**3.4**	**3.3**	**3.1**	**3.6**	**2.5**	**2.8**	**2.6**
Memorandum:									
Potential Labor Productivity[d]	2.6	1.3	1.7	2.2	2.2	2.2	1.8	2.3	2.0

Source: Congressional Budget Office.

Note: Total factor productivity (TFP) is average real output per unit of combined labor and capital services. The growth of TFP is defined as the growth of real output that is not explained by the growth of labor and capital.

a. The ratio of potential output to the potential labor force.

b. An adjustment for a conceptual change in the official measure of the gross domestic product chained price index.

c. An adjustment for the unusually rapid growth of TFP between 2001 and 2003.

d. The estimated trend in the ratio of output to hours worked in the nonfarm business sector.

The FDIC has also provided substantial assistance to financial institutions, which continue to issue new debt guaranteed by the FDIC under the Temporary Liquidity Guarantee Program. That program, which guarantees debt newly issued by banks and other financial institutions, was covering more than $250 billion of debt as of the end of January.

The Outlook through 2019

CBO expects that potential output will grow at an annual rate of 2.3 percent on average during the 2009–2019 period, or at roughly the same pace as the agency assumed in its January projections (see Table 2-4). The projections for labor input and productivity are essentially unchanged since January: The growth of potential hours worked averages 0.6 percent annually from 2009 to 2019, and the growth of total factor productivity averages 1.3 percent during the same period.[28] The projected pace of capital accumulation, as measured by growth in the capital services index, is slightly slower, averaging 2.9 percent during the period, down from 3.0 percent in January. Once the economy returns to its potential level in 2014, CBO assumes that it will continue to produce goods and services at or near its potential rate of growth.

The primary difference between the current projections and the ones published in January is the effect of the American Recovery and Reinvestment Act of 2009. Although ARRA will boost output significantly in the next several years, any short-run effects of the stimulus legislation on the business cycle will have dissipated by the end of the projection period. In the latter part of the period, the legislation reduces projected output by roughly 0.1 percent, principally through its influence on capital accumulation.

Capital accumulation is affected because the increase in government debt is expected to displace, or "crowd out," a smaller amount of private capital. That result occurs because the reduction in overall national saving dampens spending on business fixed investment and the construction of housing. Although the size of such displacement is very uncertain, CBO assumes that, in the long run, each dollar of additional federal debt crowds out about a third of a dollar's worth of private domestic capital (with the remainder of the rise in debt offset by increases in private saving and inflows of foreign capital).

Other factors, however, are expected to partially offset the negative effect of the crowding out. Many of the legislation's provisions, such as funding for improvements to roads and highways, might add to the economy's potential output in much the same way that private capital investment does. Other provisions, such as funding for grants to increase access to college education or for research and development, could raise long-term productivity by enhancing people's skills or speeding the pace of technical innovation. And still other provisions could create incentives for increased private investment. According to CBO's estimates, provisions that could add to longterm output account for between a quarter and one-third of the legislation's overall budgetary cost.

Comarison with CBO's January Forecast

In addition to the effects of the American Recovery and Reinvestment Act, the other major change since CBO presented its forecast in January is in the underlying outlook for the economy in 2009: It has worsened considerably. The labor market has deteriorated far more than had been anticipated, and the decline in business fixed investment in the fourth quarter was more rapid than had been expected. CBO also now projects a much sharper draw- down of inventories over the next several quarters, as declining production suggests that firms desire leaner inventories than had been previously thought. News of further weakness in foreign economies has also dampened the outlook, as has the sharp decline in the stock market this year.

Table 2.5. CBO's Current and Previous Economic Projections for Calendar Years 2009 to 2019

	Estimated 2008[a]	Forecast			Projected Annual Average	
		2009	2010	2011	2012-2015	2016-2019
Nominal GDP (Billions of dollars)						
March 2009	14,257	14,047	14,576	15,233	18,138 [b]	21,164 [c]
January 2009	14,304	14,241	14,591	15,347	19,077 [b]	22,500 [c]
Nominal GDP (Percentage change)						
March 2009	3.3	-1.5	3.8	4.5	4.5	3.9
January 2009	3.6	-0.4	2.5	5.2	5.6	4.2
Real GDP (Percentage change)						
March 2009	1.1	-3.0	2.9	4.0	3.6	2.3
January 2009	1.2	-2.2	1.5	4.2	3.7	2.3
GDP Price Index (Percentage change)						
March 2009	2.2	1.5	0.8	0.5	0.9	1.6
January 2009	2.4	1.8	0.9	1.0	1.8	1.9
Consumer Price Index[d] (Percentage change)						
March 2009	3.8	-0.7	1.4	1.2	1.2	1.9
January 2009	4.1	0.1	1.7	1.8	2.2	2.2
Unemployment Rate (Percent)						
March 2009	5.8	8.8	9.0	7.7	5.6	4.8
January 2009	5.7	8.3	9.0	8.0	5.7	4.8
Three-Month Treasury Bill Rate (Percent)						
March 2009	1.4	0.3	0.9	1.8	4.0	4.7
January 2009	1.4	0.2	0.6	2.1	4.5	4.7
Ten-Year Treasury Note Rate (Percent)						
March 2009	3.7	2.9	3.4	4.0	5.1	5.6
January 2009	3.7	3.0	3.2	3.6	5.2	5.4
Tax Bases (Billions of dollars)						
Economic profits						
March 2009	1,496	1,269	1,386	1,547	1,822 [b]	1,940 [c]
January 2009	1,533	1,384	1,413	1,559	2,001 [b]	2,187 [c]
Wages and salaries						
March 2009	6,543	6,496	6,743	6,953	8,315 [b]	9,709 [c]
January 2009	6,548	6,551	6,740	7,011	8,742 [b]	10,324 [c]
Tax Bases (Percentage of GDP)						
Economic profits						
March 2009	10.5	9.0	9.5	10.2	10.4	9.5
January 2009	10.7	9.7	9.7	10.2	10.6	10.0
Wages and salaries						
March 2009	45.9	46.2	46.3	45.6	45.9	45.9
January 2009	45.8	46.0	46.2	45.7	45.8	45.9
Memorandum:						
Real Potential GDP (Percentage change)						
March 2009	2.6	2.3	1.8	1.7	2.4	2.3
January 2009	2.6	2.4	2.0	1.9	2.4	2.3

Source: Congressional Budget Office; Department of Commerce, Bureau of Economic Analysis; Department of Labor, Bureau of Labor Statistics; Federal Reserve Board.

Note: GDP = gross domestic product; percentage changes are measured from one year to the next.

a. Figures for the consumer price index, the unemployment rate, and the interest rates are actual values; the other 2008 figures are estimates.
b. Level in 2015.
c. Level in 2019.
d. The consumer price index for all urban consumers.

Since January, CBO has lowered its estimates of inflation for all of the projection period. The expectation of a deeper recession and slow recovery implies high unemployment rates and a great deal of excess capacity for many years. Those factors make it likely that the United States will experience very low inflation for a long time.

For 2010 through 2015, the current projections for the growth of the CPI-U and the price index for GDP are significantly lower than the ones in January (see Table 2-5). Inflation is also lower in the latter years of the projection period because CBO assumes the long spell of excess capacity will permit the Federal Reserve to achieve a slightly lower rate of inflation on average even when the economy returns to its potential.

Comarison with Other Forecasts

Comparing CBO's forecast with others is complicated by the differences in the timing of forecasts given the rapid deterioration in economic conditions. CBO's forecast reflects information available through early March, including data on employment and unemployment in February. In contrast, the Federal Reserve's estimates were compiled in late January; the Administration's forecast was completed in early February; and the *Blue Chip* consensus was compiled in early March, but prior to the release of the February data on labor markets.

CBO's forecast has a deeper downturn in economic activity for this year than is indicated by most other forecasts, but it also has a somewhat faster rebound in 2010 and 2011. CBO's projection for the change in real GDP in 2009 (-3.0 percent) is much weaker than the Administration's (-1.2 percent) and slightly weaker than the *Blue Chip* consensus forecast (-2.6 percent) (see Table 2-6). On a fourth-quarter-to-fourth-quarter basis, CBO's projection (-1.5 percent) is below the Federal Reserve's central tendency (see Table 2-7). However, for 2010 and 2011, on average, CBO's forecast for real growth of GDP is similar to the Administration's and is stronger than the *Blue Chip* consensus forecast. CBO's forecast is at the high end of the range of estimates by the Federal Reserve for 2010 but is within the central tendency for 2011.

CBO's forecast for inflation in the near term is on the low end in comparison with the other forecasts. It is slightly lower than those of both the Administration and the *Blue Chip* consensus in 2009 and 2010 but substantially lower in 2011. CBO's inflation forecast is within the Federal Reserve's central tendency throughout the 2009–2011 period but at the low edge of that interval.

Tabl 2.6. Comparison of CBO, Administration, and *Blue Chip* Economic Projections for Calender Years 2009 to 2019

	Estimated 2008[a]	Forecast			Projected Annual Average	
		2009	2010	2011	2012-2015	2016-2019
Nominal GDP (Billions of dollars)						
CBO	14,257	14,047	14,576	15,233	18,138 [b]	21,164 [c]
Administration	14,281	14,291	14,902	15,728	19,415 [b]	23,108 [c]
Blue Chip	14,265	14,065	14,515	15,255	18,667 [b]	22,603 [c]
Nominal GDP (Percentage change)						
CBO	3.3	-1.5	3.8	4.5	4.5	3.9
Administration	3.4	0.1	4.3	5.5	5.4	4.4
Blue Chip	3.3	-1.4	3.2	5.1	5.2	4.9
Real GDP (Percentage change)						
CBO	1.1	-3.0	2.9	4.0	3.6	2.3
Administration	1.3	-1.2	3.2	4.0	3.6	2.6
Blue Chip	1.1	-2.6	1.9	3.4	3.0	2.6
GDP Price Index (Percentage change)						
CBO	2.2	1.5	0.8	0.5	0.9	1.6
Administration	2.2	1.2	1.1	1.5	1.8	1.8
Blue Chip	2.2	1.2	1.2	1.7	2.2	2.3
Consumer Price Index[d] (Percentage change)						
CBO	3.8	-0.7	1.4	1.2	1.2	1.9
Administration	3.8	-0.6	1.6	1.8	2.1	2.1
Blue Chip	3.8	-0.8	1.6	2.1	2.4	2.5
Unemployment Rate (Percent)						
CBO	5.8	8.8	9.0	7.7	5.6	4.8
Administration	5.8	8.1	7.9	7.1	5.3	5.0
Blue Chip	5.8	8.6	9.1	8.1	6.3	5.5
Three-Month Treasury Bill Rate (Percent)						
CBO	1.4	0.3	0.9	1.8	4.0	4.7
Administration	1.4	0.3	1.6	3.4	4.0	4.0
Blue Chip	1.4	0.3	1.0	2.8	4.0	4.2
Ten-Year Treasury Note Rate (Percent)						
CBO	3.7	2.9	3.4	4.0	5.1	5.6
Administration	3.7	2.8	4.0	4.8	5.2	5.2
Blue Chip	3.7	2.9	3.7	4.5	5.2	5.4

Sources: Congressional Budget Office; Office of Management and Budget; Department of Commerce, Bureau of Economic Analysis; Department of Labor, Bureau of Labor Statistics; Federal Reserve Board; and Aspen Publishers, Inc., Blue Chip Economic Indicators (March 10, 2009).

Note: GDP = gross domestic product; percentage changes are measured from one year to the next.

a. Figures for the consumer price index, the unemployment rate, and the interest rates are actual values; the other 2008 figures are estimates.

b. Level in 2015.

c. Level in 2019.

d. The consumer price index for all urban consumers.

Table 2-7. Comparison of Economic Forecasts by the Federal Reserve and CBO for Calendar Years 2009, 2010, and 2011

	Federal Reserve		
	Range	Central Tendency	CBO
2009			
Fourth Quarter to Fourth Quarter (Percentage change)			
Real GDP	-2.5 to 0.2	-1.3 to -0.5	-1.5
PCE Price Index[a]	-0.5 to 1.5	0.3 to 1.0	0.5
Core PCE Price Index[b]	0.6 to 1.5	0.9 to 1.1	0.7
Average Level, Fourth Quarter (Percent)			
Civilian Unemployment Rate	8.0 to 9.2	8.5 to 8.8	8.8
2010			
Fourth Quarter to Fourth Quarter (Percentage change)			
Real GDP	1.5 to 4.5	2.5 to 3.3	4.1
PCE Price Index[a]	0.7 to 1.8	1.0 to 1.5	1.0
Core PCE Price Index[b]	0.4 to 1.7	0.8 to 1.5	0.8
Average Level, Fourth Quarter (Percent)			
Civilian Unemployment Rate	7.0 to 9.2	8.0 to 8.3	9.0
2011			
Fourth Quarter to Fourth Quarter (Percentage change)			
Real GDP	2.3 to 5.5	3.8 to 5.0	4.1
PCE Price Index[a]	0.2 to 2.1	0.9 to 1.7	0.9
Core PCE Price Index[b]	0 to 1.8	0.7 to 1.5	0.7
Average Level, Fourth Quarter (Percent)			
Civilian Unemployment Rate	5.5 to 8.0	6.7 to 7.5	7.7

Sources: Congressional Budget Office; Federal Reserve Board, "Summary of Economic Projections for the Meeting of January 27–28, 2009" (February 18, 2009).

Notes: GDP = gross domestic product; PCE = personal consumption expenditure.

The range of estimates from the Federal Reserve reflects all views of the members of the Federal Open Market Committee. The central tendency reflects the most common views of the committee's members.

a. The PCE chained price index.

b. The PCE chained price index excluding prices for food and energy.

Reflecting the projections of low inflation and persistently high unemployment rates, interest rates for 2010 and 2011 in CBO's forecast are also generally on the low side of the range of estimates by others. Compared with the *Blue Chip* consensus estimates, CBO's forecasts of interest rates are identical in 2009, slightly lower on average in 2010, and significantly lower for 2011. (The Federal Reserve does not publish a forecast of interest rates.)

For the entire projection horizon, 2009 to 2019, CBO is estimating higher average growth than that implied by the *Blue Chip* consensus but lower growth than the estimate by the Administration. CBO projects that real GDP will be $15.3 trillion in 2019, for an average growth rate of 2.5 percent per year.[29] The *Blue-Chip's* figure is $14.9 trillion, for an average annual growth rate of 2.3 percent; and the Administration's, $15.8 trillion, for a rate of 2.8 percent.

There are smaller but still significant differences among forecasters for the average rates of unemployment, inflation, and interest rates for the latter years of the projection horizon. For 2016 to 2019, CBO expects about the same average unemployment rate as the Administration does but a lower rate than does the *Blue-Chip* consensus. Similarly, CBO's projection for inflation in those years is about the same as the Administration's but lower than that of the *Blue-Chip* consensus. Last, CBO's projections of interest rates are somewhat higher.

For the years after 2011, the Federal Reserve provides some longer-run projections, including estimates levels of real GDP growth and the unemployment rate that are sustainable in the long run and of the inflation rate that is consistent with the dual objectives of maximum employment and price stability given "appropriate monetary policy." CBO's projection of potential eco-nomic growth, at 2.6 percent five to six years from now, is within the Federal Reserve's central tendency of 2.5 percent to 2.7 percent for that time frame. CBO's projection of the unemployment rate from 2016 to 2019, at 4.8 percent, is also within the Federal Reserve's central tendency of 4.8 percent to 5.0 percent. However, CBO's projection of 1.6 percent inflation based on the price index for personal consumption expenditures is slightly below the Federal Reserve's central tendency of 1.7 percent to 2.0 percent.

APPENDIX A: CBO'S ECONOMIC PROJECTIONS FOR 2009 TO 2019

The tables in this appendix expand on the information in the body of the report by showing the Congressional Budget Office's (CBO's) year-by-year economic projections for 2009 to 2019 (by calendar year in Table A-1 and by fiscal year in Table A-2). CBO does not forecast cyclical fluctuations in its projections for years after 2011.

Instead, the projected values shown in the tables for 2012 to 2019 reflect CBO's assessment of average values for that period. That assessment takes into account economic and demographic trends but does not attempt to forecast the frequency and size of ups and downs in the business cycle.

Table A-1. CBO's Year-by-Year Forecast and Projections for Calendar Years 2009 to 2019

	Estimated	Forecast			Projected							
	2008[a]	2009	2010	2011	2012	2013	2014	2015	2016	2017	2018	2019
Nominal GDP (Billions of dollars)	14,257	14,047	14,576	15,233	15,950	16,684	17,421	18,138	18,873	19,624	20,381	21,164
Nominal GDP (Percentage change)	3.3	-1.5	3.8	4.5	4.7	4.6	4.4	4.1	4.1	4.0	3.9	3.8
Real GDP (Percentage change)	1.1	-3.0	2.9	4.0	4.1	4.0	3.5	2.7	2.5	2.4	2.3	2.2
GDP Price Index (Percentage change)	2.2	1.5	0.8	0.5	0.6	0.6	0.9	1.4	1.5	1.6	1.6	1.6
PCE Price Index[b] (Percentage change)	3.3	-0.1	1.1	1.0	0.8	0.8	1.1	1.4	1.6	1.6	1.6	1.6
Core PCE Price Index[c] (Percentage change)	2.2	1.0	0.8	0.7	0.5	0.6	1.0	1.4	1.6	1.6	1.6	1.6
Consumer Price Index[d] (Percentage change)	3.8	-0.7	1.4	1.2	1.0	1.0	1.2	1.6	1.9	1.9	1.9	1.9
Core Consumer Price Index[e] (Percentage change)	2.3	1.5	1.1	0.9	0.7	0.8	1.2	1.6	1.9	1.9	1.9	1.9
Unemployment Rate (Percent)	5.8	8.8	9.0	7.7	6.6	5.7	5.1	4.9	4.8	4.8	4.8	4.8
Three-Month Treasury Bill Rate (Percent)	1.4	0.3	0.9	1.8	3.0	3.9	4.4	4.7	4.7	4.8	4.8	4.8
Ten-Year Treasury Note Rate (Percent)	3.7	2.9	3.4	4.0	4.6	5.0	5.3	5.4	5.5	5.6	5.6	5.6
Tax Base(Billions of dollars)s												
Economic profits	1,496	1,269	1,386	1,547	1,656	1,764	1,812	1,822	1,859	1,884	1,915	1,940
Wages and salaries	6,543	6,496	6,743	6,953	7,338	7,662	7,990	8,315	8,651	8,997	9,347	9,709
Tax Base(Percentage of GDP)s												
Economic profits	10.5	9.0	9.5	10.2	10.4	10.6	10.4	10.0	9.9	9.6	9.4	9.2
Wages and salaries	45.9	46.2	46.3	45.6	46.0	45.9	45.9	45.8	45.8	45.8	45.9	45.9

Sources: Congressional Budget Office; Department of Commerce, Bureau of Economic Analysis; Department of Labor, Bureau of Labor Statistics; Federal Reserve Board.

Note: GDP = gross domestic product; PCE = personal consumption expenditure. Percentage changes are measured from one year to the next.
a. Figures for the consumer price index, the unemployment rate, and the interest rates are actual values; other 2008 figures are estimates.
b. The PCE chained price index.
c. The PCE chained price index excluding prices for food and energy.
d. The consumer price index for all urban consumers.
e. The consumer price index for all urban consumers excluding prices for food and energy.

Table A-2. CBO's Year by Year Forecast and Projections for Fiscal Years 2009 to 2019

	Actual	Forecast			Projected							
	2008	2009	2010	2011	2012	2013	2014	2015	2016	2017	2018	2019
Nominal GDP (Billions of dollars)	14,222	14,057	14,405	15,061	15,774	16,496	17,241	17,957	18,688	19,436	20,191	20,966
Nominal GDP (Percentage change)	4.3	-1.2	2.5	4.6	4.7	4.6	4.5	4.2	4.1	4.0	3.9	3.8
Real GDP (Percentage change)	1.9	-2.9	1.5	4.0	4.1	4.0	3.7	2.9	2.5	2.4	2.3	2.2
GDP Price Index (Percentage change)	2.4	1.7	0.9	0.6	0.6	0.6	0.8	1.3	1.5	1.6	1.6	1.6
PCE Price Index[a] (Percentage change)	3.7	0.2	1.0	1.0	0.8	0.8	1.0	1.3	1.6	1.6	1.6	1.6
Core PCE Price Index[b] (Percentage change)	2.2	1.3	0.8	0.7	0.6	0.6	0.9	1.3	1.6	1.6	1.6	1.6
Consumer Price Index[c] (Percentage change)	4.4	-0.5	1.2	1.3	1.0	0.9	1.1	1.5	1.9	1.9	1.9	1.9
Core Consumer Price Index[d] (Percentage change)	2.4	1.6	1.2	0.9	0.8	0.7	1.1	1.5	1.9	1.9	1.9	1.9
Unemployment Rate (Percent)	5.3	8.2	9.2	8.0	6.8	5.9	5.2	4.9	4.8	4.8	4.8	4.8
Three-Month Treasury Bill Rate (Percent)	2.1	0.3	0.8	1.6	2.7	3.7	4.4	4.6	4.7	4.7	4.8	4.8
Ten-Year Treasury Note Rate (Percent)	3.9	2.9	3.3	3.9	4.5	4.9	5.2	5.4	5.5	5.6	5.6	5.6

Table A.2. (Continued)

	Actual	Forecast			Projected							
	2008	2009	2010	2011	2012	2013	2014	2015	2016	2017	2018	2019
Tax Bases(Billions of dollars)												
Economic profits	1,563	1,285	1,340	1,512	1,630	1,740	1,807	1,816	1,852	1,877	1,909	1,933
Wages and salaries	6,521	6,500	6,647	6,901	7,258	7,579	7,909	8,232	8,566	8,910	9,258	9,617
Tax Bases (Percentage of GDP)												
Economic profits	11.0	9.1	9.3	10.0	10.3	10.5	10.5	10.1	9.9	9.7	9.5	9.2
Wages and salaries	45.9	46.2	46.1	45.8	46.0	45.9	45.9	45.8	45.8	45.8	45.9	45.9

Source: Congressional Budget Office; Department of Commerce, Bureau of Economic Analysis; Department of Labor, Bureau of Labor Statistics; Federal Reserve Board.

Note: GDP = gross domestic product; PCE = personal consumption expenditure. Percentage changes are measured from one year to the next.

a. The PCE chained price index.

b. The PCE chained price index excluding prices for food and energy.

c. The consumer price index for all urban consumers.

d. The consumer price index for all urban consumers excluding prices for food and energy.

APPENDIX B: CONTRIBUTORS TO THE REVENUE AND SPENDING PROJECTIONS

The Following Congressional Budget Office analysts prepared the revenue and spending projections in this report:

Revenue Projections	
Mark Booth	Unit Chief
David Weiner	Unit Chief
Paul Burnham	Retirement income
Grant Driessen	Excise taxes
Barbara Edwards	Social insurance taxes, Federal Reserve System earnings
Zachary Epstein	Customs duties, miscellaneous receipts
Pamela Greene	Corporate income taxes, estate and gift taxes
Ed Harris	Individual income taxes
Athiphat Muthitacharoen	Estate tax modeling
Larry Ozanne	Capital gains realizations
Kevin Perese	Tax modeling
Kristy Piccinini	Capital gains realizations
Kurt Seibert	Earned income tax credit, depreciation
Joshua Shakin	Individual income taxes
Spending Projections	
Defense, International Affairs, and Veterans' Affairs	
Sarah Jennings	Unit Chief
John Chin	International development and security, international financial institutions
Kent Christensen	Defense
Sunita D'Monte	International affairs, veterans' health care
Raymond Hall	Defense (research and development, stockpile sales, atomic energy)
David Newman	Defense (military construction and family housing, military activities in Iraq and Afghanistan and the war on terrorism), veterans' housing
Dawn Sauter Regan	Defense (military personnel)
Matthew Schmit	Military retirement, military health care
Jason Wheelock	Defense (other programs, operations and maintenance, radiation exposure compensation, energy employees' occupational illness compensation)
Camille Woodland	Veterans' readjustment benefits, reservists' educational benefits
Dwayne Wright	Veterans' compensation and pensions
Health Systems and Medicare	
Tom Bradley	Unit Chief
Stephanie Cameron	Medicare, Public Health Service
Mindy Cohen	Medicare, Public Health Service

(Continued)

Defense, International Affairs, and Veterans' Affairs	
Holly Harvey	Medicare
Jean Hearne	Medicare
Lori Housman	Medicare
Jamease Kowalczyk	Medicare, Public Health Service
Julie Lee	Medicare
Lara Robillard	Medicare, Public Health Service
Income Security and Education	
Sam Papenfuss	Unit Chief
Christina Hawley Anthony	Unemployment insurance, training programs, Administration on Aging, Smithsonian, arts and humanities, report coordinator
Chad Chirico	Housing assistance, Fannie Mae and Freddie Mac, Troubled Asset Relief Program
Sheila Dacey	Old-Age and Survivors Insurance, Social Security trust funds, Pension Benefit Guaranty Corporation
Kathleen FitzGerald	Supplemental Nutrition Assistance Program (formerly Food Stamps) and other nutrition programs
Justin Humphrey	Elementary and secondary education, Pell grants, student loans
Deborah Kalcevic	Student loans, higher education
Jonathan Morancy	Child Support Enforcement, Temporary Assistance for Needy Families, foster care, Social Services Block Grant program, child care programs, child and family services
David Rafferty	Disability Insurance, Supplemental Security Income
Jessica Sherry	Low Income Home Energy Assistance Program, refugee assistance, Pension Benefit Guaranty Corporation
Low-Income Health Programs and Prescription Drugs	
Kate Massey	Unit Chief
Julia Christensen	Food and Drug Administration, prescription drug issues
Sean Dunbar	Medicaid, State Children's Health Insurance Program, Public Health Service
Kirstin Nelson	Medicaid, Federal Employees Health Benefits program, Public Health Service
Andrea Noda	Medicare Part D, prescription drug issues, Public Health Service
Lisa Ramirez-Branum	Medicaid, prescription drug issues
Robert Stewart	Medicaid, State Children's Health Insurance Program, Indian Health Service
Ellen Werble	Food and Drug Administration, prescription drug issues, Public Health Service
Rebecca Yip	Medicare Part D, Medicaid prescription drug policy
Natural and Physical Resources	
Kim Cawley	Unit Chief
Leigh Angres	Science and space exploration, Bureau of Indian Affairs, justice
Megan Carroll	Energy, conservation and land management, air transportation
Mark Grabowicz	Justice, Postal Service

(Continued)

Kathleen Gramp	Deposit insurance, energy, Outer Continental Shelf receipts, spectrum auction receipts
Greg Hitz	Agriculture
Daniel Hoople	Community and regional development, Federal Emergency Management Agency
David Hull	Agriculture
James Langley	Agriculture
Susanne Mehlman	Pollution control and abatement, Federal Housing Administration and other housing credit programs, including Fannie Mae and Freddie Mac
Matthew Pickford	General government
Sarah Puro	Highways, Amtrak, mass transit
Deborah Reis	Recreation, water transportation, legislative branch, conservation and land management, other natural resources
Aurora Swanson	Housing finance, water resources
Susan Willie	Commerce, Small Business Administration, Universal Service Fund
Other	
Janet Airis	Unit Chief, Scorekeeping; legislative branch appropriation bill
Jeffrey Holland	Unit Chief, Projections
Edward Blau	Authorization bills
Barry Blom	Federal pay, monthly Treasury data, report coordinator
Jared Brewster	National income and product accounts, other retirement, report coordinator
Joanna Capps	Appropriation bills (Interior and the environment, Labor–Health and Human Services)
Mary Froehlich	Computer support
Wendy Kiska	Troubled Asset Relief Program
Amber Marcellino	Federal civilian retirement, other interest, report coordinator
Damien Moore	Fannie Mae and Freddie Mac, deposit insurance
Virginia Myers	Appropriation bills (Commerce–Justice, financial services, general government)
Jennifer Reynolds	Appropriation bills (Agriculture, foreign relations)
Mark Sanford	Appropriation bills (Defense, Homeland Security)
Eric Schatten	Interest on the public debt, Troubled Asset Relief Program, report coordinator
Phan Siris	Computer support
Esther Steinbock	Appropriation bills (Transportation–Housing and Urban Development, military construction and veterans' affairs, energy and water)
Patrice Watson	Database system administrator
Steve Weinberg	Deposit insurance

End Notes

[1] For CBO's previous baseline budget projections, see Congressional Budget Office, *The Budget and Economic Outlook: Fiscal Years 2009 to 2019* (January 2009).

[2] See Office of Management and Budget, *A New Era of Responsibility: Renewing America's Promise* February 26, 2009).

[3] The TARP was created by the Emergency Economic Stabilization Act of 2008 (P.L. 110-343) in October 2008 to enable the Secretary of the Treasury to purchase or insure troubled assets.

[4] The Deficit Control Act specified that mandatory spending programs whose authorizations are set to expire should be assumed to continue if they have outlays of more than $50 million in the current year and were established on or before the date when the Balanced Budget Act of 1997 was enacted. Programs established after that date are not automatically assumed to continue. The Deficit Control Act also specified that expiring excise taxes whose revenues are dedicated to trust funds should be assumed to be extended at their current rates. The law did not provide for the extension of other expiring tax provisions, even if they had been routinely extended in the past.

[5] ARRA also affected CBO's economic projections by increasing output significantly in the short run and reducing it slightly in the long run relative to what otherwise would have occurred. For discussions of the estimated economic impact of ARRA, see Chapter 2 of this report and Congressional Budget Office, "Estimated Macroeconomic Impacts of the American Recovery and Reinvestment Act of 2009," letter to the Honorable Charles E. Grassley (March 2, 2009).

[6] See Congressional Budget Office, cost estimate for the conference agreement for H.R. 1 (February 13, 2009).

[7] Those estimates do not reflect the impact of the legislation on the economy.

[8] CBO's baseline includes an estimate of the net cost of transactions for the TARP. Broadly speaking, that cost is the purchase price minus the present value (adjusted for market risk) of any estimated future earnings from holding purchased assets and the proceeds from their eventual sale.

[9] Conservatorship is the legal process in which an entity is appointed to establish control and oversight of a company to put it in a sound and solvent condition.

[10] The estimates presented in this chapter do not take into consideration any impact that the President's budgetary proposals might have on GDP or other the broad measures of economic activity.

[11] In its initial budget outline, the Administration does not present detailed information on its request for future appropriations, so CBO conducted its analysis on an aggregated basis.

[12] For discretionary programs, the Administration has compared its policy proposals with a baseline that assumes that funding for military operations in Iraq and Afghanistan continues into future years at the 2008 level of $180 billion, adjusted for inflation. CBO's baseline, however, extrapolates a lower level of war-related funding (the $66 billion currently appropriated for 2009) into future years. Thus, CBO's analysis of the President's request for defense appropriations—funding related to operations in Iraq and Afghanistan and funding not directly tied to those operations— indicates that defense spending under the President's policies would be above baseline levels.

[13] For proposals that would amend the Internal Revenue Code, CBO generally uses estimates provided by JCT.

[14] OMB included an extension of the tax provisions related to EGTRRA and JGTRRA (without modifications) in its current policy baseline.

[15] OMB included this proposal in its baseline projection of current policy.

[16] Carried interest is a component of the typical compensation received by a general partner of a private equity or hedge fund. It is generally a share of the profits on the assets under management.

[17] Current law allows firms to use losses from an unprofitable year to offset taxable income from an earlier year and receive a refund of past taxes paid. Generally, under current law, a net operating loss can be carried back to the prior two tax years.

[18] An income tax credit is refundable if the taxpayer receives a refund when the allowable credit exceeds the amount of income tax owed. Such refunds are recorded in the budget as outlays.

[19] OMB included this proposal in its baseline projection of current policy.

[20] See Congressional Budget Office, "Estimated Macroeconomic Impacts of the American Recovery and Reinvestment Act of 2009," letter to the Honorable Charles E. Grassley (March 2, 2009).

[21] Congressional Budget Office, *The Budget and Economic Outlook: Fiscal Years 2009 to 2019*

[22] Board of Governors of the Federal Reserve System, *The January 2009 Senior Loan Officer Opinion Survey on Bank Lending Practices* (February 2009).

[23] Federal Deposit Insurance Corporation, *Quarterly Banking Profile* (Fourth Quarter 2008).

[24] In an overnight index swap, one party pays the other the daily effective federal funds rate for the life of the contract in exchange for receiving a fixed rate. Therefore, the fixed rate paid for a threemonth overnight index swap contract provides a market estimate of the expected federal funds rate.

[25] Board of Governors of the Federal Reserve System, *Factors Affecting Reserve Balances of Depository Institutions and Condition Statement of Federal Reserve Banks* (statistical release H.4.1. various issues), available at www.federalreserve.gov/releases/h41/current/ h41.htm.

[26] For details, see Congressional Budget Office, "Estimated Macroeconomic Impacts of the American Recovery and Reinvestment Act of 2009."

[27] Examples of such studies include David Johnson, Jonathan Parker, and Nicholas S. Souleles, "Household Expenditure and the Income Tax Rebates of 2001," *American Economic Review,* vol. 96. no. 5 (December 2006), pp. 1589–1610; and Christian Broda and Jonathan Parker, "The Impact of the 2008 Tax Rebates on Consumer Spending: A First Look at the Evidence," *Kellogg Insight* (August 2008).

[28] Total factor productivity is average real output per unit of combined labor and capital services. Its growth is defined as the growth of real output that is not explained by the growth of labor and capital.

[29] Measured in 2000 chain-weighted dollars.

CHAPTER SOURCES

The following chapters have been previously published:

Chapter 1 – This is an edited, reformatted and augmented version of Office of Management and Budget.

Chapter 2 – This is an edited, reformatted and augmented version of Congress of the United States Congressional Budget Office, dated March 2009.

INDEX

D

N

O

P

Q

R

S

T